ALSO BY EDWARD MARRIOTT

Savage Shore

The Lost Tribe

PLAGUE

Plague

A Story of Science, Rivalry, and
the Scourge That Won't Go Away

EDWARD MARRIOTT

METROPOLITAN BOOKS
Henry Holt and Company   New York

Metropolitan Books
Henry Holt and Company, LLC
Publishers since 1866
115 West 18th Street
New York, New York 10011

Metropolitan Books ™ is a registered trademark of
Henry Holt and Company, LLC.

Originally published in the United Kingdom in 2002
under the title *The Plague Race* by Picador UK.

Library of Congress Cataloging-in-Publication data

Marriott, Edward, 1966–
   [Plague race]
   Plague : a story of science, rivalry, and the scourge that
won't go away / by Edward Marriott.—1st American ed.
     p.   cm.
   Originally published: The plague race : United Kingdom : Picador, 2002.
   Includes bibliographical references and index
   ISBN 0-8050-6680-2 (hc.)
   1. Plague—History. 2. Plague—Hong Kong (China : Special Administrative
Region)—History—19th century. I. Title.
RC172 .M374 2003
614.5'732'095125—dc21   2002026325

Henry Holt books are available for special promotions and
premiums. For details contact: Director, Special Markets.

First American Edition 2003

Designed by Kelly S. Too

Printed in the United States of America

1 3 5 7 9 10 8 6 4 2

for Grandfather

Human destiny is bound to remain a gamble, because at some unpredictable time and in some unforeseeable manner nature will strike back.

—RENÉ DUBOS, *MIRAGE OF HEALTH*, 1959

Cities are the graveyards of mankind.

—JOHN CAIRNS, BRITISH BIOCHEMIST

In observation and experiment, chance favors only the prepared mind.

—LOUIS PASTEUR

PLAGUE

PROLOGUE

LATE ONE AFTERNOON, AS THE MANGO AND BANANA SELLERS were beginning to count their day's takings and the Hong Kong street lights were stuttering into life, a monstrous rat surfaced at the intersection of Aberdeen and Bridges. The size of a small cat, it emerged from the drain on one side of the road and climbed up and out, its fur glistening and matted. The rat moved heavily, with a corpulent waddle, belly low to the ground, mouth open. It rolled its shoulders as it progressed, shifting its weight old-mannishly, as if it found covering even this short a distance hugely effortful. As the animal reached the fruit stall on the other side and lumbered to the sidewalk, the vendor began screaming. She stepped out from behind the clumps of bananas with a broom, stamping her feet till all the other stall-keepers heard her and ran to join in. Then there were six of them yelping curses, thrusting through the fruit boxes with broom handles as the rat, with sublime nonchalance, sniffed along the back edge of the sidewalk and disappeared into a hole no bigger than a small coin.

The appearance of so large a rat might be reason enough for alarm, but in these huddled streets rodents were once the sure harbinger of a swift death. A century earlier, in 1894, bubonic plague had exploded out of southern China and torn through the island colony. In the space of days, the houses were shuttered and boarded up; the only movement through the narrow alleyways was the slow shuffle of soldiers, doctors, scientists. Plague, the most feared and least understood of all contagious diseases, had returned; for the researchers gathered in the city, cracking its code was the greatest prize of all.

In Hong Kong, at the start of a global meltdown known today as the third plague pandemic, the competition narrowed to two scientists: the renowned Japanese bacteriologist Professor Shibasaburo Kitasato and his French counterpart, Dr. Alexandre Yersin. For Yersin, whose passion for research had been manifest from childhood, Hong Kong was a crucible, his defining moment. For Kitasato, confident of victory, 1894 would prove an equal crux, though for utterly different reasons.

IF EVER THERE WAS A TIME TO BE A SCIENTIST—AND PARTICULARLY a bacteriologist—it was as the nineteenth century approached its close. During the 1870s and 1880s epidemic diseases began to lose their primacy over humankind, a development that must have served both Yersin and Kitasoto as thrill and inspiration. Science was catching up, learning faster than the diseases could mutate. Leprosy, typhoid fever, malaria, tuberculosis, diphtheria, and tetanus—all these were now understood, their causal agents pinned down by the powerful new techniques of bacteriology.

Born in Switzerland, Alexandre Yersin arrived in Paris in August 1885, when he was almost twenty-two. This was the newly minted, architecturally logical and expansive metropolis of Baron Georges Eugène Haussmann, a place of broad, gleaming boulevards and avenues, a magnet for Europe's wealthiest sophisticates. And here was Yersin, struggling to get his suitcases off the train, head down as he beetled toward his first appointment, the glinting sunshine on the pale stone of the buildings little more than a distraction from the main business: his transformation from darkly intense scientific amateur to practiced and increasingly intuitive medical technician.

His timing was perfect: Less than ten days before, on July 25, Louis Pasteur, pioneering the use of rabies inoculation, had successfully cured his first patient. Over the next five years Yersin would work at the Pasteur Institute as personal assistant and *préparateur* to Pasteur's colleague, Dr. Emile Roux, in his researches on tuberculosis and diphtheria; win the 1888 Paris Medical Faculty bronze medal for his thesis on tuberculosis; spend two months on Robert Koch's Berlin bacteriology course; and, in 1890, flee his world to become a ship's doctor in the Far East, a move so sudden and unexpected that even today one hears bacteriologists muttering in sinister tones of "scandal," certain their hero had committed some shameful act that condemned him thenceforth to be always in flight.

It is more likely that he was running from something far less shadowy, that he was embracing adventure as much as escaping the constraints of his upbringing, academic life, and the social whirl of Paris. He'd always avoided parties, protesting in letters home at the pretension and vapidity of Paris society, and before long he was engineering excuses to escape: a solitary canoeing trip to the coast, "sick leave" from which he would return suspiciously tanned and relaxed.

He was a man who preferred solitude to the company of others, who never had a relationship with a woman, whose only attempt at courtship met with rebuff. Every day he wrote to his mother, and with her at least he was open, happy to express feelings of inadequacy or isolation, as if she alone would not judge.

He never knew his father—a scientist, too—who died three weeks before his birth. He was raised by women: his mother, his sister, surrounded from boyhood by the ballooning skirts of the young women who attended his mother's Swiss finishing school. To him the girls were "apes," as, throughout his life, all females would be. He had a brother, barely a year older, but it is hard to see how the two of them could have come from the same stock: The elder, Franck, was athletic, raucous, sunny; Alexandre was shy, saturnine, interior.

The shadow of his mother seems a blight: Her letters feel claustrophobic, with her constant refrain of "Why don't you marry?" and continual need for reassurance about his career path. He grew to covet his own privacy, betraying mounting irritation at the students assigned to him: "As soon as [they] have gone," he'd typically complain, "I will be happy. The laboratory will finally be mine and will be peaceful again." To his mother—a rigorous, old-school Protestant—he admitted only a single possible flirtation, and one imagines that the candidate was a young woman of whom he was certain she'd approve. Mina Schwartzenbach was a student, the niece of one of his mother's friends. Revealingly, he told his mother of the possibility before even consulting young Mina, explaining that he "might consider" courting her: the language of youthful arrogance, born of insecurity. And it was this bundle of neuroses that Mina, days later, was quick to reject. Never again—to family or colleagues—did Yersin express interest in a woman.

Likewise he spoke of his father to no one—neither schoolmates nor his mother nor his brother. Yet Alexandre senior continued to exert power: an invisible weight driving the son onward, maybe in his absence creating Yersin's manifest ambition. Psychotherapists have argued that sons deprived of fathers work harder to make their mark; Sartre, who lost his when he was two, claimed that the death "gave me my liberty," thus freeing him for artistic achievement. And so, perhaps, it was with Yersin.

TO FRIENDS, COLLABORATORS, EVEN LONGTIME COLLEAGUES, he was always simply "Yersin," his first name a mystery until publication of his obituaries in 1943. Through his fierceness, his lifelong self-imposed exile from home, his pride, and his committed friendships with children, one senses a loneliness that could only be assuaged by work, by immersion in what felt manageable.

He dressed simply and, in the handful of surviving photographs, can be seen posing stiff backed, uncertain and unsmiling.

He eschewed alcohol, secured his pocket watch to his belt loop with a length of household string, taught himself astronomy, and, in old age, grew to love airplanes. At the age of eight, in an early display of passion for scientific research, he killed his mother's cat. He secured the noose to a ceiling timber, dragged a table underneath, set out a bowl of chopped steak, and enticed the cat onward. While the animal ate he inched the noose under the chin and over the ears, and watched the rope cord divide the downy throat fur. And then, before the cat could even look up, the boy hooked his fingers under the table edge and pulled hard. Fifteen minutes later he had the animal spreadeagled on the breadboard, its belly scissored open, spleen and heart sectioned and numbered, swabbing blood, urine, and feces onto microscope slides.

The same year, his sense of destiny forming, he discovered a trunk belonging to his late father wedged behind suitcases in a far corner of the attic of his home at Morges, Switzerland. The boy as detective, sifting the past, alive to its freight and meaning, found much that was mundane—razors, shoehorns, a balding hairbrush—but also other items that seemed to speak directly to him, that felt perhaps as though his father had planted them there, certain that his son would sooner or later come looking. These were the tools of the naturalist's profession, the scalpels and calipers and microscopes his father used in his studies of insects. To the boy, turning them over and over in his hands, testing their mechanisms and examining the manufacturers' stamps in the dim attic light, they must have felt smooth, quickly warm, as if they'd not long left his father's hands.

But it was in adventure that the adult Yersin became himself, finally managing to shuck the carapace of shyness and social awkwardness that weighed so heavily on him in Europe. Among people who knew nothing of science or Paris, or of the pressures exerted on the young man by an ambitious family, Yersin flowered. He became charming, candid, humorous, relaxed. Gone was the weary boy of Paris, who'd confided morosely in his mother that he only liked one painting in the Louvre, and that for its "desolation and sadness"; in his place was an explorer in the Livingstone cast, effortlessly courageous, able to see beyond the jingoistic posturings of his colonial over-lords to the humanity in each situation and confrontation.

To begin with, his forays into the interior of French Indo-china—funded by a government anxious to map the unknown interiors of its colonial possessions—were restricted to periods of shore leave as a ship doctor, a job he held for only a year before, in December 1891, being made a colonial doctor, a post that offered almost endless scope for exploration. And it was for these escapes—becoming the first European to penetrate the interior mountains, struggling to find porters bold enough to risk facing both pirates and leeches, the adrenaline rush of knowing that any night they might be the object of rebel attack—that, increasingly, he lived. By contrast the quotidian grind of doctoring began to grate. To his mother he wrote: "You ask me if I have developed a taste for medical practice. Yes and no. I have great pleasure in curing people who come to see me but I don't really want to become a doctor, to make money out of being a doctor. . . . I find it vile and repugnant to ask money for curing people. It's a bit like saying, 'Your money or your life.'"

The maps he made during these journeys of the early 1890s were painstaking and topographically impressive, and were seized upon by contemporary geographers. On each return from the wilderness he was pushed for intelligence, the latest news on tribal rivalries, for descriptions of mountain ranges and river courses that no other white man had ever seen. Faced with such respect—as in June 1892, when he dined with the French governor in Phnom Penh—Yersin appeared genuinely nonplussed rather than calculatedly overmodest. "Everyone here," he wrote his mother even as he digested the governor's *foie gras*—"thinks I've done an extraordinary trip. I really don't believe it was that special. No one seems to believe that I've lived two months on rice alone and yet the indigenous population are forced to live on rice."

These were years of tempering, a distillation of his essence, a necessary preparation for all that was to come. In June 1893, deep in the interior, he surprised a cache of anticolonial rebels, an ambush that resulted in his single-handedly fending off the outlaws while his men fled into the jungle. Recovering in the hospital, his spirit unbroken, Yersin began to plan his next foray: his biggest-ever expedition, at the head of a team of seventy porters and soldiers, a journey that would last some three months, and during which, on account of an unexplained village fire, he would be accused of witchcraft and once again only just manage to escape with his life.

He remains a conundrum, an amalgam of the heroic and the clumsy, a man who could face up to bandits but who found even the smallest party an insufferable ordeal, for whom one rejection in love was enough to warn him off women for life. He was complex, unfathomable often even to his friends. Yet the eight-year-old capable of a chilling degree of forensic detachment would become a man of honor and courage, absolutely loyal. He was a fierce patriot and was born at a time when colonial excesses were at their most pernicious, yet he was never heard to denigrate another on grounds of race or skin color. During one period of doctoring he was robbed continually by his patients, yet found it impossible to condemn them: "We the French have always stolen from the people in Indochina, so it might be quite good that they can steal a bit of my money back."

All this, and only thirty years old: For most people, even the more adventurous of his contemporaries, such achievements would have been enough for eighty years.

BY CONTRAST, SHIBASABURO KITASATO APPEARS UNAMBIGUOUS; a man of formidable scientific intellect, he would become one of his country's first and most celebrated microbiologists. Born in a mountain village in southern Japan in 1852, he was sufficiently renowned at the age of thirty-three to be picked by the Japanese government to travel to Berlin to study under the genius tutelage of Robert Koch, the first foreigner to do so. The extension of his stay from three to six years was due to Koch's personal intervention: Kitasato's work on tetanus had been so groundbreaking that Koch successfully petitioned the Emperor of Japan for Kitasato to be allowed to remain. His return to Japan in 1892 was equally auspicious: Before leaving Koch's laboratory, the German government awarded him the title of professor, the first such honor ever accorded a foreign scientist.

And then, in the first months of 1894, bubonic plague hit Hong Kong, the world's fourth largest merchant and passenger port, a British colony. Plague, which had destroyed the European population during the fourteenth century—and had exploded in sporadic, ferocious outbreaks ever since—had returned, and at the very moment when medicine was beginning to grow complacent, to congratulate itself on the progress achieved so far in the war against disease.

Worse still, there was no cure. Terrified that plague would escape from Hong Kong and that in time nowhere would be safe, the island government appealed for help. The eminent Kitasato, by now acclaimed as the first scientist to have obtained a pure culture of the tetanus bacillus and as the pioneer of antitetanus vaccination, set sail from Japan less than a week after his government received Hong Kong's Mayday. For the Pasteur Institute in Paris only one researcher fit the bill. Yersin may have been young, but few possessed the kind of bravery and clearsightedness he had already demonstrated. On June 12, 1894, he sailed from Saigon, Hong Kong–bound.

· 1 ·

NO DISEASE IN RECORDED HISTORY HAS CARRIED THE TOTEMIC
power of plague. No disease has erupted with such violence
and eradicated populations so quickly and with such brutal efficiency, or remained so poorly understood for so long. Plague
has inspired more literature than any other epidemic, has set
humans against one another in a way normally only witnessed
during the darkest hours of war. It has transcended itself to
become emblematic of something far more invasive and apocalyptic than mere infection; the word itself—*plague*—deserves a
paragraph all its own, to be printed in twenty-six-point type, a
warning in and of itself. Time has made it more: collective
noun for any malevolent force: locusts, warplanes, hurricane

rains. And verb for the worst that one person can do to another, *to plague* being "to torment, to drive insane."

For centuries the disease was so feared that *plague* as an uttered word, as a single quiet syllable, was held to carry a unique power. Simply to murmur it was thought to risk unleashing the infection, and so, in 1745, Frederick the Great forbade his generals from using the word, insisting instead on the gentler, less-panic-inducing "foul fever." Later, pseudonyms grew ever more various, more unlikely: "typhoid pneumonia," "croupous pneumonia," "intermittent fever."

Most commonly plague was explained as an act of God, a punishment for wickedness and shortcoming. To the credulous and superstitious Europeans of the Middle Ages, the ravages of the mid-fourteenth century pandemic, the Black Death, were just retribution for any number of transgressions: heresy, lechery, avarice, episcopal decadence, the greed of kings, the drunkenness of the peasantry. And for those whose neighborhoods remained plague-free, almost anything was quakingly read as portent: heavy mist, falling stars, blasts of hot wind from the south, blood spots on freshly baked bread, a stranded whale.

Ignorance about the causes of plague created a vacuum through which wildly competing theories coursed, each with their vigorous and persuasive proponents, their noisy gainsayers. In the Middle Ages thought was split: Plague could be caught either from another person or from a "miasma," a kind of atmospheric corruption. This was an infinitely broad and accommodating category, and consequently the most popular: Corruption of the air was believed to be caused either by organic decay or by such natural calamities as earthquakes or noxious gases escaping from fissures in the ground. For those who held that contagion spread person-to-person, the only security lay in isolation. Safest still, if a certain physician from Montpellier was to be believed, was to remain blindfolded throughout the epidemic. "Instantaneous death occurs when the aerial spirit escaping from the eyes of the sick man strikes the eyes of a healthy person standing near and looking at the sick, especially when the latter are in agony."

Each time plague reared up again, this centuries-old controversy was revived. By the nineteenth century the two camps were no closer to agreement, and an outbreak lasting from 1834 to 1835—which claimed thirty-two thousand lives as it spread from Alexandria to Cairo—triggered a spate of medical publications by Europe's most respected physicians. Records survive of one doctor—a stalwart of the contagionist school—who never ventured out during the epidemic without a posse of four mounted servants to protect him from chance contact with plague cases. He wore a protective suit with a mantle of oilcloth, and covered his saddle with waxed material. When diagnosing and treating patients, he made sure never to touch their bare skin, preferring instead to dip his fingers in oil, wrap them in tobacco leaves, and only then to attempt to feel the pulse. His best efforts notwithstanding, he was dead of plague within the year.

Most physicians' attempts to understand plague amounted to little more than wild fumblings, their theories born more of prejudice and fear than educated calculation. For millennia— through the pandemics of the sixth and fourteenth centuries, through countless more localized epidemics—the disease had maintained absolute supremacy, a fixed point around which scientists and doctors flailed blindly, inventing ever more preposterous experiments to prove their hypotheses. And so, in the 1830s, during the Egyptian outbreak, French advocates of the contagionist theory devised a series of trials that, had they been conducted today, would have caused the severing of diplomatic relations, trade embargoes, and petitions to UN human rights committees. In one experiment a condemned criminal was injected with pus from a plague bubo, his progress thereafter closely monitored. His continued good health must have cheered the next criminal to be plucked from death row, since all this unfortunate had to do was sleep in a hospital cot in which another had died of plague. When, shortly afterward, he developed the listless fever, the blood-stained sputum, the bloated and cyanosed face common to all plague victims, the scientists claimed proof: Here was a disease propagated by putrefaction; the only quicker way to contract it would have been to lie alongside the decaying corpse itself.

By the late nineteenth century, the field had become crowded: With no empirical research in place and no proven technique or concrete lead, the proponents of all competing theories held equal sway. Having made little headway since the fourteenth century, authorities—depending on their religious or cultural persuasion—explained plague as any one of the following: an infection brought on by the wrath of God, by corruption of the air or soil, by overcrowding and filth, by a general or specific moral laxity, by a straightforward person-to-person contagion, by a particular alignment of stars, by a stifling climate, by proximity to putrefying corpses—as in the case of the vaults and catacombs of Cairo, where the annual Nile floods saw body parts washed past bathers, washerwomen, and children splashing in the shallows. Methods of prevention were as various as the causes: judiciously worn dried toads, amulets filled with arsenic, lockets containing camphor or eucalyptus. But the safest and simplest means of warding off plague, according to brothers George and John Thomson—working in Bombay in the early 1900s as the Hong Kong plague turned global—was to throw open the window. The "virulence of the germ," they claimed, was neutralized by a "sufficiency of fresh air."

But scientific memory can be woefully short. By the 1890s plague had been almost forgotten, part of the folklore of Dark Age horrors. Since 1835, with the Egyptian outbreak having petered out as mysteriously as it had begun, there had been only sporadic and limited episodes, meager enough in scale and effect to relegate plague to the lower division of dangerous diseases. And so the news from southern China and Hong Kong in the late spring of 1894, that plague was resurgent, came not only as a powerful jolt—a sickening sense, as with approaching war, that boundaries and all the best human efforts counted for nothing—but as the ultimate challenge: Of all diseases plague was the most dreaded. The wake-up call from Hong Kong proved to be the spur to a heroic and largely forgotten scientific endeavor and one that, moreover, resonates powerfully today. Even now plague is a disease that, as in the quiet years before 1894, is—in the words of one contemporary frontline researcher—merely dormant, "down but not out."

· 2 ·

IN THE FIVE WEEKS SINCE PLAGUE HAD BEEN CONFIRMED AND
the deaths had begun escalating, Hong Kong had been transformed. Where before had been the constant motion of liveried
porters unloading trunks from visitors from as far afield as the
United States, Singapore, London, and Japan, now there was
unholy quiet, customs posts manned by skeleton crews, the
only quayside movement visible from the deck of an approaching ship the slow shuffle onward of coffin bearers, heads down,
shoulders bowed, feet dragging eddies of dust.

From ebullience to fear, confidence to suspicion, neighbor
against neighbor, European against Chinese. For Hong Kong
in 1894, though only fifty-three years into its colonial role, was

already a port of international significance and renown: From two thousand fishermen in 1841 this "barren rock" so comprehensively damned by Britain's foreign secretary Lord Palmerston had become home to a hundred times that. Writers of tourist guidebooks spoke wonderingly of the "pleasant but mild excitement combined with feelings of contentment and security" that the fortunate visitor would experience when first approaching the island. Hoteliers, fully aware of the colony's attractions, clambered over one another to pull in customers. The Hong Kong Hotel, overlooking Victoria Harbor, boasted "Hydraulic Ascending Rooms of the latest and most approved type"; for the Windsor Hotel the draws were the architecture—"finest in the colony"—and the cuisine—"under European supervision."

Most Europeans, however, paid scant attention to either the landscape or the hotels' decor: For them a Hong Kong posting was part of a carefully judged career strategy. For Sir William Goodman, who would become chief justice of the Hong Kong Supreme Court, the decision to leave a respectable but unremarkable bar practice in the London suburbs and "look for some appointment in the Colonies" was put down to an "anxiousness about my professional outlook." For the young James Stewart Lockhart, setting sail for Hong Kong in 1879, the expectation was of fortunes to be made, claims staked, just as several of his Argyll relatives had done in the colony before him. Like Goodman, Lockhart was methodical in his ambition: two years in Guangzhou to study Cantonese— the necessary leg-up over monolingual colleagues— before his first Hong Kong government appointment. By 1894, the year plague struck, he would be acting colonial secretary, struggling to keep order when all around was panic, flight, and mob violence.

The life led by the colonial overlords was leisured and gracious, if socially restricted. The European upper classes mixed neither with other whites of lesser social standing nor with the Chinese. Instead—for reasons of climate as much as snobbery—they retreated uphill, to the cool mountainous slopes overlooking the harbor, where they built great verandaed mansions and shady arboretums. Here in the "Peak District," on vast sprinklered lawns, in front of stuccoed palaces, lifting tumblers of fresh-squeezed lemonade from silver trays, women in white dresses spent the afternoons playing croquet. Their children—those not yet old enough to have been dispatched by steamer to boarding school in England—trailed in silent lines along paths sheltered from the midday sun by camphor and high citrus trees, governesses at front and back. Come evening, with the children asleep, there would be dinner parties, concerts, bridge fours: the same faces uttering similar platitudes, with only the electric rattle of insects just beyond the screen doors to break the spell, to remind them that they were not in fact at home in comfortable Dorking or Harrow.

The maintenance of European life and custom was an uncertain process that involved a good degree of wishful thinking. For as long as they kept themselves loftily separate on the slopes of the Peak, the Europeans could persuade themselves that the other world did not exist: the Hong Kong of crowded tenement housing, where animals slept in the same rooms as their masters, where cholera was a constant menace, where a combination of careless and insanitary living, serious overcrowding,

and a high rat population was fast creating the perfect breeding
ground for plague.

Of the white population, only the workingman had inter-
course with the Chinese: It was the foot soldiers and wharf
laborers who frequented Chinese brothels; the bureaucrats and
office workers, businessmen, and more senior military ranks
used their surplus pay on European or American prostitutes.

When they grew tired of whoring, on-leave sailors and merchant seamen caroused their way through central Hong Kong,
staggering from door to door, throwing money at whichever
householder had alcohol to sell. Like wayward magnets, they
were attracted most often to the island's least salubrious quarter, the all-Chinese Taipingshan, an area so famously insanitary that, when plague erupted there in the spring of 1894, it
was impossible for anyone to feign surprise. Through here,
throughout the small hours, disheveled ships' crews of all
nationalities danced chaotically to the hornpipe, hollering out
rough approximations of a sea shanty. Their arrival in port was
dreaded by resident Europeans, and no doubt by most Chinese.
"They drink like fishes," lamented a Wesleyan missionary just
weeks before plague broke out. "They ride around in rickshaws, making the night hideous with their shouts, eat overripe
fruit from street stalls, are stricken with cholera, and die in a
few hours."

In their drive toward self-obliteration these incautious revel-
ers failed to notice the fatigue and resignation on the faces of
the Chinese who served them, who silently offered shot glasses
of hooch and, just as quietly, palmed the proffered dollars. For
behind the doorways in which they stood were buildings in

which no European—of however humble birth or expectation—would ever have countenanced living.

Taipingshan covered ten acres: 384 scrappily built brick houses wedged against a sharply sloping hillside, the "Great Peace Mountain." Because of the incline, the back of the ground floor of each dwelling was subterranean and therefore windowless; the floor was of earth, and often damp. Above were two, sometimes three stories, whose floors were fitted with rough boards through which detritus, liquid, and dust fell freely, and it was in box partitions in these upper rooms that nine or ten whole families would bed down: five or six individuals at a time, children and a cross-section of generations and all their possessions, shoehorned into a space some twelve feet square. Rooms more than fourteen feet high were subdivided both vertically and horizontally, a practice that not only provided another floor but also cast into sepulchral darkness the partitions and families below. With no chimney, the air was opaque and choking with cooking smoke, the atmosphere hot and fetid from the smoldering urns of pig fat, rendered from hogs that, deprived of their own rooting space, spent their short lives making their sties in their owners' bedrooms. What water there was came from wells that even the Chinese considered hazardous to health. In short, Taipingshan was an entire district that was not only a potent reservoir of everyday illness but a place where contagion, once started, would prove impossible to stop.

Yet, over the years, there had been warning voices. As early as 1851, only a decade into the colony's life, the colonial surgeon was using his annual report to lament the "dirty and gregarious habits of the people and the pestilential defects in the construction and situation of their dwellings." Twenty-one years later, the new appointee to the post, Dr. Philip Ayres, found that little had changed: Brothels were breeding typhoid; Chinese houses, whose construction flouted "every rule," were "not fit for pigs"; most sewage drains were simply allowed to peter out at the end of the street, excreta leaching into the sub-soil. Yet again, no action was taken: Due to opium addiction Ayres himself was held to be an unreliable witness, and his report was buried.

By 1882, when Osbert Chadwick from London's Institute of Civil Engineers was sent to Hong Kong expressly to study and report back on the worsening overcrowding and attendant chaotic sanitation, conditions had deteriorated to a point where language almost failed him. "The system of house drainage," he sighed, "is radically bad." There was a bare handful of pub-lic latrines; the water supply was inadequate; what sewage made it to drainage culverts ended up straight in the harbor. Government should shake itself to action, he counseled. "My report will show the necessity for strong and complete mea-sures of sanitation, and I trust that they will be undertaken for the immediate benefit of the public health without waiting for the necessity to be demonstrated by the irresistible logic of an epidemic."

Despite the mounting evidence in favor of a radical cleanup, the next few years were marked by bureaucratic procrastina-tion, not decisive action: the passing of a public health ordi-nance, the appointment of a sanitation board, then endless arguments over its scope and power. Then yet more ordi-nances, the insertion of careful subsidiary clauses, followed by yet another sanitary study. The "unreliable" Dr. Ayres, after an

1893 house inspection, seemed close to despair. "The floors were reeking with filth. The drainage was very bad, the smell abominable. In some of the houses were dark holes in which there were quantities of decomposing and putrid meat, fat, and bones, and one of them filled with maggots. The stench was unbearable. I found [these houses] in the same condition I had reported twenty years ago."

The cumulative effect of decades of unheeded warnings was a kind of collective numbness among the European population, an indifference heightened by the fact that, during the same period, their own health and sanitation had steadily improved. The numbers being invalided home were falling, streets in the white districts were wider, and drainage more efficient. And with this came confidence—long afternoons whiled away at the Happy Valley Racecourse, evenings at the Hong Kong Jockey Club. For government officials and doctors, civil engineers and town planners, for all those who had so effectively silenced their professional consciences, the life of these last days was an easeful, leisured existence.

AND FEW PARTIED HARDER THAN JAMES LOWSON, SUPERINtendent of the showpiece Government Civil Hospital, a giant white-porticoed monolith on the lower slopes of the Peak. Entries in his diary are brief, often telegraphic, but preciously illuminative of this life of the privileged classes.

The year started busily, as it would continue. On Saturday, January 6, 1894, Lowson, one of the colony's most gifted sportsmen, wrote, "Cricket. Made 107 + 3 for 23. Maxim Gun Corps." A week later he was skippering "Stella, Paddy May's yacht . . . came in first." There were golf tournaments, balls, nightly dinner parties, all of them noted. Friends and acquaintances were mentioned in often cursory fashion, with some abruptness, surnames only. "Atkinson left at 5.30 for Canton with Pearson and his womenkind." The flippancy discernible in that "womenkind" is evident elsewhere as well: In his description of an acquaintance being accidentally knocked over by a gun as "amusing"; in his free admission to another that he "did not care a tinker's dam [*sic*] for him"; in his dismissal of the suffering of yet another with the perfunctory "tired of life—cheer up."

Lowson was at the top of the colonial ladder, and so, when plague was first reported across the border in Canton, he would have known that this, of all medical matters, was not something happily left to a subordinate: He'd have had no choice but to investigate personally. On Saturday, May 5, a day when he would normally have been contentedly pulling on his cricket whites in preparation for a weekend at the crease, he was in Canton, conferring with worried local doctors. By Monday he was back in Hong Kong, where rumor had preceded him, and there was little he could do to stifle speculation. Plague had leaped the Chinese border. The Black Death was back. The world was no longer safe.

· 3 ·

JAMES ALFRED LOWSON WAS STILL TWO MONTHS SHORT OF HIS twenty-eighth birthday when he made his first, reluctant diagnosis of plague. From photographs he appears older, tougher skinned, suspicious. In one, the closest to an unposed snapshot that survives, he sits on the edge of what looks like a hotel bed, possibly in Canton during that early long plague weekend.

The shot has the spontaneous, rickety feel of a self-timed pose, although of course such technology was many years off. He is wearing a silk jacket, in style a Western-Chinese hybrid, with Chinese fasteners in place of buttons, and a V-cut Savile Row collar. His legs are crossed, hands folded in his lap. His hair is combed flat to his head, with a rigid, straight-ruled part.

He wears a long, down-angled moustache and is looking over the photographer's shoulder at a point high up, near the ceiling. In certain immediate ways he is unusual looking, and it is not hard to imagine how his misaligned eyes and sour-fruit mouth could make an outsider feel profoundly ill at ease and unwelcome, a fumbling gate-crasher.

On Monday, May 7, 1894, Lowson and his fellow investigators climbed aboard the ferry that would return them from Canton, down the Pearl River, to Hong Kong. They arrived back that afternoon. "In club at 6pm," his diary reads. "Rumours of plague." In the early hours of Tuesday, rumor became fact, with Lowson's positive Hong Kong identification: "1 a.m. diagnosed A. Hung as suffering from the plague and isolated him."

EXACTLY ONE WEEK LATER ALEXANDRE YERSIN——IGNORANT OF the escalating emergency in Hong Kong—arrived in Saigon anticipating a long and much needed period of rest. The previous three months had seen the most ambitious and grueling of his expeditions so far, an exploration of the uncharted region between Nha Trang and Tourane. During those weeks he had passed through lands belonging to tribes who had never before seen a white man, many of whose people had—fearing diabolical, pale-skinned witchcraft—barricaded their village gates against his approach. The report he handed to the colonial authorities was notable for its balance and restraint—despite its author's ordeal—and was also rich in detail, analysis, description: of the topography of the plains and mountains, of the customs and beliefs of each tribe he encountered, of the possibility of a colossal haul of gold, of the need for a fairer tax system.

From the report one gets the impression of a young man bent on extreme exploration, as obsessed by geographical exactitude as by notions of racial fairness. With his letters home, though, the focus narrows: His "dream," he tells his mother, is to "follow the trail of Livingstone." Yet, during this time, Yersin was, through official channels, pursuing a quite separate goal.

For at least forty years plague had been a constant menace in the southern states of China—flaring up, then abating, never completely disappearing. As early as 1850 the *Overland Friend of China,* an old-school colonial newspaper, reported that Canton "and the neighbouring towns and villages are afflicted by a malignant fever . . . [that] resembles the plague which desolated London two centuries ago. . . . We are in hopes that it will not extend to Europeans." More detail, of a more measured kind, was forthcoming in 1889, with the publication of the British government's *Imperial Maritime Customs' Annual Report,* which claimed that Yunnan Province, northwest of Canton, had "suffered annually for a period of years from the plague, a kind of malignant fever, fatal in a few days, having as one of its symptoms a hard swelling on the neck, in the armpits, or in the groin." Rats and cattle were conspicuous casualties; immunity, apparently, was conferred by altitude: Plague "rarely scales heights over 7,200 feet high."

Ever since his arrival in Indochina in 1892, Yersin—in common with every alert traveler—had been aware of the presence of plague in the region. Within weeks of his arrival he was petitioning the French governor-general, Jean-Marie de Lanessan, requesting permission to leave for Yunnan to study the disease: Clearly, he told Lanessan, himself a former doctor, prompt action was required. He could start, he pledged, as soon as he returned from his first, eagerly anticipated, journey into the Vietnamese interior.

The response from Lanessan was swift and brutal, a breathtaking demonstration of how far behind he'd left his Hippocratic roots. "There has never been plague in Yunnan," he replied flatly. "And if there were, I would deny it. We put poor old Tonkin [the northernmost region of Vietnam, bordering China's Yunnan Province] down enough without laying plague at its door as well."

Yersin, running short of time before the start of his expedition, and powerless against such determined high-level resistance, quietly withdrew, aware that another angle of attack was needed. In fact, as he later wrote in his notes for the Pasteur Institute, "Plague was no longer raging exclusively in Yunnan, but had reached Long-Tcheou and Pakhoï . . . the whole frontier of Tonkin was threatened." But alone he could not supply sufficient leverage: To Lanessan, intent above all on short-term political expediency, on the diplomacy of minimum offense, Yersin—with his irritating whine about some obscure, long-dead disease—was as a persistent mosquito, a trivial distraction from the real business of government.

Away in the mountains, at the start of a four-month trek that would take him some two hundred miles inland from coastal Nha Trang, through jungle ranges to the Mekong, and then down the great sweeping caramel river to Phnom Penh, Yersin's determination was hardening. Laboratory life, he now knew, was not for him. "My firm intention is never again to work at the Pasteur Institute. I spent enough time there . . . and now that I am far away, I can judge it more objectively. Life in a laboratory would seem impossible to me after having tasted the freedom and life of the open air."

Moreover it is clear from the laconic tone of his letters that physical danger never once threatened to overwhelm him, as it might have done with a more normal, more fearful man. Days when Yersin's party was attacked are detailed precisely, but without notable emotion. Events unfold, speak for themselves, are almost comic in their understatement. On June 24, 1893, high in the mountains, he and his men set off after a band of rebels led by one Thouk, "armed with machetes, spears, and rifles," whose plan, Yersin learned, was to massacre the French in Phan Rang. "Of course," he writes, "I had to act." A day later, his own men once again having fled, Yersin not for the first time found himself alone with the enemy. Runs his dead-pan summation: 'I only [now] had to fight the five chiefs.' His success resulted in the rebel leader's execution, which Yersin was invited to watch. "Beyond any doubt," he would write, the death of Thouk "was a gruesome sight. His head fell after the fourth saber blow. [He] did not even budge. These Annamese die with a truly impressive coolness."

BY OCTOBER 1893 YERSIN WAS BACK IN SAIGON AND GEARING UP for another assault on the governor-general. This time, how-ever, he was armed with fresh intelligence: Word had reached him that during his absence Lanessan had received an unequiv-ocal ministerial despatch from Paris, ordering him to send a plague researcher to Yunnan. All Yersin had to do was put himself forward.

Buoyed by this information, Yersin would have arrived in confident mood for his audience with the governor-general. Since his return from the mountains he'd become something of a celebrity in the colonial capital, his heroic singlehanded defeat of Thouk's rebels discussed in awed tones at dinner parties, in the marketplace, on the croquet lawn.

And Yersin, in turn, was growing visibly in presence and confidence: The shy young man of Paris, diffident in the company of his peers, had been transformed. For the first time in his life—many thousands of miles and a whole new culture from the land of his birth—he felt at home.

Yet, despite the orders from Paris, his meeting with the governor-general resulted in as much frustration as before. Lanessan, who had first questioned even the existence of plague, now used cost as his reason for obstruction.

"Who," he demanded, "will pay the bill?"

"The colony," replied Yersin, who had no reason to believe any different, and whose astonishment at the governor-general's reaction was such that he recorded the exchange verbatim in his official report. "The colony would cover it, I would think."

"If you think that," Lanessan shot back, "then you are wrong. You are very wrong."

FEW NEWS STORIES FROM ANY AGE HAVE EXCITED JOURNALISTS more than an outbreak of plague, and it took less than twenty-four hours for the first Hong Kong reporter to catch wind of

James Lowson's initial diagnosis. By midday on May 9, 1894, there would have been no one in the colony ignorant of the *Telegraph*'s front-page bulletin. "A fatal disease," the paper announced, "somewhat similar in its effects to the 'black fever,' which has carried off thousands of the natives of Canton during the past month . . . has, we regret to learn, made its appearance among the Chinese residents in the Taipingshan district."

Few diseases have ever been more feared, and so it was only inevitable that those with the most to lose should have been the quickest to voice denials. According to the *Telegraph*, the government, in the person of the registrar of deaths, had moved swiftly to quash any mention of plague, "courteously informing us that the deaths in Taipingshan district today are . . . from diarrhoea, phthisis, bronchitis, etc.; none from plague." Such, however, was the reliability of the paper's source that this was not the last word. "In Chinese circles," the report concluded, "the existence of a very fatal disease of some kind in Taipingshan is insisted upon."

A day later, with panic rising in the crowded Chinese quarter, the government was resolutely sticking to its story. On May 10, the *Hong Kong Daily Press*, without any discernible hint of irony, reported some forty deaths in Taipingshan in the previous two days, a mortality rate that the authorities apparently judged unremarkable. "On enquiry with the Registrar-General's department, we find that no suspicious deaths have been reported, and that no information has been received—although enquiries were carried out—which justifies any apprehension that an epidemic is likely to break out."

For much of the mid–nineteenth century—from 1851, a decade after the birth of the colony, till the early 1870s—the

Hong Kong Chinese, in their treatment of terminal illness, had unwittingly done pretty much all they could to breed sickness. The worst such example was the I-ts'z, a temple-cum–death house in the center of Taipingshan: Behind the shroud of blue incense in the main hall were eight cubicles, rented out to the families of the dying, where, in garments gone cheesy with sweat and feces, unattended by any kind of regular doctor, the sick would wait for death.

To the Chinese, few things were guaranteed to confer uncleanliness more effectively than proximity to someone close to death: hence the I-ts'z, where the dying were abandoned. It took the colonial authorities a good eighteen years to register properly the inhumanity and full medical horror of the I-ts'z, and that only by chance, during the course of an investigation into the death of a valued worker from the emigration depot who had expired in sub-Dickensian squalor in the spring of 1869.

The dubious honor of recording the gruesomeness of the I-ts'z fell to Alfred Lister, registrar general.

At my first visit there were, dead and alive, about nine or ten patients in the so-called hospital. One, apparently dying from emaciation and diarrhoea, was barricaded into a place just large enough to hold the board on which he lay, and not high enough to stand up in, another room contained a boarding on which lay two poor creatures half-dead, and one corpse, while the floor, which was of earth, was covered in pools of urine. The next room contained what the attendants asserted to be two corpses, but on examination one of them was found to be alive . . . the other rooms contained miserable and emaciated creations, unable to speak or move, whose rags had apparently never been changed since their admission, and whom the necessities of nature had reduced to an inexpressibly sickening condition.

Lister's revelations had repercussions far beyond the slew of ghoulish headlines in the next morning's papers. Within the ranks of the colonial bureaucracy, the search for a scapegoat was immediately triggered; when the news reached London it was held up as further evidence of the abuses of the "coolie trade." Policemen stormed the I-ts'z, removed the dead, and sent those still breathing to the Government Civil Hospital. They then forbade the building to be used as anything other than a temple, a ruling that led to a buildup of corpses and the dying on street corners, of abandoned and putrescent bodies aswarm with crawling things, slimy with decay.

The governor at the time, Richard MacDonnell, ordered action: specifically, a hospital set up for and funded by the Chinese. Raising the necessary $15,000 would not be a problem, he believed; for evidence of the "great wealth" of the Hong Kong Chinese, one need look no further than the large sums spent on "their puerile national processions and 'shows' every year." The Chinese, for their part, chose to overlook the governor's slight and came up with double: $30,000, to which the government added a further $115,000.

THE TUNG WAH HOSPITAL—TREATING PATIENTS WITH TRADI-tional Chinese methods, eschewing the Western model in every detail right down to its accounting system—opened in February 1872. For the first time in Hong Kong, Chinese medicine was made respectable. At the Tung Wah, as on most street corners, treatment was with herbs, the philosophy one of balance between yin and yang, a disequilibrium of which would spark disease. The organs were classified according to the five elements of the universe—gold for the lung, wood for the liver, water for the kidney, fire for the heart, and earth for the stomach and spleen—and could react with one another in the same way as the elements themselves. It was a system distinguished above all by curiosities: Feeling the pulse, among the most important of all diagnostic practices, was impossible with a nonconsenting female patient, and so a length of string would be tied around her wrist; the doctor, holding the other end, would somehow manage to gauge her well-being. For the Western physician witnessing such eccentricities, the reaction was invariably the same: To Dr. Philip Ayres, Chinese methods were "nothing but empiricism and quackery."

Much the same could fairly have been said of the kind of practices adopted by Dr. Ayres and his colleagues. When plague hit, the European doctors—all the while brazenly boasting of their expertise and their preeminence in the face of rampant infection—adopted a sweeping approach that spoke most eloquently about the extent of their ignorance. Furniture was burned, clothing soaked in disinfectant, interior walls whitewashed; eventually nothing but wholesale demolition of the plague district was deemed sufficient. Hardly surprising, in short, that the Tung Wah Hospital should have been driven to the point where it found itself encouraging open rebellion against the government, a move that led to swift retaliation: the mooring of a fully armed gunboat just offshore, its cannons trained on the roof of the Chinese hospital.

· 4 ·

A SOLDIER WITH A BOX CAMERA STANDS AT THE TOP OF A NAR-
row back alley. Below him, halfway down the sharp incline,
between houses shuttered and barred, are ten others: sleeves
rolled up, white helmets brilliant in the heat, smoking pipes to
disguise the stench of the work. The soldier raises the camera
to his eye, composes the shot. As he presses the shutter, he
thinks perhaps that this could be home, that the old Chinese
woman looking on, dismayed as her clothes are plunged into
disinfectant, could be his own grandmother, the street itself a
slum in any northern town. And yet the scene feels reassuringly
foreign, too, the plague he and his military fellows are engaged
in fighting is so clearly the product of Oriental neglect and slat-

ternly Chinese housekeeping. He puts his camera away and reaches for his broom, roused to action by the sudden hollering of the color sergeant—the thought might cross his mind that they deserve all this, the intrusion, their homes turned upside-down, the forced entry and eviction. They should consider themselves lucky.

The soldier and the three hundred or so other plague fighters from the Shropshire Light Infantry did not know that less than a week into the epidemic, something close to panic was infecting high command. Safe in the cocoon of his orders—to search every house, douse clothing and bedding and furniture with disinfectant, to ignore any plea or protestation from the householders—the soldier would have been unaware of the wild fumbling that distinguished the government's first attempts at curbing the spread of disease. On May 11, two days after the first apocalyptic headline, James Lowson and Philip Ayres—the colony's most senior doctors, and a pair united in their distaste for political doublespeak—were called as witnesses before an extraordinary meeting of the sanitation board. Their joint report detailed their visit the day before to the Tung Wah, where they'd rooted out no less than twenty cases of plague. And still—despite Lowson's firsthand testimony from Canton, where he'd seen the hospitals filled to their entrance halls with the moaning and feverish, all displaying identical symptoms to those now dying in Hong Kong—the committee chairman remained skeptically aloof. Throughout, he studiously avoided using the word *plague,* as if just to utter it might bring it into being. Instead, the transcripts show him opting for laborious euphemisms: *epidemic, endemic disease, contagious disease.*

He need not have bothered. Fearing Chinese reprisals for the forced "cleansing" of their homes, European doctors had taken to carrying revolvers on their rounds, their pockets weighty and percussive with shells. In New York, Buenos Aires, and London, owners of shipping lines were tracing nervous fingers across the maritime charts, looking at alternative Far Eastern harbors: Shanghai, Saigon, Manila. The word was out: Hong Kong was unsafe, had become within the space of days a leprous brother, excluded from the international family.

It must have been at least in part an effort at wresting back some measure of control that led Sir William Robinson, governor of the colony since 1891, to put out a plea for help. Plague was looming unmanageable, that much he could see. And despite their bold assertions to the contrary, his own doctors clearly understood little of its mechanics, causes, or how it spread. To his cry for assistance, the world's finest responded: Professor Shibasaburo Kitasato, celebrated for his discovery of the tetanus bacillus; and Dr. Alexandre Yersin, explorer of the dark Indochinese interior, diphtheria pioneer, and as rough-edged a maverick as Kitasato was sleek, proper, and establishment.

The two men were similar in only one regard: the quality of their professional commitment and dedication. Kitasato was eleven years older and, from photographs taken during his time in Hong Kong, appears a somewhat dour forty-two-year-old; the thirty-one-year-old Yersin, by contrast, seems serious but not without humility, some sense of his place in things. One snapshot shows the Japanese and eight European doctors, posed for a team photograph, Kitasato sitting right in the center. More than anything the photograph bespeaks the welcome Kitasato—or "the Professor," as the colony's newspapers would deferentially refer to him—received from Hong Kong's foremost physicians. Flanking the lone Japanese are Ayres, the extravagantly mustachioed colonial surgeon; Lowson, Kitasato's greatest champion and ally; and six other top surgeons and doctors. What pervades is an air of quiet self-congratulation. Kitasato's pose is slouched, his head tilted back and eyes half closed, the straw boater at rest casually in his lap, his fingertips caressing the brim.

To European eyes, accustomed to the slighter build of most Chinese, Kitasato was comically stocky, even freakish. One newspaper early on described him as "a short-haired and profound-looking gentleman with a very large head." Yet, despite his outsize cranium, Kitasato's personality, appearance, and professional approach appealed to the Hong Kong establishment. Not being French, he was thus removed from the region's intense Anglo-French colonial rivalry. This of course was an advantage, as no doubt was his penchant for the severely formal uniform of starched white collar and morning coat in the laboratory. To Lowson, who hosted him regularly at dinner, Kitasato was simply "a good chap."

Kitasato arrived as part of a substantial expedition, accompanied by trunks of laboratory equipment, microscopes, slides, and pressure sterilizers. At his side were two highly qualified and eager deputies—Professor Tanemichi Aoyama and Dr. Tohiu Ishigama—as well as three experienced assistants. The disembarkation of Kitasato's entourage would have caused a rare commotion at the quayside. The mere appearance of a boat with noticeably foreign lines and markings, the porters busy on deck as they handed ashore a line of dark leather trunks would have been instantly remarkable: the last month had seen total shutdown of port traffic, as shipping lines from across the world diverted their vessels from Hong Kong. Compared to the sporadic and lethargic motion of the floating hearse on its way to and from the burial pits, the bustle and industry of Kitasato's boat would have seemed thrilling, an occasion of hope and consequence.

YERSIN HAD RETURNED TO SAIGON FROM THE MOUNTAINS ON May 17, and learned immediately that plague had made the leap from China to Hong Kong. Clearly, with the breaching of the defenses of such a vital international port, his old petition—to study plague at its Yunnan frontier—was now obsolete, and a new plan was needed. In the memoir he kept of those plague months he wrote—laboring over the sentences in a precise schoolbook hand, with looping ascenders and perfectly balanced ballooning *f*s—"The first thing I shall have to do in the study of plague is to look for its microbe; it is now evident that an initial microbiological study on plague will be much easier in Hong Kong than in Yunnan."

With scarcely a break to debrief his expedition team or take a shower after the hard hike out of the jungle, Yersin hurried to the governor's official residence. Since his last stay in Saigon, there had been a welcome change in the colonial hierarchy: Governor-General Jean-Marie de Lanessan had been replaced, and his successor, Laurent Chavassieux, seemed to be a man who shared none of his predecessor's taste for willful obstruction. No doubt he'd still have been rehearsing his revised pitch to Chavassieux when he arrived at the sentried gates, only to be informed that the governor had just left for a tour up-country. Yersin, undeterred, "convinced M Chavassieux will see things in the same light," set off in pursuit.

Some two weeks later in Qui Nonh, a fishermen's village on the way north to Hanoi, Yersin finally managed to track down Chavassieux. This is Vietnam's magnificent, and still largely unspoiled, tropical east coast; and here Yersin, on the pale-sand village square, the ground littered with shredded coconut husks, surrounded by a wall of curious faces, was at last able to put to effect all the arguments he'd spent so long reviewing. Chavassieux's answer was frustratingly equivocal: While he professed to see the merit in Yersin's argument, he refused to send him to Hong Kong without confirmation from Paris. Furthermore he would make no decision until he had heard the latest from Yunnan. So go to Hanoi, he ordered Yersin: Await orders there.

In Hanoi, Yersin's predicament was further complicated. In the hope of securing allies, he headed straight for the main hospital, to the chief of operations for health services for the entire Indochinese colony. This man—referred to by Yersin simply as "Trucy," no first name—knew Yersin well, and would have had a good idea of the explorer-scientist's capabilities and enthusiasms; he agreed to send a telegram to Paris supporting his bid to go to Hong Kong. The response was immediate and forthright: Orders remained unchanged; a plague researcher was required in Yunnan, not Hong Kong, a job Chavassieux had earmarked for Yersin. And, as a colonial service doctor, he had no choice but to leave at once. No further delays would be tolerated.

Still Yersin hesitated, pondering his next move. If his experience of bureaucracy had taught him anything, it was to trust only his own judgment. Six days into his stay in Hanoi, the orders from the high command in Paris still in place, he wrote his mother that not only did Yunnan currently contain "only a few isolated cases of plague," but it was also home, comically, to "a colonel who fears the epidemic more than bullets, and who would like me to go there to attend him . . . which does not enter my mission at all."

And so Yersin, having no wish to end up as personal physician to a hypochondriac army officer, sent a telegram to his friend Albert Calmette, a Pasteur Institute–trained scientist now colonial secretary of state for health. Calmette, who'd later go on to pioneer a tuberculosis vaccine, was Yersin's contemporary and also one of the few men with whom he felt properly relaxed. Yersin outlined the crisis, concluding by asking Calmette to appeal directly to the Foreign Ministry over the heads of the colonial authorities in Hanoi. This was his last chance, and he knew it.

On June 9 a messenger arrived, breathless, at Yersin's Hanoi hotel. The message was brief, succinct. Calmette had prevailed: Paris had agreed. Yersin, as the Pasteur Institute's official researcher, would be going to Hong Kong after all.

The bureaucratic maneuverings had cost Yersin vital laboratory time in Hong Kong, where plague was now claiming at least a hundred new cases a day. As time went on, research was becoming increasingly hazardous. It was as well that Yersin, for the moment, remained ignorant of the other major threat to his work: the presence of a sizable, well-connected, and fully equipped Japanese plague team that, by the time Yersin finally set sail eastward, had already disembarked at Hong Kong Harbor.

· 5 ·

IT WAS ONLY WHEN HE WOKE TO THE SOUND OF THE TELEPHONE
that he knew he'd been sleeping at all. The night was hot and
windless; even with all the windows of the small apartment
open there was no breeze, and he'd lain down naked beside his
sleeping wife, slick with sweat.

After he lay there a while, motionless, his newborn daughter
snoring gently in the cot at the end of the bed, Mohanlal felt
the heat become tolerable. But at this point he also became
aware of voices in the street below. He reached for his watch:
One-thirty.

Noise at this hour was not unheard of in Surat, and on any
other night he'd have rolled on his side and buried his head

under the pillow. But this felt different: There was shouting, high-pitched argument, people clamoring to be heard. Across the road he heard a window bang shut.

He swung his legs off the bed and walked to the window. From the balcony, under a sputtering orange streetlamp, he could make out a huddle of some thirty or so men. Despite the shrillness of their shouts, the palpable tension, this did not look like a brewing fight. There were hands on shoulders, wild gesticulations, a proximity that felt like brotherhood.

Puzzled, he stepped back inside. To block the noise he closed the windows behind him and, as compensation, opened the front door instead. In the whitewashed stairwell of the apartment house it was blessedly cool, and as he made his way back to bed he hoped that he would finally be able to sleep.

Yet he lay awake for what seemed hours, alive to his wife's every murmur, to each catch in his little girl's breathing. He heard the voices in the street fade, then die. In a yard somewhere a dog began barking. And then the telephone rang, breaking into a sleep he'd been certain he'd never have, rousing him shakily from the bed.

"Yes?" His voice was barely a whisper.

"Don't drink the water. It's not safe." A long pause. "The water."

"Who is this?" He was suddenly awake. He looked across at his still-sleeping wife, cupped a hand over the receiver. "It's three in the morning."

"Never mind that. Do as I say. The water is poisoned."

"Why?" he whispered back, but even as he was speaking he heard a click on the line, then the echo of his own voice, loud in his ear.

He unplugged the phone and lay back on the bed, his heart hammering. His wife had not stirred. Her forehead was a matte sheen; her pulse flickered in the hollow of her neck, between the knuckles of her collarbones. He felt himself merge with the bed, liquid with heat. He laid his watch on his chest, no longer hoping for sleep, knowing that before long his daughter would wake, crying to be fed.

When he heard the jangle of a telephone he was up again, a towel grabbed around him, before remembering that of course his was now disconnected. He heard the ringing tone twice more—the noise bright through the wall—and then came old Banjeri's croaked hello. "Water," he kept saying, and then, louder, "Do not . . . never again."

"What . . . who's that?" His wife's voice, behind him, sounded blurred. He looked around. Her hand was raised to her face, but her eyes were still closed.

Across the stairwell he heard a door open. Mohanlal reached for his raincoat, threw the towel into a corner. He lifted the latch and closed the apartment door softly behind him.

"What's all this?" Mohanlal called out to his neighbor, a diamond cutter who was coming out of his apartment hitching up his trousers, rubbing his eyes. "What have you heard?"

"You had a telephone call?" The diamond cutter turned toward him, one hand on the banister.

"Yes. What is it? A practical joke?"

"The water. Is that what you heard?" They were close now, their voices lowered.

Mohanlal nodded. "So you had it too. You believe it?"

The diamond cutter scratched his chin with a long fingernail, an audible stubble rasp. "Who would do it? The Muslims? Not even they, I think."

Interrupting them came the clunk of another apartment door closing. They turned to see Banjeri shuffle into the hallway. The gold weave of his slippers caught the light, glittered. He gave a tiny nod, barely acknowledgment, and stayed where he was, arms folded. Mohanlal and the diamond cutter, sensing that deference was required, walked across to him.

"Mr. Banjeri," they said in unison.

"I have lived too long," the old man answered mournfully. "When a man I do not know telephones me at three in the morning to tell me that poison now flows from my tap, then I would rather not be alive."

The three men looked at one another in silence. Mohanlal was thinking of his wife: Fearing her panic, he hoped she would sleep through, waking in the morning to plausible explanations, to the unmasking of some ineffectual hoaxer.

"We want to keep calm," he said, as much to himself as the others. "How could the water be poisoned? The whole city's water?"

"It is impossible," Banjeri nodded, tugging at a pendulous, liverish earlobe. "I agree with you. But how to be sure?"

"I tell you who would know," said the diamond cutter. "Dr. Shah. Mohanlal, you are a newspaper man: The doctor respects you. He does not listen to me. You go and ask him."

Banjeri touched Mohanlal's shoulder. 'Good idea. Do it now.'

Mohanlal looked at his watch. Five-thirty. Behind other apartment doors he could hear early-morning noises: coughing, the gargle of a plug. He gave a little bow and walked off down the hallway. He stopped at the fourth door, next to an embossed brass nameplate: Dr. Ramesh Shah, followed by a long string of initials. He rang the doorbell. Nothing. He waited, then tried again. Still no response. He put his ear to the wood, but all he could hear was the muffled echo of other early risers, too indistinct to be coming from the doctor's apartment. Then suddenly, and with shocking force, he found himself banging his fist against the door. All around him doors opened.

"Come out, Shah," Mohanlal shouted. "Out of there."

His neighbors were staring at him, men and women with sleep-tangled hair, wearing bathrobes. He knelt down, put an eye to the mail box. Inside a strip of light fell sideways across the passageway; the floor was strewn with books and clothes; the bed was stripped clean of sheets.

He stood up. His wife was standing in the entrance of their apartment, the baby against her shoulder. "Mohanlal," she began, but he raised a hand.

"Everybody, listen. The doctor is gone. Why has he gone? Since when did he ever go anywhere? I do not like it. Something bad is happening."

IN THE CITY OF SURAT—A SPRAWL OF DIAMOND PLANTS AND textile factories, of squalor remarkable even by Indian standards—the summer of 1994 had been extreme. First the heat, then nearly three months of rain—July through September—which saw the caramel-brown Tapti River breach its banks and roll through most of town, forcing families onto their rooftops with what possessions they could salvage. And, when the floodwaters withdrew, there was no white dove, no olive branch, just the sweet stench of decay: in every street bloated and split-open cows; dogs with sausage-fat swollen tongues; goats with flies feasting on every blackened and distended orifice.

By the third week of September the floodwaters had mostly receded, leaving the streets ankle thick in coagulant ooze. Householders tentatively climbed down from their rooftops, negotiating uncertainly the slime that had once been their living-room floors. Worst hit was the working-class neighborhood at the north end of the city—an area of low-built, rough concrete houses known as Ved Road, for the north-south artery through its clogged heart—and here, on September 21, a young man and woman mysteriously collapsed and died within hours of each other. By the end of the day, two more were dead. The symptoms of all were identical—high fever, vomiting, breathlessness—but, in every case death had come too swiftly for a second medical opinion to be sought. Puzzled and not a little unnerved, none of the attending general practitioners attempted a diagnosis.

By the evening of Wednesday, September 21, eight people were registered suddenly dead, although speculation—stoked by whispers and frenetic muttered confidences—had pumped the figure to nearer one hundred. To every death—both real and reported—there was a common theme: The afflicted were all young, or at least in early middle age, struck down "in their prime." By seven that evening there was a growing crowd outside the New Civil Hospital, the city's largest. Wards were filled close to capacity; the wail of ambulance sirens was audible across town. In the main lobby—a huge concrete-pillared concourse, with rusty splashes of betel phlegm along the bottom of every wall—crowds were fighting to get to the drug counters. On the balcony above, a line of doctors scanned the melee— dressed head to toe in white, their faces masked, only their dark eyes visible.

THE GOVERNMENT-FUNDED NEW CIVIL HOSPITAL WAS THEN, and remains, a bleakly ugly and unpromising forum for medicine. Built in 1972 of poured concrete—now chipped and crumbling—it sprawls across five or six acres of burned-red, rubbish-strewn wasteland. The design seems ill-thought-out and confusing, with related departments often a ten-minute walk from one another, along endless elevated walkways, past beggar women and their sad-eyed, ragged children. There were 750 beds here, roughly half of which—except for an epidemic season—lay empty, testament above all to the patients' parlous recovery rate: The ratio of deaths to admissions, according to the hospital's own figures, had been on the rise since 1981. No one out of choice, however grave his condition, would allow himself to be transferred here; but treatment was free, and most could not afford a private hospital.

The elevators were broken, desks piled high with sheaves of yellowing paper. Outside the scorched grass was littered with vast lumps of concrete embedded in the ground at strange angles, as if they'd fallen from the sky.

Dr. Shailendra Vajpeyee, a big man, heftily built, hair brilliantined to a glossy black, was the hospital's medical superintendent, the official in charge in September 1994. On Monday, September 19, three patients, all malaria suspects, were admitted; two died before the night was out. By Wednesday morning senior doctors were muttering about pneumonia, and the third patient, his breathing becoming harsher and more erratic, was stretchered at a run to the X-ray room, where pneumonia was duly diagnosed and treatment begun. That afternoon another patient was admitted—symptoms identical, the same breathlessness, high fever, sputum-filled cough—and prescribed the same drug regimen. When neither responded, something close to panic set in.

"Within hours," Vajpeyee said, "eight or nine patients died. And if that was not bad enough, no one had any idea of the cause." An emergency meeting was called. The hospital's most senior doctors, surgeons, and administrators argued furiously. It was dengue fever, insisted one; a mutant strain of malaria, claimed another. A third carried news from a nearby charity hospital, where two more people had died, both with the same symptoms. Finally, into a room suddenly silent, one of the doctors spoke softly, with certainty: "The plague."

Vajpeyee shrugged. "What did we know? Only that a large number of people had died in a very short time. That we probably were witnessing the tip of an epidemic. So what could it be? There is a rule of thumb: Always suspect the worst, the most dangerous disease. And there is none more dangerous than plague."

The mention of plague had thrown the room into turmoil. Doctors fought to be heard. Wasn't plague a disease of the past? Imagine the damage to India's reputation if it had in fact resurfaced! Wasn't it possible, posited the head of the medicine department, struggling to control his floundering subordinates, that an outbreak had been triggered by an earthquake the year before in the neighboring state of Maharashtra? The link between geological disturbance and plague, he went on, was well known. When this assertion was met with silence, he ordered his doctors to the hospital library. Read the textbooks! he barked. Then back here.

The plague textbooks were hard to find, wedged behind more recent publications on AIDS, malaria, and tuberculosis. Two were unearthed, one twelve years old, the other twenty-two: Both were blotched with insect excreta; when opened, the pages coughed dust. The volumes were forced flat, indexes thumbed for "clinical features." Both texts differentiated pneumonic from bubonic plague. Pneumonic plague, the quicker-acting and more swiftly fatal, was marked by "a chill, followed by fever, cough, and splinting of the chest, with the production of the sputum that soon becomes bloody. . . . Progress of the disease is rapid, with extensive lung consolidation, septicaemia, prostration, mental confusion, subcutaneous haemorrhages due to intravascular coagulation, and shock, with death ensuing in two or three days." The advice was unequivocal: Treatment— large doses of the antibiotic tetracycline—should begin immediately.

For the hospital management this was proof enough: From this moment on, doctors were ordered, anything resembling pneumonia would be treated as plague. The doctors returned to their offices and wards somberly, in silence. Warned of the dangers of contagion, they raided the stores for surgical masks; when supplies ran out, they covered their mouths and noses with handkerchiefs. Those with access to operating theaters stole in for surgical gloves; all covered their heads, leaving only the narrowest slits for eyes. By midnight on September 21, twenty-five new patients had been admitted; seventy-two hours later there would be more than four hundred.

By the next morning, with Surat's morning newspapers claiming a death toll between three and four hundred, figures repeated unquestioningly by the BBC World Service, all normal life in the city had ceased. Shops remained shut; street vendors' stands stayed empty. Buses out of town were loaded beyond capacity with families, women and children wedged inside, men on the roof. Fights broke out on the station concourse as people tried to force themselves inside cars already solid with refugees; women covered their mouths with folds of sari, the men with any rag that came to hand. There were vehicles of all kinds on the roads—pickups, scooters, Bajaj rickshaw taxis, goods trucks—but nothing was moving. Amid bleating horns, the dust and heat and desperation rose thick; the air was metallic, sour.

At the hospital soldiers were posted outside the plague wards: Two patients had already attempted escape. The militia were under orders to use force, and carried automatic rifles and full clips of shells. The outbreak, Vajpeyee admitted, caught the hospital completely unprepared: Most years the run of infectious diseases was at least predictable; plague, or so they'd imagined, had died years before.

"So we had to go on what we had heard, what we had read," he said, clasping and unclasping his hands. "For no one had seen the disease itself. All I could remember was that it killed ten, thirteen million people here in India between 1896 and sometime in the 1930s. Before antibiotics, of course. That even a small epidemic could wipe out several hundred."

The hospital, by now designated the official plague center, resorted to ferocious regimens of antibiotics—streptomycin, tetracycline, chloramphenicol—injected and in capsules, aware that pneumonic plague acted fast. "If you get treatment within six hours," Vajpeyee said, "then mostly likely you can save the patient. After twelve hours, chances are fifty-fifty. After twenty-four hours, the outlook is very bleak." And so, as fast as surplus drugs became available, they were trucked to pharmacists across the city, distributed door-to-door: a whole army of the white coated and masked, bearing handfuls of miracle dust, whose mechanism was to most a mystery, that were nonetheless accepted and consumed on faith.

DURING THOSE FIRST DAYS VAJPEYEE SLEPT LITTLE. WHENEVER he returned home from the hospital, his telephone would start ringing. "Friends, anybody who knew me. They all called me on the telephone. They wanted to know if they should stay in the city. I told them that nobody could guarantee that they would be safe either if they left or if they stayed. 'Look at me,' I told them. 'I am working here with my patients. I am staying. If you want to leave us, well, that is up to you.'" Of all his acquaintances, he nodded, allowing himself a quiet smile, not one joined the half-million-strong exodus from the city.

"But," he added, "I do not wish to give the wrong impression. There is a side to this story that gives me no pride at all. On those first days, when the panic in the city was very large, and many thousands were fleeing, people tried to go to their family doctors for help. These are private practitioners, you understand, and they have clinics on every street corner. But when their patients needed them, they were not there: All such clinics were closed. Why? Because the doctors had been the first to flee, driving far from town as soon as they heard that plague had broken out. And I ask you: What were the people to think then?"

· 6 ·

IT SITS BECALMED, ITS REFLECTION A DARK SHADOW ON THE still water. It fills most of the frame, though the rough grain of the print and the lack of sharp detail make one suspect that the photograph was once part of a broader shot, cropped for focus. It is a vessel, but one unlike any other. In harsh and geometric monochrome, it appears forbidding, almost predatory. There is no fore- or afterdeck, just a straight-line vertical—blinding white, of wood or plate metal—from gunwale to roof gutter. Into these walls are cut windows of varying shapes and sizes, but all black and featureless, with no visible frames or glass. Near bow and stern the windows are wider, squatter; amidships they shrink to arrow slits, close together. The roof is pitched, with fifteen or so stovepipe chimneys. There is a flagpole but no flag. With the dark mountains behind, the ship appears ghostly and alone. It would, one cannot help thinking, make an excellent penitentiary, reserved for the most determined and malign recidivists.

Little wonder, then, that this malevolent-looking hulk, pressed into service at the start of May 1894 as a floating plague hospital, should have become an object of terror. Moored some three hundred yards off the Hong Kong waterfront, *Hygeia*—a name redolent more of wishful thinking than any proven curative powers—was immediately designated a dedicated treatment center for plague-stricken Chinese. This was straightforward racial segregation, however vigorously Dr. James Lowson, superintendent of the Government Civil Hospital, tried to justify it on medical grounds. Lowson argued against allowing the Chinese to be treated in their own hospital, the Tung Wah, claiming that it would be impossible to prevent contagion spreading into the community. Far safer for everyone, he told the assembled doctors and colonial officials at an extraordinary meeting of the sanitation committee, for the diseased to be out of sight, offshore, from where there would be no escape.

As *Hygeia* filled up with the moaning, feverish, and dying—and not one Chinese doctor accepted Lowson's "invitation" to inspect the facilities and conditions on board—opposition hardened into something darker, more indicative of the underlying hatred the Chinese had always felt for their colonial masters. In front of the busy streets of Hong Kong, like a lone actor on the stage of a packed amphitheater, lay the *Hygeia*—a constant reminder of all that was unequal and unjust about this two-tier society. And as they stared from their tenements and back alleys out across the water to the spectral white hulk, the Chinese began to tell one another that something far worse than medicine was being practiced by the European doctors on board, those men in white coats whose masked faces would occasionally flash into focus at the windows, then slip into darkness again.

The most insistent of all such rumors was the first story to gain currency: that *Hygeia* was a hospital in name only, and was shortly to become a sinister form of plague laboratory, with the end product a "new and certain cure for the plague," whose raw materials were the livers of Chinese children. Anticipating a military-swift conscription of schoolchildren, mothers withdrew their offspring from classes: By mid-May more than half the Chinese schools, bereft of pupils, were closed. Other fantasists claimed that an industrial-scale infanticide was planned, with the government aiming to bury alive some twenty thousand babies, although no reason for such barbarism was ever given. Feeling themselves cornered and overpowered, the Chinese began their own form of disease prevention, which involved long and raucous street processions, headed by the portered likeness of a Chinese deity, and accompanied by the machine-gun rattle of firecrackers. In this atmosphere of mutual suspicion it took little to stoke the flames of paranoia, and newspaper reporters, true to type, did their bit. "Is it a fact," enquired a "correspondent" of the *Hong Kong Telegraph*, "that a Chinese woman was sent on board the Hygeia by the Sanitary Authorities supposed to be suffering from the plague, but which proved to be a case of pregnancy? And is it true that the mistake was not found out until it was too late to save the patient's life?"

It was not long before every gesture of the colonial government in the direction of hygiene was greeted with clamorous animosity by the Chinese. The efforts of the three hundred volunteers from the Shropshire Light Infantry to act as plague monitors, inspecting houses in the most crowded Chinese quarters, incited violent clashes. By May 21 one of the accompanying sanitary inspectors had even gone so far as to plead his case before the magistrates' court: Attempting to enter a house, he had been driven back by a mob hurling rocks and bricks. The accused—three housewives—were found guilty and fined.

Even on the rare occasions when the soldiers' work progressed smoothly—when the targeted house turned out to be abandoned, its inhabitants fled north into China—it was repulsive, grueling labor. They'd rise at dawn, then head out from their barracks at seven-thirty, armed with buckets and limewash, trailed by a reluctant posse of press-ganged "coolies." They'd start on the ground floor, scrubbing furniture and clothing, scouring pots and frying pans, then move upstairs. According to an anonymous witness, the decrepitude beggared description, and tested to the full the vocabulary of disgust:

> All paper was torn off the walls and woodwork, and then, in all its nakedness, you saw the filth of these dwellings. Vermin of all sorts were found crawling everywhere, and heaps of rubbish and filth lay disregarded in odd corners. . . . Water was brought in buckets from the cookhouse, and a commencement was made of getting the floor clean. It is impossible to give any conception of the filth which was then swept down the stairs—it must have been seen to be believed.

News of British soldiers kicking down doors in the Chinese quarters of Hong Kong, hurling furniture into the street, and slooshing the furniture with acrid detergent, spread quickly to Canton, the closest mainland-Chinese city and the one from which most Hong Kong Chinese families originated. Within days, a slew of posters had gone up all over the city warning that the entire European population faced massacre should anyone dare condemn Cantonese dwellings on grounds of health. To compound this, word was put about that the despised foreigners were also distributing poisoned scent bags. No European felt safe; two female missionaries, guilty of nothing more than attempting to stretcher a plague victim to the hospital, were hounded and stoned.

Chinese leaders in Hong Kong, fearing army reprisals, opted in the end for opposition of an altogether more decorous, fittingly British, nature. On May 22 a delegation arrived on foot at the great porticoed entrance to Government House with a written petition containing four demands: an end to the enforced military inspection of their houses; that plague sufferers might be allowed free passage home to Canton; that those remaining be treated exclusively in the Tung Wah, their own hospital; and that henceforth the funereal hulk *Hygeia* no longer be an epidemic hospital for the Chinese.

Most Chinese no doubt regarded the petition as a ludicrous piece of window dressing, not least the clause requesting unhindered return to Canton. For, throughout May, Chinese from all over the colony—with or without permission—had been fleeing in the thousands. Official figures, tallied at quayside, listed 76,036 people as having quit Hong Kong that month, with only 42,390 arrivals—a shortfall of more than thirty-three thousand. As May became June, the graph rose ever faster, forcing construction work and manufacturing, shipping and food production to a point near closedown. The Hong Kong Rope Works shut its doors, dismissed its few remaining staff, as did the Lee Yuen Sugar Refinery. Mail boats, fearful of touching land, tethered postal bags to buoys, turning for the open sea before the pickup launch was even within hailing distance. By the beginning of June, this once-bustling harbor lay abandoned, the only figures on the docks the white-uniformed soldiers, the only water traffic the solitary, low-slung coffin barge on its continual passage to and from the burial pits.

Within two weeks of the start of the epidemic, the main hospitals—the Government Civil Hospital, under Lowson, and the Chinese community's Tung Wah—reached capacity. Backing down under pressure from the Chinese, the government pledged to cease sending Chinese plague patients to the *Hygeia,* and instead pressed into service an arguably far more pestilential venue, an abandoned glass factory in Kennedy Town, whose only conceivable merit was its proximity to the burial pits. Firsthand accounts make it clear that this was not a building in which any man would have willingly chosen to spend his time. Lowson's diary entry for May 24 contains a retrospective scribble, and despite the passage of some four decades, he remembers scenes that "baffled description. When I think of it now, I wonder how anyone came out of it alive."

A photograph from one of the first days of the factory's life as a plague hospital shows a long room with bare floorboards, just wide enough to allow a walkway between two rows of bodies. Some thirty men are visible, lying on their backs on reed mats. Their heads are turned toward the photographer, eyes glassy, cheeks sunken. They are covered with a variety of rags and army-issue blankets. It must have been hot—this was the eve of monsoon season, and the windows along both walls are thrown open—yet the patients, icy with rising fever, clutch their clothing around them. Men lie on their sides, hands between legs for warmth. Nowhere is there any sign of medicine, or of any doctor.

The comparison between the derelict glass factory, designated Chinese only, and another temporary hospital—set up on May 14 in the Kennedy Town police station for Europeans who might become afflicted as well as those Chinese willing to submit to Western medicine—could not have been starker. Both were in the same neighborhood, but there any similarity ended. The police station, according to one source, was "surrounded by a wide verandah, open on all sides [and] is admirably suited to the purpose. Everything and everywhere is clean, bright, and cheerful. The officer in charge is radiant, and the sisters from the Civil Hospital, who take turns at this work, are the embodiment of kind activity and considerate attention." There was no shortage of bedding, food, and medicine, and all the patients appeared optimistic of recovery. The glass factory, by contrast, was "decayed and ruinous," filled with "moribund" patients, all of whom "seemed occupied with dying." Overcrowding was so severe that patients lay half on top of one another, "impatiently resenting the overlapping hand or foot of the next neighbour." There was no sign of food, "either administered or in preparation." When night came the sick silently covered their faces with their blankets, a motion that spoke most eloquently of despair, of the fact that few expected to see dawn.

As the death toll continued to rise, so the white population did its best to remain aloof. Thus far, after all, plague had confined itself to the "native classes"—clear testimony to the causal link between moral decay and disease. But, while on one level reassuring, the racial bias of the contagion had a lamentable side effect for the colonial classes. "The scare among the Chinese was spreading to the private coolies and house 'boys,'" one witness complained. "Many left without giving any warning, and Europeans began to fear they would find themselves without servants." Even wealth—of which there was no more certain marker than a mansion on the prestigious, airy upper slopes of Victoria Peak—was no protection against the loss of staff, for a new rumor had caught fire among the Chinese that the plague had been caused not by "filth," as the Europeans kept insisting, but by the methods of construction of the Peak Railway, the funicular tramline that cut straight from the heart of the business district to the summit of Victoria Peak, 1,825 feet above. The rails, it was claimed, had not been laid on traditional wooden sleepers but on the yielding bodies of Chinese babies: Plague was the gods' inevitable punishment for such wickedness.

Yet a far bleaker scenario now lay in prospect for the colonial classes. "Soon," railed an editorial in the *Hong Kong Telegraph*, "every European will have to wash his own shirt and pull his own rickshaw!" And it would have been with just this kind of doomsday in mind that the worshipers gathered at Saint John's Cathedral on Sunday, June 3, to hear a special prayer for deliverance from plague, and to ruminate on the Reverend R. F. Cobbold's sermon on Ezekiel 8:19—"For I have no pleasure in the death of him that dieth, said the Lord God; wherefore turn yourselves and live ye." Unknown to Cobbold and his packed and uncommonly prayerful congregation, however, the first two white men to contract plague were at that very moment breathing their last in the sepulchral gloom of the *Hygeia*—their presence on the Chinese-only ship clear evidence of the shortage of hospital beds—their last memory of the fading world the clank-clank of the anchor chain and the whisper, like the spirits of the world to come, of the harbor swell against the hull.

TO THOSE BLESSED WITH THE GIFT OF RETROSPECTIVE WISDOM, plague came as no great surprise. To some Chinese it was necessary to look no further than the forests where, for the first time in thirty years, the bamboo had flowered prodigiously: a certain omen of ill. To the Europeans, who'd have scorned such a belief as wayward superstition, the roots of the disease were more various, though scarcely more accurate or scientific.

Dr. Alexander Rennie, consular surgeon for Canton and the first white man to report on the epidemic, proposed that plague was triggered by contaminated and insufficient water, poor ventilation, but above all by "filth." As reassurance to his readers, he dismissed any notion that it might be contagious, certainly outside the crowded Chinese neighborhoods. This theory was expanded by the governor of Hong Kong, Sir William Robinson, who added the bold and entirely unsubstantiated coda that it was the recent drought that had caused the outbreak, since the consequent depletion of reservoirs had meant less water for cleaning streets, drains, and houses. Dr.

James Lowson was broadly of the same opinion, although he—like Rennie emphasizing the causal role of "poverty and dirt"—credited a few days of heavy rain with the ability to flush out the "poison . . . [which] is not infectious or contagious." Others, like Royal Navy surgeon Herbert Penny, were less sure as to plague's contagiousness: Most likely, he contended, the disease was carried in clothing and transmitted through contact.

In nonscientific circles opinions were no less erratic. Within days of the first case, the correspondence columns of the newspapers filled with a clamor of competing theories, all equally convinced of their own validity, all equally wayward. Tobacco, wrote one reader, was a "simple preventative," and should be made freely available to all soldiers—a claim that at least had its historical precedent: Chewing tobacco leaves was used in Stuart times as a plague prophylactic, and Pepys wrote in his diary that, during the 1665 London plague, "an ill conception of myself and my smell . . . forced [me] to buy some roll tobacco to smell and chaw, which took away the apprehension." So efficacious was the weed held to be that, in times of plague, even schoolchildren were forced to partake: An Eton schoolboy is recorded as being "never whipped so much in his life as he was one morning for not smoking."

While there was no propagandist in Hong Kong who would have dared suggest such an extreme punishment for a simple refusal to inhale, there was a consensus in favor of an approach that was altogether more wanton. Taipingshan, the overcrowded Chinese district at the center of the epidemic, should be demolished; better still, wrote one reader in the first week of June, burned to the ground. "It is quite clear the poisonous gas issues from certain particular localities . . . the only sure measure to stamp out plague is to burn down infected houses."

"Sir," countered another voice, "It is rumoured that Taipingshan is to be utterly demolished. Cui bono? Such a measure would have as much effect in curing or even preventing the plague as whitewashing the walls; that is, none whatever. It isn't in the walls, nor yet in the bricks. It is in the filth-saturated soil," a state of affairs he laid unequivocally at the government's door for introducing a drainage system "which not one in thirty of the population for generations to come but will abuse; that is, as soon as the pipes are laid they proceed to choke or break them and consequently the soil gets saturated."

The signs—the proliferation of ever-wilder theories, their misplaced rage and whiff of recrimination—pointed to a community under siege. All that was needed now was a scapegoat, and the Europeans were of one voice: immigrants. Plague, hollered the press, was "due to the vast influx of the filthy mendicants and coolies . . . imagine this lot all huddled together . . . reeking with filth, many of them diseased." The only solution—propounded in language beloved of xenophobic despots down the ages—was to "purify" the island by expelling the infected. As this racist rhetoric was reaching its shrill climax the two foreign scientists, Professor Shibasaburo Kitasato and Dr. Alexandre Yersin, were stepping straight into an atmosphere so charged with distrust and venom that it might have been wartime.

· 7 ·

THERE ARE FEW CLUES REGARDING THE INTRICACIES OF Kitasato's character. He wrote sparingly and, unlike Yersin, kept his rages and passions to himself: No diary or letters survive in the public domain. From his published papers and speeches comes a sense of an austere professional, secure in his methodology and diagnoses, whose interest in the culture of Chinese Hong Kong was proscribed and oversimplified. Unlike Yersin, whose reaction to the lives of the Chinese—in all their undisguised squalor and otherness—was both fascinated and horrified, Kitasato responded to what he saw with economy and detachment. Speaking to the Private Hygiene Society of Japan at the end of 1894, he compressed six or so weeks of observation into a hundred words of blunt description. Chinese houses, he instructed his audience, were "constructed on top of each other, with box-like rooms that are generally very small, without sunshine. I wonder why they do not live in larger rooms."

Kitasato was pragmatic, private, fiercely competitive. And he arrived in Hong Kong confident of victory, that the prize of plague was within his grasp. He'd taken no chances: His backup team was of the highest caliber. Among them were the renowned pathologist Professor Aoyama from the Tokyo Medical School, who was a top government official, and the bacteriologist Dr. Ishigama, appointed Kitasato's chief assistant.

Kitasato and his team began their stay in Hong Kong at the residence of the Japanese consul. Here, in pale-columned splendor, served green tea by deferential Chinese footmen, Kitasato heard the labored and minutely formal expressions of the emperor's, and the colony's, pleasure at his safe arrival. One can picture him—his appearance assembled from the handful of portraits that survive—as resolute despite travel fatigue, his mustache maybe a little bushier than the usual tight crop, his small eyes behind the circular steel-rimmed spectacles darker, more tired.

Before long, Kitasato had installed his team in the Hong Kong Hotel. He had reached the colony mid-monsoon; at night—as on most summer nights in the city then and now—the rain hammered on the groove-tiled roofs of the colony's villas and tenements, its shanties and hospitals. June is the island's hottest and wettest month, with rainfall during those four weeks regularly topping sixteen inches, and temperatures well into the hundreds. In 1894 the monsoon started early; before the end of May, soldiers on cleanup parties were often seen in full waterproofs—oilskins and sou'westers—hurrying under cover with each new cloudburst, the strength of the downpour releasing a knee-level haze. On May 28 the temperature had reached such a pitch that, in the temporary hospital in the derelict glass factory, windows were left permanently open, and from those whose hinges were too seized to move, the glass was punched clear.

EARLY ON THE MORNING OF JUNE 13, KITASATO LED HIS TEAM TO a fleet of waiting rickshaws and—in his punctilious but limited English—ordered the drivers to take them to the Government Civil Hospital, where he was scheduled to meet Dr. James Lowson. With the monsoon exploding suddenly into life again, he pulled his raincoat tight about him, lifting his patent leather shoes from the rising pool of water in the footwell. He'd have become quickly confused, too, disoriented by the endless switchbacks as the rickshaws struggled up the incline. After a while, the view was of roofs—the cramped back-to-backs of Taipingshan—then the harbor beyond, looking less than turquoise now through the blear of rain. And finally, at an elevation of some generosity and airiness, there appeared the grand vista of the Government Civil Hospital itself, classical in ambition and design, fronted by a gracious, curving driveway, distinguished architecturally by the vaulted colonnade through which, as the rain finally eased, a huddle of white-coated men now came running.

At their head was a tall, pale-skinned, and mustached European, big bony hand outstretched. As he approached, Kitasato—climbing down from his rickshaw and beating the rainwater from his coat—noticed Lowson's distinguishing feature, a misaligned right eye that, veering wide, gave the impression that he was somehow not seeing the person in front of him at all. In serious mood—as in formal photographs, straight backed and sober—this effect was heightened, but now, as he bounded across the gravel, grinning broadly despite the tension and grief of the past few weeks, there was no mistaking his pleasure and relief as he greeted Kitasato and vigorously pumped his hand.

Later, in a report he wrote for the *Lancet*, Kitasato publicly acknowledged his gratitude to Lowson, who "put everything at our disposal in the most friendly spirit." This was a magnificent understatement: Lowson in fact did everything but prostrate himself at Kitasato's feet; had he had a cloak he would have laid it across the puddles that glittered in the hospital driveway. For this Scottish-born medic, raised in the small east coast town of Forfar, educated at the University of Edinburgh, and still only twenty-eight at the start of the plague epidemic, the chance to work alongside such an eminent figure would until this moment have seemed laughably remote. Certainly, like all ambitious young doctors, Lowson would have read of Kitasato's groundbreaking tuberculosis work and would no doubt have agreed with the *British Medical Journal*'s encomium that the Japanese scientist was, "next to Koch, the greatest bacteriologist in the world." And, now that Kitasato was finally here, Lowson would have felt his own excitement building: If, as he believed, Kitasato was destined to go down in history as the conqueror of plague, he, as Kitasato's right-hand man, would also be showered with glory.

Lowson outlined his plans. He had, he explained, reserved rooms in one of the temporary plague hospitals for use as Kitasato's laboratory and autopsy suite. He'd have put considerable effort into arranging this, determined that Kitasato should have the very best facilities in the cleanest of the hospitals. In the end he'd chosen the hospital set up in the Kennedy Town police station. Though never intended to be anything other than a police headquarters, the building—Lowson told Kitasato as they shared a rickshaw across town—made a superlative hospital.

Arriving for the first time, Kitasato would have been struck above all by the contrast between the hospital and the neighborhood that surrounded it. From the central district of Victoria, with its whitewashed merchants' headquarters and spacious quayside offices, he had passed through cramped and abandoned Taipingshan—the houses now boarded up and shuttered, an occasional ghostly face at a high window, piles of rubbish smoking in the streets and side alleys—and on westward, the houses growing ever more ramshackle and only partially roofed, rotting corpses lying in gutters, their unclothed limbs askew. By the time the doctors reached the hospital, they were in a landscape almost entirely devoid of buildings, with the scrubby lower slopes of Mount Davis ahead of them, on which a group of men was at work. It looked like earthworks, some kind of construction.

Lowson leaned toward Kitasato. "Plague pits," he explained. "Gravediggers."

As they began their tour of the hospital, Lowson did his best to concentrate on the positive: He glossed over the conspicuous failure in medication, in particular his own doubtful concoction prescribed for all the plague victims, which consisted of beaten eggs, frothed milk, and an unspecified "stimulant." Instead he focused on the Kennedy Town hospital's supposed selling points: the abundance of fresh air; the "hopeful and cheerful" patients, almost all Chinese, many of whom were said to be "full of merriment"; the sufficiency of bedding, medicine, and food; the overflow cots on a section of shady veranda; the availability of clean water, gas, even the use of a telephone. Yet, only one year later, sitting down to write his official plague report, Lowson—no longer anxious to impress any visiting dignitaries—spoke plainly of the site's shortcomings. Being close to Mount Davis may have provided convenient access to the plague pits, he said, but trees on the nearby slopes "made [the hospital] a hunting ground for flies and mosquitoes which sometimes added greatly to our patients' sufferings. The arrangements of the rooms," he added sourly, "also left much to be desired."

Kitasato's first impressions, however, were highly favorable, and he ordered his team to begin immediately unpacking his equipment—microscopes, slide trays, sets of scalpels and scissors, pressure sterilizers, surgical gloves and masks. Mirroring the layout of an established laboratory, he set up tables along all walls, to form an extended workbench, leaving room in the middle for the dissection of corpses. And all the while, hovering in the background, unable to conceal his boyish excitement, was Lowson, chattering to the professor's back as the older man uncased his instruments and screwed together lenses, recounting the story so far: the wild rumors, the forced inspections of houses, the ensuing riots.

It had been, Lowson informed Kitasato—moving closer now, his voice lowering to a whisper—a terrible month, with Hong Kong as if under siege, the disease itself almost a bombardment, forcing people to hide away, fearful and suspicious, trusting no one. Chinese and Western doctors shared almost no common ground. When the European physicians insisted on isolating plague patients—preferably on the offshore hulk *Hygeia*—the Chinese told one another that the vessel, once full, was going to sail for Europe, where the bodies would be ground into powder and fed as prophylactic medicine to the Continent's nobility. In their efforts to prevent this happening, they did everything they could to keep the rate of infection secret. The moment a military search party arrived in a street, corpses would be smuggled from house to house; on one occasion, with every exit barred and the soldiers closing in, a plague corpse was propped up at a mah-jongg game, eyes fixed strangely on the ceiling, claw hand outstretched, tiles in an untouched pile before it.

Of the most pressing concern to Kitasato, however, was having unfettered access to corpses to conduct experiments, but he understood already that this would not be straightforward: The Chinese—who did not believe that the cause of medicine was advanced by cutting open bodies—would not willingly countenance dismemberment of their dead. Lowson, who'd sensed Kitasato's growing disquiet as his laboratory preparations neared their end, did his best to reassure him. There was a loophole, he explained, which would guarantee access to cadavers: According to hospital regulations, doctors were obliged to carry out postmortems, without necessarily consulting the family of the deceased. The rioting, the brick throwing and stoning that this had already engendered would not, said Lowson, prevent postmortems being attempted.

Kitasato—not a man to scare easily—suddenly felt frightened. A rare clue to his feelings survives in the text of a speech made shortly after his return home. Detailing the obstacles to autopsy—the certain Chinese opposition, the gulf between the different cultural and medical approaches to contagion—he breathed deeply and told it straight. "If the Chinese had found out about the post-mortem examinations, we would have been beaten to death on the spot." Clearly Lowson's placating words, his assurances of round-the-clock guards and extra medical support, did little to set Kitasato's mind at peace.

And so it was in a darkly reflective mood that Kitasato led his team back that evening to the Hong Kong Hotel. Lowson had expressed a wish to escort Kitasato back to his own residence, to install him and his colleagues in the palatial but seldom-used guest wing. But Kitasato had been adamant: He did not wish to impose on Dr. Lowson's kindness. It is not hard to picture the solitary bacteriologist, before retiring for the night, succumbing to the temptation to ride the elevator—"of the latest and most approved type"—to the top of its climb. Before him was the harbor, black and deserted now, the palest shadow through the rain marking the position of the *Hygeia;* inland were the hills and city through which plague was stalking malignantly. Kitasato sensed that his arrival in Hong Kong at this moment was indeed—as Lowson had breathlessly intoned all afternoon—the start of something epic. The red carpet had been laid out before him; all he had to do was take the first step.

· 8 ·

MOHANLAL PUT AN ARM AROUND HIS WIFE, GUIDED HER BACK into their apartment, and closed the door. He knew that his neighbors would be wanting to speak to him—to probe further, as at previous moments of community tension, assuming that as a newspaperman he had access to some kind of privileged knowledge—but there were things, first, that he needed to discuss with his wife.

He tried to lead her to the table, but she pulled away from him; the baby began to cry, little yelping stabs that made it impossible to think, splintered his thoughts. He put a hand over his eyes.

"Couldn't you feed her?" His voice came out strained, reedy.

She sat on the edge of the bed, did as he said. The baby quietened, and he felt the pressure in his head subside. But still his wife would not look at him.

"Hetal," he pleaded. "Are you trying to punish me? What have I done?"

"It is not you," she muttered, speaking so softly he had to kneel close to hear the words. "I am frightened. What is going on?"

"I do not know. But look, I am going to find out." He would get to the office, telephone her from there. "And I will come back for lunch. We can talk then."

He heard the noise of the street—the shouting and the car horns, the angry whine of scooters—before he'd even reached the front door of the apartment house. Once he was outside, an astonishing sight greeted him: It was only six-thirty, but the road was impassable. At the corner two buses were wedged nose to nose, the drivers shouting at each other through the windshields. They were blocking the side road, but there was no possibility of movement: Behind each, and on all sides, were trucks, scooters, cars, jammed bumper to bumper. Only pedestrians appeared to be moving and that, uncertainly: Mohanlal saw a man and a woman climb onto the hood of an old Datsun, only to stop the moment they had done so, looking around, shaking their heads. Under the man's mask he could see that he was shouting, the cotton gauze over his mouth wet, gathering dirt.

Normally he'd have taken his scooter to work, but one look at the melee before him was enough to persuade him to pocket his keys again and push through on foot. Elbows and shoulders jabbed and jostled him; the old-curry smell of sweat and panic assaulted his senses. Yet, in the middle of it, there was a sudden silence; the shouting fell away, and into the space he heard his own voice, rising over the dust and blue diesel.

"What is this? What is happening?"

And back came a chorus of voices. "Plague. We're leaving this place. Everyone is dying."

"Plague?" he yelled back, but all was clamor again. He pushed onward, more desperately now, aiming to reach the corner where he knew of a cut-through. He kept his head down, but felt himself crowded on all sides: black eyes, the ghostly white slashes of masks, hands clawing at his clothing. He clutched his briefcase to his chest: half shield, half battering ram.

At the corner garbage was banked high in the entrance to the cut-through: a deliberate obstruction, he guessed. The stench, even so early in the morning, was fetid and vinegary, but he launched himself up it anyway, feeling it yield underfoot, each handhold a sugary mash of banana skin and sodden cardboard, moldering fruit husks and empty ant-infested tins. At the top, as an ultimate deterrent, lay the skewed-legged corpse of a mongrel pup, both eyes gone, bright red sockets swarming with flies. Looking away, covering his mouth, Mohanlal almost tripped. He reached the bottom at a run, skidding on some unseen ooze.

And then he ran, pelted from doorways with husks of bread and old fruit; from a top window an arc of dishwater caught him on the side of the face.

The newspaper office was besieged, angry fists demanding information, as if the reporters inside weren't already doing all they could. He pulled out his security pass, but as soon as he did so hands clawed at him, and he closed it tight in his fist again.

Unable to progress, and still some ten yards from the door, he shouted for the guard, hollering his name till the peaked cap with the gilt portcullis turned toward him and the guard reached out a long arm over the heads of the crowd and pulled Mohanlal through.

It was scarcely calmer in the newsroom. Normally at this hour—ninety minutes or so from deadline for the afternoon edition—there was a quiet hubbub, the percussion of type-writer keys, the shouts of the copyboys. Today, though, all the reporters and subeditors were gathered in a tight group in the middle of the newsroom, the editor standing on a chair, facing them. He looked up when he saw Mohanlal.

"So you made it. We're just wrapping up. What have you heard?"

"Plague, poisoned water, you name it."

"It's plague, for sure," said one of the junior reporters, spooling through his notepad. "You seen the morning papers?"

The discussion became general, chaotic. The editor stepped out of his chair and gestured to Mohanlal, who pushed through the crowd. The older man crossed the newsroom, entered the glass cubicle at the far end, and waited for Mohanlal to join him. Mohanlal closed the door and took the proffered chair.

"Well," the editor sighed, sinking heavily into the chair behind his desk. "Have we all gone crazy?"

"I'm sorry?" Mohanlal answered. "Crazy?"

"I had a call this morning from Vadilal—remember him? He's on the *New York Times* now—and guess what he said? Between three and four thousand have died in Surat these last two days. On good authority, he said. It was all I could do to make him hold off for a day. Where does he get those figures?"

"There's a doctor who lives in my building. I tried to get hold of him this morning, but he wasn't there. This is the first time he's gone anywhere. That causes me concern."

"He's not the only one." The editor's eye was twitching. He pressed two fingers to the side of his face. "We've been getting reports all morning of doctors having fled. In Katargam the people have burned down a doctor's surgery. Smashed it to pieces, then threw a match into the petrol tank of his Bajaj."

"What do they say down at the New Civil Hospital?" Mohanlal asked, barely hearing what the editor had said. "How many dead have they got down there?"

"It's plague, all right," the editor said wearily. "What do the morning papers say? Fifty? The hospital doesn't know any better than that."

"But what about Vadilal? The New York figures?"

"That," he said, leaning forward over his bank of telephones, the blotting pad, and strewn pens, "is what I want you to find out."

Back at his desk, before even clearing the papers off his chair to sit down, Mohanlal telephoned home. He stood, receiver crooked in his shoulder, gazing numbly at the disorder that was his professional life—a half-eaten *nan*, an ashtray full of teabags, a three-foot pile of old newspapers—and waited as the line crackled and clicked. It rang, then went on ringing. He imagined his wife bathing the baby or fixing a bottle. He knew she'd be there, since he'd made her promise to await his call. Yet it rang and rang. Another reporter approached him, wanting a name and telephone number, and Mohanlal leafed through his contacts book, scribbled the number, then put the receiver to his ear again. It was still ringing. He held the phone at arm's length, as if it had some kind of animate nature of its own, as if perhaps it knew what was happening at the other end. And then, abruptly, he dropped it back in the cradle.

An hour later, a headache building, he was climbing the stairwell of his apartment house. The door to his apartment was locked, and it took him some time to find his key. When he let himself in, it looked as if little had changed: bed still unmade, far window open, his daughter's toys in a basket by the bathroom.

"Hetal," he called out. "I'm here. It's me."

He stopped. In the middle of the bed was a sheet of paper, torn roughly from one of his notebooks. He grabbed it, held it to the light.

"Dearest one," he read, and had to stop, the tears blurring his vision. He wiped his eyes on his sleeve, took a deep breath, and looked down at the paper again. "We have gone," the note continued. "I know you wanted us to wait, but I am frightened. People are dying here. Even the doctors have gone. I know you have to stay and I don't expect you to follow us. We both love you. Let us all pray that this thing is over soon."

· 9 ·

ON FRIDAY, JUNE 15, 1894, A SMALL CARGO FREIGHTER SAILED silently into the Hong Kong harbor. No crowds awaited its arrival; no soldiers ran up the jetty to grab the hawsers as they were thrown overboard; ashore, in the shadow of the customs houses, no rickshaws began jostling one another, suddenly eager for custom. It was ten in the morning, a rare break in the rain, and the hillsides above town were veined with red-clay streams, every dry gulch now frothing and coursing, sweeping down through town, where choked gutters spilled into the alleys, carrying with them every kind of debris, fruit husks, excrement.

On board, a lone white man was kneeling beside three tan leather suitcases. He checked the locks, tightened the straps, then stood and gestured to the crew. As he watched, the cases were lowered by hand onto the jetty. He was the last off the boat and, as he stood there, arms around the shoulders of his two assistants—one Chinese, the other Vietnamese—the vessel that had taken him across the typhoon-whipped South China Sea pushed off into the wind to begin its perilous voyage home.

Simply getting to this point had taken many months of patient, persistent lobbying. Dr. Alexandre Yersin—buttoning his coat against a fresh squall, sensing the jetty rock queasily under him as he led the way to shore—had in fact made his first attempt to reach southern China a long two years ago. Yersin had heard and read much about Hong Kong's preeminence as an international port; he would have been poorly prepared for the desolation that greeted him. His first report, dated three days later and addressed to the governor-general in Hanoi, spoke of the colony being "completely changed": Exploring deserted streets, he had to pick his way through tableaux of Revelations-style horror: corpses abandoned in the middle of the street, festering mounds of dead rats at every turn. Aware of the gruesome novelty of what he was witnessing, he took photographs, pasting the prints in the back of his notebook. Beneath a shot of a narrow street—piles of rubble in the foreground, steps climbing away between shuttered houses—he wrote in his precise, copybook hand, "*Quartier du Taipingshan. Rue murée et évacuée à cause de nombreux cas de peste.*" Without the caption, and with no background knowledge, the picture would make no sense: It is of nothing, of an absence. And yet this is precisely the point—here is a place where human beings once lived and from which disease had routed them. The peeling handbills, the splintered windows, the doors hanging crooked from their hinges: This is all that remains.

Yersin was in epidemic territory and would have expected to find the colony sober and quiet, but the complete absence of any kind of reception party was mystifying. Surely, the French consul had received a dispatch from Saigon announcing his arrival in Hong Kong. Why, then, was there no one to welcome him? With the wind getting up and rain beginning to sting his face, he shouted to his helpers, and together they hauled the cases to the lee of the customs house.

Climbing uphill from the shore, finally inside a rickshaw, Yersin worried about the effect of the rain: All his equipment was cased, but this was rain as he'd seldom seen it, a cacophonous drilling on roofs, and he imagined it forcing through the seams of the leather, working its way into all the parts. The moment the embassy came in sight—tricolor snapping spray in the gale—he leaned out of his rickshaw and yelled. The cases! Get them under cover!

At the door stood a solitary footman. He told Yersin to wait where he was, and disappeared inside. When he finally returned, it was with instructions that only Yersin should enter: His two servants should remain with the luggage. Inside, without the cooling effect of the downpour, the claustrophobic warmth of the monsoon soon became overwhelming, and Yersin's clothes stuck to his skin. He followed the footman along pale wood floors, down corridors rendered penumbrous by the storm outside. Finally his guide came to a halt beside a vast mahogany door. He knocked, twisted the brass knob, and pointed Yersin inside.

Yersin, used to the pattern of petition and rebuff that had marked his dealings these last two years with the governor-general, was by now feeling markedly anxious. Granted, this time he had no shortage of governmental backup: Dr. Albert Calmette, colonial secretary for health, was on Yersin's side, and so the likelihood of a bald rejection was slim indeed. Far more likely was an oblique coldness, a disinterest in the goals of science, an inability to see beyond the narrow exigencies of political expediency.

He cannot have been much encouraged to find that the official behind the ostentatiously lacquered slab desk was not the consul at all, but his stand-in, the *chancelier d'ambassade,* Bourgeois. Whatever his shortcomings in status, however, the official had at least set time aside for Yersin. "He was expecting me," Yersin wrote in his report for the Pasteur Institute in Paris with a discernible hint of relief, a sense that, from this point on, the ride would be easier. And, as Bourgeois listed the introductions made so far, he confirmed Yersin's optimism. Messages with news of Yersin's imminent arrival had been sent to both the colonial secretary, James Stewart Lockhart, and Hong Kong's colonial surgeon Dr. Philip Ayres. Yersin should see them immediately; they would arrange laboratory space, maybe even assistants.

Bourgeois's next words, however, were heavy with warning. "And how is your English, my friend?"

Yersin shook his head. "Not good." The sole other language he spoke was Vietnamese, and that only after years of study and enforced application. He had never visited Britain, and from elementary school English lessons could remember only the most rudimentary greetings and farewells.

"Then you will find nothing easy. The English do not speak French, and will not comprehend your failure to speak their language. I am afraid they will think you most rude and undiplomatic."

Accustomed as he was to setbacks, Yersin would not have seen this one coming. He had expected to find danger in Hong Kong but not the bureaucratic frustrations of the past two years. Now it looked as if the pattern was set to continue. And there was more.

Bourgeois coughed, waited till Yersin looked up again. "As you know, we are not on good terms with the British. This is not new, but it will most certainly affect your work here." He paused. Yersin whispered, "I understand."

"I fear that your very presence here," Bourgeois continued, "despite the fact that it was the British government which requested help, and that it was our own Pasteur Institute which sent you, will be construed by the Hong Kong doctors as criticism."

Yersin felt anger rise within him. "Criticism? How so, exactly?"

"Because it implies that their lot are no good. Why else would you have come this far?"

As Yersin left the embassy—"well-informed," as he later noted, "but terribly ill-at-ease"—he put a hand inside his jacket. He pulled out a letter, the result of a chance encounter back in Haiphong. It was a note of introduction from a Dr. Lefèvre to Father Vigano, an Italian missionary who had lived in Hong Kong for some thirty years. This introduction—downplayed in Yersin's correspondence and reports—would prove crucial.

When they met, the two men developed an instant rapport, and Vigano, no doubt sensing Yersin's state of friendlessness, canceled all other engagements. "He is happy," Yersin wrote, "to put himself immediately at my disposal, to accompany me everywhere on my official visits and to the plague hospitals." To Yersin's relief, Vigano was also an impressive linguist, speaking fluent English and French. As for age, Vigano must have been at least in his sixties—twice Yersin's years—for, as Yersin records, he had long ago served as an "artillery officer in the Italian army," and in 1859 had been awarded the Légion d'Honneur for his part in the Franco-Italian effort to repulse the Austrians from northern Italy at the Battle of Solferino. As a result of this, Vigano had "retained a French heart and French feelings."

And so Yersin and Vigano proceeded together. They forced a frenetic pace, with the Frenchman hungry to get to work. First, they searched out Dr. Philip Ayres, colonial surgeon, a man nearer Vigano's age than Yersin's: a man so tall he had to duck to get through doorways, whose extravagant wisps of mustache—unruly and wild-tendriled in a fashion unlikely to be permitted in any hospital today—marked him as a maverick, disinclined to defer mindlessly to higher authority. It had after all been he whose strident and damning report on the state of the colony's sanitation in 1872 had been so deliberately ignored, and whose gloomy predictions were now, two decades later, proving daily ever more prescient.

Ayres had been looking forward to Yersin's arrival ever

since his letter from Bourgeois, and he greeted his new visitors with enthusiasm. Blithely he attempted to speak on behalf of the entire medical community, assuring Yersin "of all assistance from the civilian doctors who form the colonial health board."

By now Yersin was questioning the validity of Bourgeois's gloomy predictions, for the rest of the day produced no encounter that was anything other than encouraging. Vigano introduced him to a score of Portuguese and English doctors who struck Yersin, to a man, as "friendly," "open-minded," "interested," and "most agreeable."

It was late by the time Yersin and Vigano finished their last call, and, with the streets deserted and corner noodle bars all closed—their owners either dead or in hiding or fled to China—they dined in Yersin's hotel. Already Yersin—a jungle explorer accustomed more to hammock than laundered sheets—was looking for a way out, anxious to spend his nights researching, not sequestered in some mute-corridored hotel, far from the epidemic streets. But as yet no such opening had arisen. His best bet was to wait until tomorrow, when he'd scheduled meetings with the two most influential men in the colony—the governor, Sir William Robinson, and Dr. James Lowson. If Robinson could offer nothing, no doubt Lowson—grateful to have a bacteriologist of Yersin's caliber on his side—would go out of his way to make him welcome at his own hospital. Rest assured, Vigano told Yersin, by this time tomorrow you will have your rooms.

Yersin slept well that night. His natural optimism—badly knocked by Bourgeois's initial doom-laden prognosis—had returned. As he reviewed the day's events, he recalled with relief how few of Bourgeois's remarks had proved correct.

Only one matter gave him pause. Toward the end of his meeting with Frederic Stedman, an English doctor, he had been taken aside. Stedman's face had become grave, as if about to offer condolences. According to Stedman, Yersin wrote, "a Japanese mission has been here for several days, studying plague." And they'd already had results: Shibasaburo Kitasato, the leader of the team, had discovered a bacillus after only twenty-four hours' work. Yersin kept his feelings to himself. In none of his writings does he speak of his reaction, but in a later update for the governor-general underscored the word "*bacille*" and added, in heavy pencil, a prominent exclamation point.

Early the next morning, Saturday, June 16, Yersin and Vigano presented themselves at Government House. This was, and remains, an impressive piece of white-stuccoed Victorian real estate, built at the same time and with similar ambition as the Government Civil Hospital: Both speak of pomp, of the stately and unquestioned colonial project, and it is unlikely that Yersin—by now in urgent need of official assistance—would have approached the baize-smooth lawns and marble white frontage without at least a twinge of apprehension.

He need not have worried. Sir William Robinson was far from intimidating. Official portraits show an uncanny and rather comical likeness to King Edward VII, who would succeed his mother, Queen Victoria, as British monarch some seven years later. Both men were tall, heftily built, and barrel chested; but it was their large heads and identical beards that consolidated the resemblance.

Robinson, nearing retirement at fifty-eight, was almost as well traveled as his royal lookalike. A career colonial administrator, he had served as governor in a score of other British territories, including Barbados and the Bahamas. But nothing in his career had prepared him for the administrative and human catastrophe that was now Hong Kong, or—as the most senior official responsible—for the collapse in his own standing that had accompanied it. The very day of his meeting with Yersin, the *Hong Kong Telegraph*—the colony's biggest-circulation daily—reported the latest word on the streets, "that Sir William Robinson is really a Frenchman, and has (perhaps on account of the Franco-Chinese war of 1884–85) gone to the trouble of purchasing the Hong Kong governorship with the special object of introducing the plague and deliberately killing off the whole Chinese community."

By the time Yersin and Vigano arrived on the governor's doorstep shortly after breakfast, Robinson would already have been well acquainted with the contents of the morning papers. Yet, in Yersin's brief account, there is no suggestion that the governor allowed the latest flurry of malicious gossip to affect his professional cool. Robinson, wrote Yersin in his report for the Pasteur Institute, "receives us with his habitual courtesy." And this was no empty display of manners: Robinson took the trouble to personally guarantee Yersin "that the doors of all the plague hospitals be open to [him]."

Robinson's influence, however, extended only so far: The doctor with ultimate responsibility for the plague hospitals was Lowson, the irascible skew-eyed Scot, and so it was to the Government Civil Hospital that Yersin and Vigano hurried first. Approaching the building's sweeping colonnaded facade— as Kitasato had done just three days earlier—Yersin would have had no idea how significant a figure Lowson would prove, or to what degree he possessed the authority to make or break the careers of the colony's doctors and researchers. The very last thing Yersin would have suspected was the relish that Lowson derived from the exercise of this power.

YERSIN AND VIGANO WERE USHERED INTO LOWSON'S OFFICE together, and Vigano, as before, made the introductions. Lowson leaned across the desk, proffering a cold hand that gripped Yersin's with a surprising and unsettling force. He uttered a single French word—a lackadaisical, drawled *"Bonjour,"* heavy with ironic emphasis—before lapsing back into English.

"I should tell you," he said, clasping his hands behind his head, "that I don't have much time. It's not a good moment, right now. *Comprenez?*"

Vigano turned to Yersin and translated for him.

"But," Yersin interjected, "I understood that Dr. Lowson would be expecting me."

"My dear fellow," Lowson replied, a thin smile just discernible under his mustache, "we are in the middle of the biggest epidemic this island has ever seen. I spend my days rushing from one emergency to the next. You must forgive me if I fail to read the odd missive."

Vigano, without interrupting, answered straight back. "Dr. Yersin is from the Pasteur Institute in Paris. As I'm sure you are aware, he is one of the world's most distinguished bacteriologists. He is here on invitation to study the plague. And the governor," he added darkly, "has already assured him of every possible assistance."

Lowson glanced from Vigano to Yersin. He nodded slowly, narrowed his eyes. "You are aware that there is already a

Japanese bacteriologist in Hong Kong? You will have heard of him, I feel sure—Shibasaburo Kitasato, a professor. He truly *is* world famous."

"Yes," said Yersin, "I have heard that he is here. And I would be happy to work alongside him. We could join forces, combine our expertise."

Lowson shook his head. "Professor Kitasato has come with five assistants. He is settled into his work. And—as I'm sure you have heard—he has already struck gold. He has found the bacillus that causes plague." He paused, looking hard at Yersin. "I wired the *Lancet* only yesterday."

Yersin sat in silence, absorbing this latest news. On the desk a carriage clock ticked loudly. He looked at his hands. Once the *Lancet*—one of the world's best-respected medical journals— published Kitasato's findings, hearsay would become fact, with Kitasato confirmed as the plague pioneer. And yet, something in him rebelled against the speed of Kitasato's announcement. Plague had remained an enigma for centuries; surely it would not reveal its secrets in forty-eight hours?

Yersin looked up at Lowson again. "In that case," he said, taking a deep breath, "I offer my sincerest congratulations to the professor. But I would still most strongly request some laboratory space of my own, ideally a room in one of the plague hospitals."

"I think," Lowson replied, "that Professor Kitasato has taken the last available space. As you will understand, I made sure he had the very best."

Yersin, disappointment turning to fury, rose abruptly to his feet. Vigano reached out, put a hand on his arm. "*Attends,*" he murmured. To Lowson, gently, he said, "A simple room would suffice. Dr. Yersin, as you know, is traveling alone. He is not greedy for space."

Lowson drummed his fingers on the tabletop, his long nails loud as tap shoes on the lacquer. He addressed a point over their heads, his focus jittery. "Not this morning. Impossible. Later on I will take you around the hospitals. Afternoon, it'll have to be. Three o'clock. And now," he finished, standing up from his desk and, without pausing to shake hands, striding toward the door, "you will have to excuse me. I have an epidemic on my hands."

OF ALL THE CLUES TO THE STRANGE BREW OF PASSION AND MIS-anthropy that was James Lowson, his diary for 1894 is the most compelling. The original was guarded by his granddaughter in Australia, but a sole microfilm copy exists in the archives of a small medical science museum in Taipingshan—a building erected in the aftermath of plague as the colony's first and desperately needed pathology institute. Through the densely written pages—and the careful paste-ins of endless newspaper clippings—comes a sense of a man in the grip not only of a thrilling emergency but also of his own powerful prejudices, his own quite particular and unbending view of the world.

The difference in attitude and approach toward Kitasato and Yersin was immediately obvious, and—though Yersin's writings led one to suspect as much—shocking in its lack of professional impartiality. For June 14, the entry read, "Kitasato discovered bacillus. Kitasato and Aoyama to dinner—good chaps." In the coming weeks he recorded numerous other dinners with the Japanese team, as well as the odd "tiffin" (officer corps slang for "snack"). Yersin received no such hospitality. Whenever he made an appearance in Lowson's journal it was seldom by name: On June 16, the day the Scot grudgingly assented to show him the various plague hospitals, the entry read baldly, "Took Frenchman around." Within the space of a few hours, Yersin had been reduced to a faceless nonentity, distinguishable only by nationality. His presence, Lowson's cursory scribble implied, was an irritation, although thankfully one that could be quickly pushed aside. He would have to fend for himself.

The reasons for Lowson's animosity toward Yersin were harder to gauge. But there were clues. Despite a calculated and sustained tone of scientific detachment, his fifty-eight-page report on the epidemic expended considerable energy justifying his own failure to make any kind of discovery:

> It may be thought that we surely had enough time to make some efforts in the direction of discovering bacilli. I can only say that after a day of from twelve to eighteen hours hard and exciting work in the trying heat of a Hong Kong summer none of the men who had to bear the brunt of medical supervision, and who had to look forward to a prolonged mental strain, were much inclined to start work with the microscope by gaslight.

His and his doctors' labors were the real work, necessitating bravery on a scale not required of the men of science: "In the Egyptian epidemic in 1843 half of the French physicians in Cairo perished from the plague; and in the Russian epidemic in 1879 . . . the first three medical men who were in attendance on the sick died, as did numerous attendants. These were the somewhat appalling figures when the epidemic broke out."

As he warmed to his theme, his sense of resentment became more pronounced. "Some of us," he complained, "must regret that our time, being taken up by practical work in connection with the treatment of the plague—for which no fame is secured—we had so little time to look to the more purely scientific side of the question." And Yersin—in Lowson's eyes by far the less impressive of the two foreign scientists—made an easy target for his bitterness.

Unlike Kitasato, Yersin was profoundly dissimilar to Lowson: where the Frenchman was socially reserved, Lowson was gregarious, indiscreet, a successful and popular sportsman, who spent most evenings—at least before the outbreak of plague—drinking at his club or dining with friends. And, as his diary shows, he had little time for difference, for those whose approach was more circumspect than his own. An official who disagreed with Lowson on an aspect of treatment is described as "not listening . . . I cleared out." Later Lowson accuses the members of the sanitation committee of doing "nothing but complaining and making idiotic comments," while "we doctors were fed up at having all the dangerous work to do and never one minute off duty." Even Sir William Robinson does not escape Lowson's vitriol: At one point, for reasons unspecified, he and Colonial Secretary Lockhart are described as "making themselves obnoxious—bloody fools."

It is quite possible that Lowson was in plain language a snob, who found himself pawing the ground before the statesman-scientist Kitasato but simply did not register Yersin's presence as significant. Kitasato was a welcome guest, Yersin an interloper; Kitasato merited his support and hospitality, Yersin manifestly did not. And there was no doubt in Lowson's mind who would ultimately prevail: How, he'd have asked himself, could anyone in his right mind equate this mumbling, undersize Frenchman with the brooding, mysterious genius that was Kitasato? There was simply no contest.

AT THREE THE SAME SATURDAY AFTERNOON—FIVE WEEKS INTO the epidemic, with some eighty thousand Chinese now having fled to China, and the death rate showing little sign of slowing—Yersin and Vigano presented themselves once more at Lowson's office. He, no doubt keen to shoehorn the promised hospital tour into as short a period as possible, ushered them immediately into waiting rickshaws. They careered down the hairpins from the Government Civil Hospital as the monsoon swept in again. Out on the rain-smooth water, huddled in the back of a partially covered rowboat commandeered as ferry, Yersin saw a pale racing just off the stern: white dolphins, oblivious to the chaos and panic in the world above, chasing their wake.

They came alongside the *Hygeia*. Yersin's first impressions have not survived—in his Pasteur report he remarked only that there were eight patients on board, all English soldiers, making it something less than a quarter full—but it is hard to imagine that the very fact of a hospital ship, especially one this empty, did not strike him as at least a touch surreal. He'd have noted the long line of achingly black, featureless windows, the lack of any open deck space, rust bleeding from the anchor port. Glancing up at the roof, he'd have wondered too about ventilation: The six stovepipe chimneys were clearly for braziers; the three rooftop vents appeared to be stuck shut. And he'd have looked back, across the quarter mile of water they'd crossed to reach the vessel, and wondered just how much such an isolated hospital could ever perform its function.

Hygeia had a wedge of steps, riveted in place, from deck to water, and Yersin and Vigano stepped from the gunwale of the rowboat and climbed toward the half-size door in the ship's side through which Lowson, a moment earlier, had disappeared. Once inside, their eyes would have taken a while to adjust to the gloom. And then came the intermittent groaning, the whisper of doctors and attendants, the rubber-wheeled hum of the medicine cart; he saw the shivering, fetal-crouched forms. Lowson, in conversation with another doctor, let Yersin and Vigano stand ignored at the entrance before turning abruptly on his heel and hurrying them around the beds.

The *Hygeia* patients, Yersin wrote, "appeared to be convalescing." All eight, having made it through the first week of infection, were likely to recover: a sample highly unrepresentative of the *pestifères* as a whole, some 80 percent of whom never survived. Yersin paused beside each one, lifting aside the bedclothes and bandages to examine the buboes, the bruise-dark swellings in groin and neck and armpit that were the distinguishing marks of bubonic plague. At each slight movement, even the final lifting of the bandage, Yersin was struck by the flash of pain in the men's eyes, the limbs tensing, then loosening, the hands grabbing at the sheet and bed frame. Within five minutes, ten at the outside, he would have finished his round; at the door Lowson was waiting impatiently; the boatman's hands were already on the oars.

For half an hour, heading into the wind, they kept parallel to the shore and made slow progress. Yersin wanted to offer assistance to their boatman, who was continually knocked sideways by ever-bigger waves, but Lowson made it clear that the three Europeans should be above such petty acts of charity: He'd ordered Yersin and Vigano into the covered stern, from where he now barked instructions at the boatman in nursery English, clapping his hands for emphasis. As they progressed, he shouted out the names of landmarks on the mainland.

"Government House, Harbour Office, GPO," he hollered above the crash of waves against the bow. He gesticulated wildly. "Peak Tram, Happy Valley, Kellett Island gunpowder depot."

Yersin found himself drifting into reverie, this ponderous boat passage the first time for reflection since his arrival. They were heading for the northwestern tip of the island, to the Kennedy Town district, where, in the former-police-barracks-turned-hospital, Kitasato and his team were at work. Lowson had indicated, though pointedly made no promise, that there might be a room here where Yersin could base himself, and this appealed to Yersin. As former pupils of Louis Pasteur and Robert Koch, he and Kitasato would be sure to adopt quite different approaches to research, but this could only benefit the work: They'd be targeting the same problems from different but complementary angles.

They landed with a jolt, riding heavy against the pilings of the Belchers Bay jetty. Along the entire length of the dock only one other vessel was moored, and it took a brief glance for Yersin to know its purpose: Coffins were being unloaded, passed from ship to land along a line of barefoot, shaven-headed workers, their stripped torsos polished with sweat, ragged soaking trousers held up with twine. Beyond the jetty, on a patch of rutted mud, stood a horse and cart, the animal with its head hung low, mouth afroth. A track led away from the shore, climbing up a sparsely wooded hillside. Halfway up, Yersin spotted tiny figures, working at what seemed like a chalk quarry: The excavations had exposed a pure-white scar in the landscape.

"Burial pits," said Lowson, watching him. "Quicklime. We get them under as soon as we can."

From the jetty they walked, turning their heads from the stench as they passed the coffin cart, aware suddenly of a crescendoing whine of insects, turning to see a crust of flies around the lid of the topmost coffin. The hospital, some fifteen minutes later, was unmistakable: a red cross flying from the flagpole; a group of nurses in white dresses and starched caps in conversation on the grass at the foot of the main steps. From what Yersin could see, a veranda encircled the entire building, and on this extra cots had been assembled. The two-story building was of brick—a rich clay red, darkened by the rain. It reminded him of the country lodge of a Vietnamese colonial official.

The nursing staff, Lowson explained as they approached, were all European, and the patients billeted here were those happy to accept Western medicine; the rest—the majority, all those who refused to submit to the methods of white doctors— being divided between the nearby glass factory and the Tung Wah hospital, based in Taipingshan, the epicenter of the epidemic.

The moment he stepped through the main entrance, Yersin knew that this was where he wanted to work. From the very first glance inside, it seemed the antithesis of the cramped and diseased central district, with its oozing, glassy-eyed corpses and gutters blocked with dead rats, with its abandoned houses and smoking pyres of clothes and broken chairs. What he was looking at now was the model of a field hospital: polished wood floors, large windows affording ample breeze, a surfeit of beds. In a far corner, under an open window, he even saw a patient smiling at the nurse bending over him.

A POLICEMAN WAS STANDING IN FRONT OF A LARGE, DARK wood door. Lowson stopped, shook his hand, and, turning, pointed at Yersin, then Vigano. The policeman nodded, somber. Yersin could see his jaw muscles working, flickers of tension under the skin. He noticed his revolver, his riot stick, the fatigue in his eyes. The policeman nodded once more and picked a key from the loop on his belt, then slotted it into the lock. He opened the door, directing Yersin and Vigano to follow Lowson.

They were in a dark passageway now, windows shuttered. Yersin heard the key turn in the lock behind him then Lowson, at the front, splutter what sounded like curses. He heard him rattle at something, then, cursing again, give up and knock loudly.

"Kitasato!" Lowson shouted, but before he had a chance to cry out further, the door opened and light flooded into the passage. Yersin could see a diminutive, bespectacled Japanese, whose hand was now being vigorously pumped by Lowson. He wore a white cotton suit, surgical mask, and gloves. Behind him were workbenches with microscopes and slide trays. Just

visible around the doorjamb were the white feet of a corpse, tag
tied around a toe.

Yersin and Vigano followed Lowson into the room. Two
Japanese researchers in long white coats were bent over the
corpse. The chest had been sheared open and Yersin saw the
astonishing scarlet of the interior organs. One of the men was
working away with a scalpel, up to his forearm in blood, while
the other held out a white enamel bowl. It seemed to Yersin,
though he was too far away to be sure, that they were extracting
slices of lung, an approach that perplexed him: Why, he
puzzled, would any scientist have imagined the mechanism of
the disease to be found in the lungs, rather than in the plague
swellings themselves?

In his Pasteur report Yersin made special note of his astonishment. "I am surprised to see," he wrote, "that they are not
even examining the bubo; rather, they are minutely investigating the heart, the lungs, the liver, the spleen, etc." This bewilderment doubled when he saw Kitasato go on to place the
samples under his microscope. Announcing that he could find
no evidence of "his bacillus, [Kitasato] declares that the patient
died of typhoid fever and not the plague!"

The longer Yersin's encounter with Kitasato went on, the
more skeptical he became of his competitor's approach. Doubtless the intensity of his rivalry made it inevitable that he should
look for flaws; certainly it would seem that, from the moment
he first confronted Kitasato—deliberately belittling him in his
notes as *"Monsieur"* rather than *"Professeur"*—Yersin was
determined to strip away the aura of invincibility with which
Lowson had all day been lovingly garlanding him. In the end,

however, he could easily have afforded a less defensive posture: Invited by Kitasato to have a look through the microscope, Yersin saw not only the typhoid bacilli that Kitasato had claimed were there, but smaller, scarcer bacteria. For the first time a buoyant note, a palpable sense that the prize is yet to be seized, enters his writing. "I refrain, however, from any comment." There is triumph here, excitement, and not a little relief.

Encouraged to find himself suddenly on a more level footing with Kitasato—notwithstanding the latter's settled and impressive surroundings, and the industrious bustle of his assistants—Yersin, emboldened, approached him directly. Of this, the pivotal moment of their relations, a detailed first-person account is needed, but the only one that survives—Yersin's—runs to a mere three hundred words. In all Kitasato's writings there is scant mention of Yersin, and one can only conclude that he was consciously airbrushed from the photograph of memory, as if all Kitasato noticed was himself, his own work and his own circle of intimates: Even Lowson, his most loyal champion, is referred to at one point as "a British quarantine officer," a post that he not only never held, but was also way beneath him. In Yersin's account there follows the telling detail that, "as [the Japanese] know neither English nor French, I try to converse with them in German." Yersin, a shy man, was making a deliberate effort to extend a cordial hand to Kitasato. He spoke in the spirit of scientific collaboration, knowing his German to be worse than ropy, yet confident that Kitasato would reply in the same willing and cooperative spirit.

What he would never have expected was ridicule. Barely had he finished his stumbling opening remarks than the Japanese scientists, without even the most cursory response, began "laughing among themselves." And then, to a man, they turned their backs on him.

· 10 ·

HE COULD SMELL THE KEROSENE BEFORE HE REACHED THE door; by the time he was on the street, a wad of rupees in his back pocket, leaving home with nothing but the clothes in which he stood, the reek was overpowering. The road had cleared a little since dawn, and the air was charged with a different atmosphere: less panic, more fury. Vehicles were actually moving now, albeit at a crawl: Scooters carried whole families, a flatbed the residents of an entire apartment house. Across the street, cutting through the growl and whine of engines, came the sound of breaking glass.

Mohanlal elbowed through, ducking under the neck of a motionless, oblivious cow. He heard the splinter of glass again, followed by a yelp that sounded like war: pure vengeful emotion. His way barred, he climbed over the hood of a Toyota, the metal scalding his hands, sensing the fender give underfoot as he sprang to the far sidewalk. Looking up, he saw that what had once been the office of his neighbor, Dr. Ramesh Shah, was now a disintegrating shell, the windows gone, door shredded. Inside, glass was strewn across the desk and the waiting-room chairs. A man was pouring kerosene from a soda bottle, his face expressionless. He lifted the bottle, sprayed an arc across the wall.

"Stop!" Mohanlal screamed. "What are you doing?"

Another man, ax in hand, met his eye. His lips were wet, his teeth red from betel juice. "He is a rich man, and a coward. He deserves nothing."

Mohanlal stepped into Shah's destroyed office; glass, like so much harmless candy, crunched underfoot. "You can't burn it down. The whole block will go. Give me the kerosene." He held out his hand. The whole scene seemed suddenly out of reach, beyond surreal: He felt nothing, not the terror he'd expected, just a sense of being underwater, every sound muffled. He watched his hand, the kerosene, his adversary, all this in silence. Then suddenly, and to his astonishment, the other man shoved the bottle at him, and the sound burst riotously back on. Everyone was shouting. Mohanlal, clutching the bottle, his shirtfront drenched, stepped backward, almost tripping, onto the sidewalk. Before he'd even had a chance to turn, the men inside were bent to work again. Mohanlal saw the ax raised high, a flurry of papers, a chair in midair. And he ran.

His head was full of overheard conversation, fragments that turned his normally dispassionate reporter's brain to panic:

"No one is left," "If you stay, you die," "You know how much the bus . . . ," "Forget the train," "But the doctors. . . ." Then his attention was drawn by a crowd gathered on a patch of garbage-strewn wasteland. Those people, in dramatic contrast to everyone else, were stationary, gathered in a circle, facing inward: Their very stillness was astonishing, and he found himself breaking away from the road to pick his way across the mud toward them.

Closing in, he glimpsed the flash of a spade, and his first thought was: cover-up. Someone has died, and they're interring him, they're trying to avoid being hospitalized themselves. But when he stood at the edge of the group, and looked through the heads to the center, he saw no sheeted corpse, just a growing hole in the ground.

"We're burying it," said one man. He coughed: His mask filled, collapsed. Mohanlal thought he saw blood on the material, and he knew what this meant, that the lungs were now infected. He took a step back.

"Burying?" he repeated. "Burying what?"

"Squirrel," came another voice. "We found it dead. It died of plague. So we bury it."

"And you," shouted yet another, "are you a doctor? Are we all doomed now? Will no one get out of this place alive?"

Mohanlal, regretting the curiosity that had brought him thus far, backed farther off. "No," he said. "I'm not a doctor. But this is plague. You've heard that, right?"

"It is the city's fault," barked out a voice, and to this there was a murmur of approval. "All the garbage, the filth. No wonder we have plague."

. . .

AS PLAGUE SPREAD IN SURAT, FEAR BRED RECRIMINATION: WE
ourselves are to blame, said some; others raged at God; leftists
blamed the rich, the diamond entrepreneurs and textile million-
aires whose imported smoked-glass-windowed limousines were
the first to hit the potholed streets out of town. The medical
fraternity hardly set a better example: While the majority of
doctors fled, a band of their colleagues chose instead denial,
announcing a reward of three hundred thousand rupees to anyone able to demonstrate that the epidemic was not plague. To
those who stayed on, like sixty-year-old Dr. Sudha Trivedi, the
cause of most grief was the universal lack of compassion, evidence of a dark hole, corrupted and grotesque, where the community should have had a beating heart.

As a medic herself, a specialist in health education, what
wounded Trivedi most deeply was witnessing fellow doctors
choose their own safety over the lives of their patients. Some
six years later, as she remembered those weeks—folding and
unfolding her soft hands in the lap of her sari—her gaze drifted
toward the window. From this height—six stories, across the
guano-spattered roofs of other apartment buildings—the Tapti
was clearly visible, almost a half-mile wide, approaching the
ocean. Crossing the river on the way over there had been large
white blocks, floating like miniature icebergs; only when the
wind gusted them clear of the surface did they reveal themselves to be chunks of polystyrene. Now, in Trivedi's dark eyes,
there was a pale stripe: The river's reflection, and it spoke
of her connection to this place, where her grandparents and

great-grandparents had lived, but whose people, more recently, had caused her such disappointment.

"It was a bad thing, a very unfortunate thing," she said, and her voice trembled. "When I heard that the doctors had disappeared from the city, I literally got pain in my heart. I do not expect anything of the uneducated people, but of the medical person I do expect integrity. Everyone loves his own life—that of course is the first thing. But medical people have to think of others. And that did not happen."

Yet even the medics, in those first days, were at a loss. Trivedi's first reaction was to assume mistaken diagnosis. "I thought it could never be plague. I'm sixty years old, and I'd never seen a plague case, so I rushed to the hospital to see the patients. Of course I had read about plague in books, but I admit I had no idea what it looked like."

What she, in common with most Suratis, possessed in abundance, however, was a reservoir of family memories of the last time, close to a century before, that plague had struck. Stories told by her grandfather, great-aunt, and father had become folklore: Her great-aunt in particular, widowed before she had children, had assumed almost mythic status in the intervening decades. Trivedi's eyes sparked alight. "She was the only woman to carry a dead body on her shoulders," she said, raising her hands above her head to mimic her aunt's pioneering bravery. "This was a time when nobody was ready to help anybody, but my auntie did not think like this: She served people without pause for herself. She worked like a man, and they had no remedies back then, no rescue teams, no government help. And she did not get the plague." But her mercy had gone hand-in-hand with a fierce sense of judgment. "She believed that plague was God's anger at those who did not have good conduct of their lives."

Trivedi, who stopped short of such a brutal assessment, had wasted no time spreading the modern message: that plague was treatable and not an occasion for panic; that "it was a postflood calamity and we should not be afraid of it"; that, however fearful, people should not abandon their homes. "Don't run around," she told them. "You will spread the disease." And all the while, as she walked the streets handing out strips of tetracycline tablets, administering calm, a small voice nagged at the back of her brain: You thought plague was dead. You were wrong. In the end, deprived of any other solace, she prayed that plague, once over, would never return. "We were attacked by this disease because we were unaware of it. But we know of its dangers: We have put our hand in the fire and will not do it again. That is what I pray."

FOR CLOSE TO A WEEK THE EXISTENCE OF PLAGUE WAS FURIously contested. There was no question that the situation was extremely serious, and the Surat authorities, witnessing the extraordinary scenes of panic on the roads out of town, vainly struggled for control. In midexodus people were "advised" not to leave, but to "confine themselves" to their houses, and this very suggestion, with its note of emergency quarantine, no doubt propelled even the last remaining waverers into flight.

Conscious of the dangers of loose talk, the municipal commissioner warned that it was a criminal offense to spread rumors. In what was pitched as a precautionary measure, hawkers with roadside stands were forbidden to sell fruit, vegetables, and juices. Confusion ruled: Within the space of twelve hours, and by impeccable sources, the existence of plague was first confirmed and then, with equal ferocity, denied. The confirmation came from the Surat authorities, who offered as backup the assurance that "plague is infectious but curable"; denial, however, issued from higher up still, from the national government in Delhi. "There is nothing serious in Surat," gambled the minister with responsibility for Gujarat State— adopting the same ostrich approach as the governor of French Indochina had done with Alexandre Yersin in the early 1890s— "and if there is you can hang me." Yet, even as these words were being spoken, the prime minister was ordering twenty-four-hour surveillance of Surat: a "this-is-Houston"-style control room with phone banks and computer screens, and instructions to document all evidence. Plague was the meltdown scenario, and it was looking ever more plausible with each hour that passed.

AT THE NEW CIVIL HOSPITAL, PLAGUE CAUGHT THE ENTIRE staff unprepared. The store rooms were empty of filter masks—an everyday surgical requirement as well as a necessity for treating plague patients. It took nine days for all staff members to receive them, and almost a month before every doctor had a gown, gloves, and goggles. Equally serious, the hospital's laundry and incinerator were broken down for the entire duration of the epidemic: The subsequent inquiry noted "open-air burning of hospital mattresses and bedsheets used by suspected plague patients just behind the hospital." Few elevators were working; X-ray and electrocardiograph machines had been awaiting repair for weeks; and patients' records were kept in such an illegible scrawl that follow-up monitoring—for which home visits should have been mandatory—was impossible.

Scarcely surprising then that, five days into the epidemic, with the hospital stretched way beyond its meager limits, sixty-eight patients—plague suspects all—fled the compound. The language of those charged with their apprehension spoke of warfare, of something altogether darker and more malevolent. "They are living bombs," muttered the chief of the health department, "and we have to locate them at any cost."

IN THE BACK ALLEYS OFF VED ROAD—WHERE THE FIRST corpse, weeping blood from nose and eyes, was stumbled upon—the chaos of those first few days was vividly and swiftly remembered. Until that point plague had been a disease of the past, no more relevant to the residents of Ved Road than the last viceroy, or Gandhi: a point of drama from history, now long forgotten. Even a young doctor, like Chetan Acharya, walking today through the plague district, admitted that, the moment he heard the first rumors, he'd gone straight to his medical dictionaries. The rest of the population, with no information but the whispers of neighbors on which to rely, chose flight; the bolder few, and those with no place to go, opted to stay, and what action they took spoke more of hope than of either knowledge or experience.

For Hitnath Zha, an orange-robed, sandalwood-scented social worker, the cause of plague was rats, and he'd spent the small hours of the first plague night setting traps all around the house. For the entire next week, in concert with his neighbors, he'd boycotted fresh fruit and vegetables. The one rat he managed to snare he bagged and carried far from his house, burying it deep in waste ground, working in the heat with mask and gloves, the earth soft and dark as molasses after the rain and the flood.

Plague hit Surat at its weakest moment. The floodwaters had barely receded; corpses of drowned animals lay like abandoned meal sacks in the roads and alleys; mud lay six inches deep on the living room floors of houses. And yet, with entire neighborhoods suddenly on the move, and every sense of safety long gone, there were still those who chose to remain. A young man and his grandfather—the same sad-dog eyes, hawk nose—recalled their own decision.

"We had nowhere to go," the younger man said, shrugging. "I am born and brought up in Surat, my grandfather too. The migrants, the diamond and textile workers, they could all go back home. But for us, this is our home."

Had they been more watchful or knowledgeable, they might have spotted the warning signs, the harbingers of epidemic: the floodwaters whose grime mark even now, six years later, was visible halfway up the concrete walls; the sewage-corrupted grain silos; the vultures that perched high on the telegraph poles. It was not until their community watchman, a nocturnal security guard, was found unconscious on a neighbor's doorstep one morning—only an hour from death, his gums and lips bleeding and livid—that a dreadful scenario began to present itself, a situation for which no one was in any way prepared.

The usual theories proliferated, all uncannily reminiscent of the fourteenth century: Plague had broken out because

drinking water was poisoned by sewage; because of some efflu-
ent secreted by rat corpses; because of an unnamed airborne
contaminant. And, as in the Middle Ages, those who fled—the
majority—were stoned as they entered each new town. For
days, their calves bandaged against the maulings of wild dogs,
they went without food. For water, they pillaged wells or, late
at night, stole into backyards, emptying faucets straight into
their mouths.

IT WAS DARK. DR. CHETAN ACHARYA WAS TALKING AS HE DROVE,
lights off. He turned off Ved Road onto a rough track, and the
light seemed suddenly to fade.

"All this," he said softly, "it is a very recent memory for the
people here. At least ten *lakhs,* one million people, were
affected by the flood alone, even before we were hit by plague.
It was a terrible calamity. And what coverage did that receive in
the world media? Nothing. If just ten people in the U.S. had
been caught in floods, just imagine the cameras, the commentators."

He fell silent. Ahead was a dry riverbed, then a steep bank.
Farther on was a landfill site, garbage glowing palely. The light
was almost gone. He stopped the car.

"I am lost," he said. He turned the headlights on, and a cow,
dazzled by the glare, stared back. On every horizon electricity
glowed orange: There was no sunset. Dark shapes loomed,
then receded. He shoved the car into reverse and turned. His
tracks were still visible in the dirt.

· 11 ·

MORE THAN ANY OTHER DISEASE, PLAGUE HAS CHANGED THE
course of history. It has surged across continents, leaped
oceans, operated according to its own ferocious and apparently
random rules. For thousands of years it remained a mystery,
and there is today still much about its mechanism that is
unknown. Of all diseases, plague—even in this age of AIDS,
Ebola, resurgent tuberculosis, and malaria—still retains a unique
potency, and for good reason. Europe, in the fourteenth century, lost a quarter of its population to plague, and this in turn
altered the Continent's entire economic structure: Before 1346
overpopulation had meant that only skilled professionals—
teachers of Latin, farm managers—were in short supply; come

plague, there were suddenly no men to drive ploughs or sweep floors. Professors became carpenters, linguists became wheelwrights. Two and a half centuries later, plague scythed down half a million in northern Spain; subsequent outbreaks in the seventeenth century doubled that total, bringing Spain's seemingly unassailable political and economic dominance to an abrupt end.

The history of plague is the story of humanity—wild and unpredictable, bloody and brooding, intimately connected to the lives of the animals that serve and stalk us and to the crops we cultivate, dependent on season and rainfall and ecological disturbance, but not without the possibility of redemption, cure, and deliverance. Plague has been part of the English lexicon ever since the publication of the King James Bible in 1611, though whether the "plague of the Philistines" referred to in the first book of Samuel was bubonic remains uncertain: What is beyond doubt is that, for seventeenth-century Europeans, with three centuries of plague behind them, no disease held greater force, and it would therefore have been the inevitable translators' choice, the only credible synonym for large-scale pestilence.

In other texts, references to plague were better documented and less ambiguous. The earliest Chinese description dates from A.D. 610; the next, which comes some thirty years later, includes the significant observation that plague was common in Kwangtung—a province of Canton—but rare in the interior. The implication is clear: Plague first hit China early in the seventh century, some two generations after it broke into the Mediterranean basin in 542. Both epidemics are now seen as part of the same continuum: the transnational outbreak known to modern historians as the first pandemic.

From the eighth century until the Middle Ages, plague remained quiescent, at least in Christian Europe, and it is this pattern of dormancy and then explosion that continues to cause scientists such concern: If past behavior is a guide to future volatility, then plague remains an uncertain, looming threat. And nowhere, it seems, is safe. The second pandemic, which precipitated such a shakedown in European order during the Middle Ages, effected much the same in China. The numbers are astonishing: From 123 million in 1200, China's population dropped to a mere 65 million by 1393; the intervening years had seen a double invasion—first the Mongol hordes, then plague—which between them had wreaked a formidable destruction, the worse, in the case of plague, for being so little understood.

Imagine a physician in Caffa in 1346, in Smyrna in the mid–eighteenth century or in Hong Kong in 1894: His town is in the grip of plague and he recognizes the need for action, but has no idea what to prescribe, to advise. Efforts at control were furious but wayward: The only common factor was the desire to do *something*, since the alternative—despair, apathy, nihilism—was unimaginable. By the early nineteenth century the thinking had simplified: Plague, as an 1819 select committee in the British Parliament reported, was "a disease communicable by contact only," and what modifications this hypothesis underwent over the next hundred years were at best nominal. Instructions to plague fighters in Bombay in 1898 defined the disease as "essentially associated with unsanitary conditions in human habitations, the chief of which are accumulations of filth, overcrowding and absence of light and ventilation"; it was "mainly conveyed from place to place by individuals in their person, clothing and personal effects." To these, and to thousands of other such claims, there were at least partial truths, and quarantine, it was hoped, was a broad-enough approach to be effective. The requirements were certainly rigorous: Ships arriving from ports suspected of plague had to anchor in a scheduled port for forty days, during which time no communication with land was allowed. Yet plague—through mechanisms that remained frustratingly opaque—continued to elude such border controls.

Its longevity as a threat and its refusal to surrender its secrets meant that plague long ago became an inevitable human crisis. Writers as diverse as Giovanni Boccaccio, Geoffrey Chaucer, and William Langland all treated plague, and the very real possibility of sudden and unglorious death, as the mirror-side of life: an act of God, like a freak storm or drought. And there were other consequences for literature: Scholars have even suggested that the decay of Latin as a *lingua franca* among educated Europeans, and the rise of national languages as a medium for serious writing, was hastened by the death from plague of swaths of clerics and teachers. Artists, too, became bleaker in their vision: The serenity of Giotto was replaced, in the work of many painters, by the common use of motifs such as the Dance of Death. The effervescence and buoyancy of the thirteenth century—which saw the joyous construction of many of Europe's finest cathedrals—gave way to a more troubled, interior age.

· 12 ·

RIDICULED BY THE JAPANESE, BARELY TOLERATED BY JAMES Lowson, Yersin found himself in a deeply uncomfortable and uncertain situation. From his brief tour around the Kennedy Town police barracks, he'd have quickly registered that, despite Lowson's earlier indications, no rooms remained unoccupied. He needed laboratory space, and required it in or close to Kennedy Town, since it was here, on the western corner of the island, that the plague pits were located and in this location, therefore, that he stood most chance of gaining access to the corpses he needed for autopsy work. Faced with a suddenly implacable Lowson, he'd have insisted that provision be found for him. He spoke of his own medical duty, of the obligations of doctors in general, coming close as he dared to direct accusation. And then, quite unexpectedly, Lowson relented.

There was, he told Yersin, one possibility, but it would require a restricted and modest use of space. On the first-floor gallery—an area through which orderlies and other hospital staff could pass freely—there was just enough room to set up a workbench. Yersin, he said, could work there. And with that— just a gesture roofward to indicate the approximate location of Yersin's quarters—Lowson swept from the cool wood interior to the monsoon heat outside, his white coat afloat behind him, barking for his rickshaw, relieved, at least for the moment, to be rid of his troublesome Frenchman.

For the next few days Yersin saw little of Lowson, and even less of Kitasato who, though at work in the same hospital, kept himself and his team cloistered away in their rooms, squirreling out only at dusk to hurry back to their hotel. Doubtless Lowson, as the doctor in charge of the plague hospitals, was extremely pressed: It was his responsibility to oversee all treatment, to discuss and decide on diagnoses, to steer a diplomatic course between the open distrust and venom of the Chinese and the righteous Victorian determination of the colonial authorities. And it was he—as his twenty-three-page letter at the end of May to the British foreign secretary in London showed— who was behind such questionable practices as eucalyptus-oil-soaked handkerchiefs for all "sisters [nurses] and attendants"; whose research had led him to conclude erroneously that plague was "not infectious or contagious," and "probably more chemical than bacterial"; who had struggled so hard to recruit hospital attendants after "the Chinese amahs and boys [had] simply fled"; and for whom the burden of work was so great that "only by slaving night and day [was I] enabled to carry on."

Yersin rose early the following morning, two days since his arrival on the island, anxious to begin work as soon as possible. The day, however, did not start well: At eight o'clock, he came out of the hotel with his pressure sterilizer and microscope cases, and as he waited on the sidewalk for a rickshaw, one of his assistants fled down the street. Dust eddied in his wake; a lone soldier, out on a morning patrol, shouted after him but made no effort, in the already claustrophobic heat, to follow. Yersin's first reaction was to assume ignorance—"at first I think that [he ran away] out of fear for the plague"—but there must have been something in the Chinese boy's demeanor—a failure to meet his eye that morning, shirt collar too soon sodden with sweat—that made him reassess. Instinctively he reached inside his jacket for his wallet. When he opened it, the boy's abrupt flight made perfect sense: Seventy-five piasters, a substantial wad of notes, were missing.

On the way to Kennedy Town, Yersin turned over the incident in his mind. From his writings, surprisingly little rancor is detectable: For a prouder man, such a betrayal might have triggered a vengeful hunt for the culprit; Yersin, focused solely on the work ahead, saw only "inconvenience. . . . I was counting on this Chinese person as an interpreter with his compatriots." Yet one wonders at his professed sangfroid. Friendless enough before, Yersin would now—whatever his subsequent editorializing—have felt exposed as never before. He could rely on no one, not even those in his pay, and for any human being—no matter how assured—there can be few bleaker realizations.

The whole of that day, Sunday, June 17, Yersin worked alone, at his side his sole remaining retainer: the Vietnamese boy who'd accompanied him on his later jungle expeditions. Over the next few hours he took delivery of a number of guinea pigs and mice—experimental animals, all intended for the same unlovely end—and installed his equipment. Recalling the gleaming ranks of optical and surgical instruments that had proliferated along every inch of Kitasato's research space, Yersin must have felt acutely his own conspicuous lack of hardware. He had microscopes, scalpels, and autoclaves—two-piece, cylindrical pressure sterilizers, their curved steel dulled to pewter by the humidity—but, laid out in front of him, the entire array would have occupied less than half the benchtop.

His next step was obvious and should have been straightforward. "More than anything," he wrote of this moment, "I would like to perform an autopsy." Only by excavating the plague swellings from a fresh corpse, and sliding a smear under the microscope, could he begin investigating the infective agent. He'd have heard of the difficulties in obtaining fresh corpses—Lowson's taste for the macabre was such that he'd have had few qualms about detailing the lengths to which the Chinese were likely to go to prevent dissection of their dead relatives—but he was also aware that Kitasato, as far as he could tell, had no shortage. Once set up, therefore, Yersin would have lost no time in dispatching his assistant to the doctor in charge of the temporary plague hospital. His request would have been simple: The next death you have, ensure I get first look.

And then he waited, confident that within a couple of hours at most he'd be standing, scalpel glinting between fingertips, over a bloated and gaseous blue-black corpse. He had learned of the symptoms from Lowson, who listed them with lurid relish. It is clear from the reports the Scot went on to write—one for the British foreign secretary in London, another for the Hong Kong governor—that the more extreme the case the more acute his sense of thrill. The bubo, "present in ninety per cent of cases, is generally exquisitely tender"; the tongue furred white, turning "absolutely black before death"; victims were pictured lying on "miserable sodden matting soaked with abominations," their tongues "black and protruding," limbs in spasm. And so Yersin would have been expecting the worst, the most gargoylish contortions in death, the most fetid, subhuman odors.

What he could not have expected was the response he got. Within minutes his assistant reappeared with the news that "[no autopsies] will be carried out today." His reaction to this rebuff is not recorded. Even at this stage it is possible that—despite Lowson's undisguised favoritism—Yersin's suspicions were not yet aroused, and indeed he was before long given an encouraging update. A doctor approached carrying a tray of test tubes containing blood samples from patients: He could at least start somewhere.

For the rest of that first day, Yersin blurred slides with blood and squinted at them through his microscope, inching the smears under the bulb of his lens till his eyes had trouble focusing. Sometime—maybe this day, possibly later—he broke from his work and walked outside, following the death carts to the plague pits on the lower slopes of Mount Davis. He had his box camera with him, and here, as elsewhere, and as if aware of the momentousness of the times, he recorded what he saw. The print that survives of the burial ground seems artificially dark, like those early-movie attempts at creating the effect of night, but shows clearly the industrial scale of the burial program. A pile of newly quarried chalk white slabs occupies the immediate foreground. The incline rises sharply, and, cut into the receding hillside, are row upon row of gravestones, divided level from level by broad steps of freshly turned earth. To the uneducated eye, the gradations look as neat as rice paddies in the dry season, awaiting rain and hoe.

Returning to his laboratory, Yersin bent over his microscope once more. By now he had examined the blood from "several patients." The results had been uniform and negative. Nowhere did he discover anything out of the ordinary—no bacillus, no microbe, no infective agent.

Kitasato, by contrast, was at that very moment claiming spectacular results. In his report of July 15, addressed to the Japanese interior minister and later published in the *Tokyo Medical School Journal*, he records June 14—when Yersin's boat was still a full day's sail from Hong Kong waters—as the date of his first autopsy. The dissection was carried out by his pathologist, Professor Tanemichi Aoyama, on a corpse some eleven hours old. Lungs, spleen, liver, buboes, and blood from the heart were removed. In all, Kitasato wrote, "I found a great deal of bacilli." He filled a syringe with the blood and injected it into two laboratory mice: They died two days later. "Day after day," Kitasato recorded, "I took blood from plague patients for examination and found the same bacilli."

Kitasato was triumphant: The mechanism of plague, the causal bacillus, was his, and already, as the ultimate stamp of official acceptance, the internationally renowned weekly medical journal *Lancet* had accepted his findings, which were now due for imminent publication. And yet Yersin, working in parallel, examining blood samples from no doubt the same plague victims, had found no such bacillus: The bacteria he'd spotted under Kitasato's microscope that first day were, he now felt sure, unrelated to plague, and in his workbook he wrote simply, "no results." Clearly, they could not both be right.

· 13 ·

TAKE A GENEROUS SHEET OF PAPER, COLORED PENS, ENOUGH
space to lay it all flat. Sketch the outline of the continents, the
globe unfolded. And then, with the first pen—red, for the start
of the conflagration—draw a line from southern China to
Hong Kong. It is 1894, and slowly, as the summer lengthens, the
thin red line inches on: Amoy, Macao, Foochow. By 1896 it has
reached Bombay, and here, to signify a shift of pace, the color
changes. In purple now, lines claw outward, to St. Petersburg,
Yokohama, Nagasaki. Within India, an interior web of infection grows, drawn black because the toll here is worse than anywhere, and accelerating—55,000 deaths in 1897, 117,000 the
next year, 135,000 in the twelve months after that. Before the

old century has passed, a spray of yellow, like bullet tracks, hits Europe—Oporto, Lisbon, Trieste. And now we have a tangled tapestry, with the Atlantic suddenly enmeshed—Ascunción, Corrientes, Formosa. The map is a riot of color. Connections, like a rampantly expanding railroad network, are proliferating and fusing, spawning, always moving.

Such was the speed of the spread of the third pandemic that, within six years, every continent on earth was affected. In 1900 it struck Africa, Australia, New Zealand, London, Cardiff, Astrakhan in Russia and, finally, the west coast of the United States. And it is this last that, to this day, retains the scent of scandal: A pattern, begun in Hong Kong in 1894, was repeated six years later as if preprogrammed, on the far side of the world.

PORT AUTHORITIES ACROSS THE UNITED STATES HAD BEEN ON the lookout for plague ever since news had reached them from Hong Kong. Quarantine officers were trained and expectant, and so, when the SS *Nippon Maru* sailed through the Golden Gate on Tuesday, June 27, 1899—at the end of a journey begun in Hong Kong—it was immediately impounded. The vessel was searched, and eleven Japanese stowaways were discovered. The next day, when the crew was shifted to Angel Island quarantine station, two of the stowaways were found to be missing. Some days later, their corpses, buoyed by *Nippon Maru* life preservers, were spotted drifting in San Francisco Bay. Autopsy results were unequivocal: Both men carried plague.

For a time all was quiet, and week by week, public health officials breathed easier. Then, on Tuesday, March 6, 1900—

some nine months after the two stowaways were brought in, blue lipped and swollen, from the chop of the bay—a man's body was stretchered, blanket over his head, from the basement of Chinatown's Globe Hotel. Because the victim had died alone, his death unwitnessed, an autopsy was ordered. The physician on duty noted dark bruiselike groin swellings and reported his suspicions to the city health officer. Hours later, a second examination was carried out, this time by the health board's bacteriologist. His report was clear, if reluctant: The man had, in his opinion, died of plague.

Plague had never before hit the United States, and the American establishment, like the European classes in Hong Kong six years earlier, reacted with instant fury. Rather than welcome the city's efforts to curb infection through quarantine, the forces of big business instead opted for ridicule. The investigations of federal quarantine officer Dr. J. J. Kinyoun were lampooned in the *San Francisco Bulletin*: "Have you heard of the deadly bacillus, / Scourge of a populous land, / Bacillus that threatens to kill us, / When found in a Chinaman's gland?" Kinyoun's experimental animals were, the anonymous poet went on, "living and thriving," which was in fact naked falsehood—two guinea pigs and a rat, all injected with plague tissue, had already died. But the pressure worked: Within forty-eight hours, the hastily imposed quarantine of Chinatown was lifted.

What took its place—a sly racism, couched in scientific language—was also reminiscent of Hong Kong in 1894. Soldiers were posted at strategic exit points from the city, with orders to examine anyone—but most particularly anyone Chinese—attempting to leave. By May, with the existence of plague finally accepted by the city health board, antiplague regulations were hurriedly implemented. At the very best, these were unconstitutional: One forbade "Orientals or members of other races particularly susceptible to the disease" from using trains, streetcars, or ferries. And then, as if this were not indignity enough, the health board drew up proposals to evacuate all Chinese to detention camps on Angel Island and—as in Hong Kong—demolish their homes and restaurants, hotels and stores, swinging the heavy ball until nothing was left standing.

Everywhere was confusion, misinformation, obfuscation. The state governor—at a time when the death toll was nearing a hundred—claimed that "plague did not nor ever did exist in California" and, in January 1901, even went so far as to question Kinyoun's working methods, claiming that he had isolated the bacillus not from plague victims but from unnamed imported cultures. Unable to leave it at that, the governor went on to propose that the transportation of plague cultures without high-level permission should be a crime punishable by life imprisonment and that, moreover, it should be a felony to broadcast the presence of plague.

With the San Francisco Medical Society, the U.S. Marine Hospital Service, and the city health board all admitting the existence of plague—and the Chinese, the Merchants' Association, and most newspapers issuing equally vociferous denials—rumors flew wild and unchecked. Plague, some said, had died out in the Middle Ages. According to others it belonged to the days of Charlemagne, before the "common people" had soap; it was, alternatively, an "oriental" disease, peculiar to "rice eaters"; and, concurred the majority, whatever its mechanism or cause, it certainly never attacked Caucasians.

The last victim of this first San Francisco epidemic was a thirty-three-year-old woman from Concord, California. It was February 29, 1904, and 122 people had died, in every case the cause of death the subject of strenuous dispute. The denial of plague had persisted throughout, and went to the very top: Eugene Schmitz, mayor from 1901, even refused to approve the printing of health department statistics, and did his utmost to shift from office the four members of his health board who continued to claim that plague was alive in the city. And then, for a while at least, plague, like a wily heavyweight, pulled back. Those who'd argued against its existence began tentatively to congratulate themselves, proving clearly that no lessons had been learned, for the disease had retreated as if of its own accord, and not as the result of any coherent hygiene drive. This was a mistake that the United States would not make again. Plague, as it would yet discover, never willingly renounces a claim on new territory: Once it has its claws in, it does not loosen its hold.

ON JUNE 18, 1894, THREE DAYS AFTER HIS ARRIVAL IN HONG KONG, Alexandre Yersin wrote what would be the first of three bulletins to the French governor-general in Indochina. The original draft survives and—with its hurried excisions and additions, its stutters of ink and wayward punctuation—speaks most strikingly of urgency, of an electric freshness, of the thrill of being so close to the solution of medicine's most intractable problem. It speaks, too, of the force of Yersin's ambition: Two sentences outlining the work of Shibasaburo Kitasato and his team have been forcefully struck through, almost as if Yersin were trying to will his competitors into nonexistence. The edited bulletin, therefore, would have reached the governor-general with no mention of the Japanese bacteriologist.

The bulletin is also rich in description; like an imaginative novelist, Yersin knew the value of the telling detail. He writes of the contents of Chinese houses being carted to the shore and burned; of the dwellings' barbaric cleansing, which saw soldiers using "steam pumps" to "flood them with torrents of salted water"; of the ninety-five centimeters of concrete poured over each interred corpse; of streets deserted save for the occasional shuffle-past of stretcher-bearers. Walking the streets he noticed few pedestrians, but "many dead rats lying on the ground."

SHORTLY AFTER DAWN THAT SAME DAY, ALEXANDRE YERSIN HAD swabbed down his workbench and set up his equipment in preparation for what he hoped would be a day far more productive and revelatory than the last. As the morning passed, however, it became apparent that this was not to be: Each time he tracked down the doctor in charge and requested an autopsy—his English for this phrase at least now polished and swift, no longer a target for ridicule—he was told that "they are reserved for the Japanese." "I thought I had the same rights as them, but it seems I was wrong." But, as yet, he assumed nothing more sinister than favoritism.

And so that second day was spent much as the first: in endless microscopic examination of blood samples, each of which revealed the same uniform blank. His growing sense of frustration cannot have been eased by the acceleration in the rate of infection, and from the windows of the Kennedy Town hospital he'd have seen the first concrete evidence of this buildup: the hasty construction of a series of grass-and-pole longhouses, which were filling with patients as fast as they could be assembled.

At some moment during the day he stood up from his microscope and walked across the patch of grass and mud that separated the two hospitals. Arriving at the new hospital, with its pallid attendants and strange and unexpected aroma of grass cuttings, he would have been polite, yet insistent, and no doubt done his best to omit mention of the rebuffs he'd so far received. But here too, as if by conspiracy, no autopsies were allowed him. As before, he was permitted to take blood samples, and returned across the uneven ground in the gathering dusk to prepare the slides with a leaden hand, by now expecting and finding nothing—no foreign agent, no squirming microscopic evidence of the bacterium he knew to be there, but which he'd so far been prevented from tracking down.

The next day, June 19, Yersin was at his workbench at five in the morning. In his notes and letters he offers no explanation for such an early start, but it is likely that he slept poorly back at his hotel, unable to find rest as he picked over the indignities of the day before. Yersin was a proud man, scrupulous in his dealings with others, and the hostility he'd encountered would no doubt have wounded and infuriated him. And so the small hours found him groping for his clothes, holding a match to his bedside lantern, standing outside in the absolute dark and silence of the night while his hotelier disappeared for a rickshaw. He arrived at the hospital with dawn still an hour away, found the doctor on duty, and requested—for the twentieth time— clearance for the mortuary. And, once again, he was refused.

It was another five hours before the Japanese team arrived at the hospital, a fact that deepened Yersin's already pronounced sense of grievance. "There is obviously," he would write in his report for the Pasteur Institute, "preferential treatment in this." As the day progressed, his indignation found another focus, this time the stream of casual visitors he was forced to welcome: Returning from a tour of the hospital, or from a discussion with one of the doctors, he'd find "people touching my laboratory animals and my culture tubes." For a man happiest working alone, this was an intolerable level of intrusion, and he determined to find a space that would offer him more privacy, more "independence."

WHILE YERSIN WAS RUMINATING HIS NEXT MOVE, THE HONG Kong governor—facing an emergency for which his previous Caribbean postings had left him woefully underprepared—sat down to compose a comprehensive bulletin to his overlords in London. From the first case of plague in the colony, the imperial government's anxiety had been palpable, and on June 16, Robinson found himself opening, no doubt with considerable trepidation, a telegram from the marquess of Ripon, British foreign secretary, demanding news of the "progress of bubonic plague, . . . names of any Europeans dying or attacked," a summary of "the effect on Finances" and confirmation that the disease had—as was rumored—spread from China. "If so," Ripon ended darkly, "what measures did you take against its introduction?"

Robinson, having already fired off some thirteen updates—brief dispatches all, most often simply a tally of numbers, totals dead or fled, names of streets and neighborhoods now abandoned—clearly decided that a far more expansive account was now required. And, in thirty-seven numbered and finely detailed paragraphs, he chronicled the damage so far, and the action taken.

Lest the foreign secretary assume any kind of sloth or incompetence on his part, Robinson began by stressing the fleetness and dynamism of the legislation and medical response he'd already set in train—feats all the more impressive when one considered, went the implication, that he'd first heard of the outbreak only on May 15, on his return from an eight-week leave of absence in Japan. At this point Robinson lost no time in explaining how he'd promptly set up a new sanitation committee, who "have since acted with extraordinary energy and efficiency": Hospitals had been "at once established."

His upbeat tone evaporated, however, when detailing the effect plague had had on the island colony itself. "Without exaggeration I may assert that so far as trade and commerce are concerned the plague has assumed the importance of an unexampled calamity." The price of foodstuffs was up 50 percent; steamers bound for San Francisco, Honolulu, and Vancouver had banned Chinese passengers from boarding; mail ships from England, France, and Germany were not even entering the harbor, let alone taking on cargo. At least a tenth of the building stock, Robinson estimated, was destined for demolition.

And yet there was hope. From Japan—noble empire, loyal ally, whose hospitality Robinson had so recently and sumptuously enjoyed—had just arrived a party of "experts." The reference is brief—three lines at most—and avoids any reference to Yersin, but the implication is unmistakable. "The Japanese experts," Robinson wrote, "claim to have discovered the Bacillus of the plague and the medical staff admit the claim." Here was diagnosis, officially verified, sanctioned, and approved at the highest level: The end of disease, even cure—ran Robinson's soothing subtext—was in sight.

ALONE AND FRIENDLESS, YERSIN MUST HAVE BEEN OVERJOYED at the arrival in his laboratory that day of his sole ally, the elderly Italian missionary Father Vigano. The visit was unannounced, and even before Vigano had had time to pull up a chair, Yersin began unburdening himself. His position was untenable, he said: A scientist needed quiet, to be spared interruption. But more than this, he needed unfettered access to research materials. And, Yersin lamented, he had neither.

Between them, they devised a solution. "We decide," Yersin wrote, "that what is best for me is to have a little straw hut built next to the big straw hut hospital," an emergency shelter that had just been erected near the Kennedy Town police station. They shook hands. Vigano rested an arm across Yersin's shoulder; together they gazed out in silence at the blur of white coats outside the makeshift hospital, the grooved and beaten earth that served as the entrance area, the ever-growing pile of pale wood coffins outside the main door. What about permission? Yersin queried, his initial euphoria subsiding. What likelihood was there that the authorities, who had defied him thus far, would suddenly grant him this kind of extraordinary planning permission? What chance at all?

It had grown late. Outside the hospital Vigano's rickshaw was waiting, driver slumped, snoring, across the seat. As they stepped outside it started to rain. There was a tremor of thunder, and the driver spluttered awake. Before Yersin and Vigano could reach the rickshaw, water was coursing afresh underfoot; veins of lightning flashed across the wet ground.

YERSIN DOES NOT RECORD HOW HE WAS ABLE TO BUILD HIS hut, but securing permission cannot have been straightforward. Red tape was a speciality of colonial government, and the stranger the request, the more desks it would have had to cross. And his mood cannot have been much improved the next morning, Wednesday, June 20, when he learned of the contents of the *China Mail*.

Under the headline DISCOVERY OF THE PLAGUE BACILLUS, there appeared an obsequious account of an interview with Kitasato and Aoyama. The unnamed interviewer's predisposition was plain from the start. "It was a wise measure of the Japanese government to send these scientists here," the article began, before proceeding at length to list Kitasato's professional credentials: his doctorate at Tokyo University, the seven years spent at Robert Koch's bacteriology institute in Berlin, the triumphant return home in 1892, and the establishment of his own laboratory.

Yersin, unable to read much English, had to rely on Vigano for translation, and listened quaveringly, alert for every nuance.

How much did Kitasato know? How close was he? "The two experts," he heard, "have identified the Hong Kong plague with bubonic typhus." There was reference to abundant plague bacilli being discovered in the blood of patients, a finding directly contradicted by Yersin's microscope work, which had uncovered no such bacteria. Kitasato and Aoyama, the writer concluded, were working on an account of their findings, publication of which was breathlessly awaited:

> Their final official report, whenever it may be ready, will no doubt prove of great value not only to the Japanese but also to the Hong Kong government; and the University of Berlin may be congratulated on having furnished Hong Kong, and we may say the scientific world, with such able, painstaking, and scientifically cautious observers as Professor Kitasato and Professor Aoyama.

YERSIN, FIVE DAYS IN, BEGAN TO PLOT REBELLION. WITH retreat unthinkable, he and Vigano would have sat down and traded ideas, casting about for a way through, some method of evading the restrictions under which Yersin's work was beginning to suffocate.

Yersin was in no doubt about what he needed: unfettered access to cadavers. Yet, without official permission, there seemed no way of achieving this. All corpses were guarded by soldiers; between death and burial there was not one moment when an unauthorized person was able to breach security. Worse, the hospital mortuary was, in Yersin's words, "a sort of cellar," outside which, for twenty-four hours a day, naval conscripts stood sentry. The plan that Yersin and Vigano eventually devised was exquisite in its simplicity, though it ran the ultimate risk: If they were discovered, Yersin would most likely be expelled from Hong Kong. His future with the Pasteur Institute would have been in shreds, his career as good as over.

· 14 ·

BORDER GUARDS, CUSTOMS OFFICIALS, SOLDIERS, POLICEMEN: given the right inducement, all have been known to bend the rules. Over a number of days, Yersin took to passing by the naval sentries who guarded the mortuary, nodding acknowledgment after the first few times, calling out a greeting after that. Fighting to overcome his own reluctance at exposing his poor English, he'd have stopped and attempted small talk, seldom getting beyond the first stock pleasantries, but sensing the sentries beginning to soften.

Returning with Father Vigano to his workbench—only to find the English wife of one of the doctors reaching and cooing into the guinea pig cage, ordering her to leave in language affronted and bellicose—he tore off a clean sheet of graph paper and began to list his expenses. The first-day theft of seventy-five piasters had left him tight for money, and the cost of building his own laboratory hut was going to restrict him further, but he now knew that he had no choice: He could wait no longer to start his autopsy work. And, with the authorities refusing him access, only one option remained. He would bribe the sailors guarding the mortuary. He'd take his scalpel to what bodies he could reach, then retreat fast. It was far from ideal, but he could see no other way.

Choosing to operate outside the law was certain to be perilous. If word got out among the Chinese that Yersin was smuggling himself into the mortuary and desecrating the bodies of their relatives, he'd be lucky to escape Hong Kong alive. By the third week in June, Chinese fears had reached a histrionic pitch, and little provocation was required to ignite a fresh riot. According to the Chinese viceroy of Canton—in a letter to the Hong Kong authorities dated just two days earlier—treatment of plague victims was barbarous: They were taken to "the glass room, fumigated with sulphur, and given iced water to drink." No visits from relatives were permitted. After death, victims were "collected in a house," until they were "buried in lime." Anyone sick was ejected from his or her home, and the building and all contents "destroyed." The immediate efforts of the Hong Kong colonial surgeon, Philip Ayres, and the police chief, Francis May, to correct these rumors—by explaining that quicklime "only hastens the decomposition of the flesh and does not affect the bones of the dead"; that immediate burial was "a precaution used in all civilised countries" when dealing with deaths from "infectious disease"; that shutting up plague houses had saved "many lives"; and that, finally, "the people were unspeakably grateful for the forethought of the officials in thus providing for their safety"—had scant effect. Yersin would have known that, by even contemplating tampering with the bodies of the dead, he would be risking his life.

He approached the mortuary cautiously. The sentries, accustomed to him by now, greeted him warmly. They knew about his problems gaining access to corpses, and quizzed him on his progress. Yersin and Vigano accepted these initial pleasantries, shook hands, and lowered their voices. Vigano, without prompting from Yersin, explained the situation. How would it be, he suggested, if we offered a little money to help you with your job? Yersin, leaning close, added a further inducement: a "tip" for each bubo that he was able to remove.

To Yersin's surprise, the sentries agreed "immediately": There is no mention in Yersin's notes of any bargaining having taken place, and so one must assume that the men were now on friendly enough terms with Yersin to think little of helping him out. The men unlocked the mortuary and showed him in. He pulled the heavy door shut behind him, and Vigano, alert for any suspicious movement, waited outside with the sentries.

Inside, in soupy darkness, Yersin groped toward the stack of coffins. Closest, he'd been told, were coffins not yet hammered shut: He had to remove the lid of one of these, conduct whatever hurried autopsy he had the stomach for, shove the lid back, and run for daylight again. His eyes adjusted: Head-height grilles, half-gummed with mud, threw rods of ashen light across the cellar. He rattled the first coffin: no movement. The second, however, was loose, and the top slid easily sideways. In the ghostly light, and under a rough scatter of calcium oxide, or quicklime, the face of the cadaver appeared bleached of color. Open eyes were filled with powder pale as talcum; the cheeks were hollow; the mouth yawned open, revealing contracted gums. Against this the tongue—hardened, stuck to the roof of the mouth—was weirdly black. With no knowledge of the disease, a susceptible mind might have guessed at witchcraft, that the person who'd inhabited the body had offended the ancestors, the spirits, and so incurred the ultimate curse.

Yersin drew his scalpel, cleared the neck of quicklime. The glands here were engorged and purplish black, and he sliced effortlessly into the soft skin, carving a ring around the swelling. The smell, even through the handkerchief he held to his face, made him cry out in shock and clutch his throat. Unsteady now, he managed to cut the bubo free and drop it into his sample tin. Holding his breath, he turned for the stairs. Back at his workbench, his heart banging in his throat, he allowed himself to look tentatively around. No one was pointing his way; nothing seemed out of the ordinary. A yelp of relief escaped from him; he lowered his head, suddenly self-conscious.

He knew that he had been lucky, but he would never know quite how fine he'd cut it: That same day, most likely at the very moment Yersin was in the mortuary, James Lowson—as was his habit—paid an extended visit to Kitasato and his team. Lowson's diary, brief as ever, notes, "Japs hard at work." The garrulous Scot would most likely have spent a good hour or more complimenting Kitasato on his progress so far, quizzing him for an update, discussing the telegram he'd wired to the *Lancet* five days before, musing over when they might expect to see final printed proof of Kitasato's pioneer status. Lowson would have also used the opportunity once more to extend an offer of hospitality, this time a weekend dinner at the Peak Hotel, with its panoramic view over Victoria, the docks, the islands, and the faraway ocean.

Yersin too was now working intently, with renewed vigor and purpose. He had returned to his workbench and started simply: Onto a fresh slide he smeared pus from the stolen plague swelling, and shuffled the slide onto his microscope tray. "At first glance," he noted "*une véritable purée de microbes,*" a result that differed strikingly from the blank readings he'd obtained from the blood samples.

In the space of six hours, Yersin's mood had been transformed. After a despondent morning he was now squinting down his microscope at what had every appearance of being the elusive bacillus. His writing became staccato; extraneous detail fell away. Without lifting his head from the eyepiece, he made notes on the pad at his elbow. "Squat little rods, rounded ends, some discoloration." From the same sample he took further smears, preparing cultures with which he injected mice and guinea pigs. And then, fearing nothing, he ran back to the mortuary. Once again the sentries let him through and asked no questions. He excavated two more buboes, then returned to his workbench. By now, staring down the tube at the busy clusters—like tiny boats, seen from the height of clouds, jostling at the start of a race—he felt confidence growing. "There is every chance that my microbe discovered in the pus of the plague swellings rather than, like Kitasato's quite distinct organism, in the blood is that of the plague, but I do not yet have the right to affirm that." The circumspection, one senses, was a professional reflex, and not true to his feelings: Far more telling is that possessive pronoun, the prominent "my." The discovery, Yersin knew, could be his, and he wired the *Lancet* immediately with news of his findings. The only obstacle was that Kitasato was just a hairbreadth from official recognition, awaiting only the publication of the next issue of the same journal for his achievement to be endorsed. Yersin would have known this, yet there is no trace of resentment in his writing. The truth, he must have felt confident, would come out. For now all he had to do was keep his research pure and his methods transparent. Right would prevail.

FROM TODAY'S STANDARDS AND VIEWPOINT, THERE IS SOME-thing quaint, even otherworldly, about Yersin. In the face of enormous pressure—wrestling bandits in the Vietnamese jungle, standing alone and virtually friendless against the Hong Kong medical establishment—he retained a preternatural calm, in his frustration never resorting to name-calling. He was fueled above all, one senses, by the conviction of the rightness of his own calling, against which obstructions of the kind he met in Hong Kong faded into insignificance. When he signed letters to his mother as "Dr. Yersin," it was an indication of the degree to which he felt defined by his profession, his calling. Thus, in the caption for the photograph he'd have taken of him outside the *paillotte*, the high-roofed grass hut he was now planning, he would write, "*Le docteur Yersin à l'entrée de sa paillotte.*" And this in the back pages of his own notebook—never a published work, intended for but a handful of readers, mostly colleagues who'd have needed no such information anyway.

It took Yersin barely twenty-four hours to have the hut assembled. Permission came through on Thursday, June 21, and Yersin "speedily made an agreement with a Chinese entrepreneur" to act as builder. For seventy-five piasters—the exact sum of which he had been robbed—he ordered a construction big enough to serve both as living quarters and laboratory space. The frame would be bamboo and timber; the roof and walls grass; the floor would sit on stilts, a good foot clear of the ground. From the front door, sheltered from the sun by a corner veranda, he could look out at the Kennedy Town hospital in which Kitasato was so comfortably installed. In the photograph Yersin stands white-suited, hand on hip, proprietorial: Despite the swiftness of its construction, the hut has an air of permanence about it. The walls are supported from all sides by hefty timbers, set at acute angles like guy ropes. For Yersin, most importantly, it spelled freedom, autonomy: Here he could work at his own pace, subservient to no one.

By Friday he was in, his trunk of clothes transferred by rickshaw from the hotel, his microscopes and pressure sterilizers arranged along a workbench that still smelled strongly of fresh-cut timber. Along another wall were his caged laboratory animals—mice, guinea pigs, rabbits, rats—scratching, snuffling, musky. He made a simple bed for himself—bamboo slats, a single blanket—and swept the floor. Outside the rain appeared to be dissolving the little remaining grass, creating one long sweep of marsh. Mosquitoes, he knew, were inevitable in such "swampy" conditions, and that first night he was "literally devoured by them." Yet he remained buoyant. "This nonetheless does not stop me rejoicing that I am at last at home."

After the initial euphoria of his first clandestine autopsy, it became clear to him that to continue his work properly he would need legitimate and full access to corpses: Hurried autopsies would create rushed results, and this research was too important to be conducted illegally, in secret, and under constant threat of exposure. While the hut was still in midconstruction, Yersin had applied for another autopsy and was refused again, "even though there were three to be done." Aware there was a side to this that he no doubt only partially understood, but conscious too that such preferential treatment ran quite against the spirit of scientific collaboration, he took a rickshaw to the residence of the French consul and to him, in language deliberate and measured, dictated a demand that he wished the consul to pass on to the colonial governor, Sir William Robinson.

Two days later, after more than a week of rebuff, clearance finally came through, and the swiftness of this turnaround raised in Yersin's the same suspicions it would have in any alert mind. To the governor, clearly, there was no reason whatever why Yersin should not have been allowed the same access to autopsies as the Japanese team, and he lost no time in agreeing to Yersin's request. Resistance to Yersin, then, must have come from lower down the chain of command. The decision to obstruct Yersin had been taken by Lowson, and him alone.

Lowson's slipperiness did not stop there. On Saturday, June 23, the day Yersin received the authorization he should have had at the start—enabling him "to perform one out of every two autopsies"—a yet bleaker realization dawned. The reason that Yersin had thus far been barred from performing autopsies was, he writes, that "the Japanese bought them all." They had, in other words, secured this exclusive access by bribing either Lowson or the government. Yersin nowhere explains how he came to this conclusion—whether through sentries' intelligence, a deduction made by Vigano, or some doctor's careless indiscretion—but it must have hit him hard. Yersin's disrespect for Kitasato by this point was such that even bribery did not surprise him. "What I am less able to understand is that Dr. Lowson could have approved such a disloyal procedure."

There was more. Once Yersin had started his autopsies— building a body of evidence, methodically examining different tissue for the prevalence of the bacillus—he received an unexpected visit from Lowson. For the first time the Scottish doctor was friendly, even ingratiating. He stooped a little as he entered the cool, dark interior of Yersin's workhut, smiling as he looked around, complimenting Yersin on the professionalism of his facilities. And then he noticed the microscopes.

"May I?" he asked, fixing Yersin with his one good eye.

Yersin nodded, directing Lowson to a chair.

"And in this one?" Lowson queried, adjusting the eyepiece, one hand on the slide.

"The microbe," Yersin told him, warming to Lowson's interest. "From the bubo."

Lowson got up, moved to the next microscope. "And this?"

"The same."

"So this is where you find the bacillus? In the bubo? Nowhere else?"

Yersin nodded. "And Professor Kitasato?" he began to say, but Lowson was already at the door, composing his good-byes.

. . .

MUCH LATER, ADDING THE FOOTNOTES TO HIS REPORT FOR THE
Pasteur Institute, Yersin would look back on the uncharacteristic and unexpected interest that Lowson had suddenly shown in
his work. With hindsight, there was an unrelenting logic to it—
Lowson's initial opposition, the endless assistance and hospitality offered to Kitasato, then the sudden and perplexing interest
in his own research.

"Dr. Lowson," Yersin wrote,

> has shown himself too much an ally of the Japanese. He should
> have been more reserved. It is he who, after having seen my
> preparations, advised the Japanese to research the microbe
> in the bubo. He himself assured me, as well as several other
> people, that the microbe isolated first by the Japanese did not
> resemble mine in any way. It was a much longer bacillus.

THOUGH THERE WAS MUCH THAT SEPARATED YERSIN FROM THE
Japanese team—both in temperament and approach—in one
aspect at least there was little to differentiate between them.
They carried out their work with a single-minded disregard for
their own safety, with a bravery that bordered on foolhardiness.
In part this was explained by their very ignorance: If plague
was a disease of "filth," then scientists operating in sterile conditions were certain to remain unaffected. Yet already this theory was looking unstable: Two English soldiers, men regarded
as the washed-white and upright antithesis of the pestilential

"Oriental," had died of plague. And it would not be long before two of Kitasato's team would also be struck down.

The account that survives is that of Professor Aoyama, Kitasato's pathologist and second-in-command, a man as perplexed by Hong Kong's climate—"It is warm and there is never snow"—as he was repelled by the living conditions of the majority of its inhabitants. In some houses, he wrote, there was "dust and filth several inches thick on the floor, matted together like felt." Hygiene was equally lamentable: "I have seen many women who have candidly confessed that they have not even wiped themselves down with a damp cloth for years and I saw no reason to doubt their words." On June 28 he sat down to lunch after a morning of autopsies "and strangely enough it did not taste good to me." Plague—disease of the primitive Other—had laid its chill finger on him.

Aoyama lost no time in examining himself: "pain in the left axillary space, . . . several glands enlarged, . . . sensation of burning heat along the whole back." By evening he was running a temperature of over one hundred degrees. For the next two weeks he was "practically unconscious."

The most telling observation came near the end of the report, although neither he nor Lowson were sufficiently equipped to draw any conclusions. In many patients, Aoyama recorded,

I often saw on the places uncovered by clothing—face, hands, the instep of the foot—round, light, red, numerous, often times somewhat prominent spots about the size of a lentil which, as a rule, grow pale upon pressure; some of these were truly hemmorhagic. Dr. Lowson assured me that they were caused by mosquitoes, and the patients said so too. I asked several of the sick whether the mosquito bites caused such circumcised, round reddish spots, before being taken sick. They all answered my question in the negative, and wondered themselves that, after they were taken sick by the pest, all mosquito bites made red spots.

Aoyama settled for the closest solution to hand. There was no experimental followup, no control groups for comparison, but then the scientist—recovering from a two-week plague coma—can't have been in any shape to attempt further research. And it was thus that he limped home to Tokyo, his notebook filled with supposition and half-truth, incomplete data and bold conclusion, to be greeted as a national hero.

TO SCIENTISTS ACROSS THE WORLD, PLAGUE IN HONG KONG WAS a drama that—through journals, newspaper reports, letters from colleagues, and grapevine murmurs—became increasingly gripping as the epidemic wore on. The fullest record, the most avid week-by-week commentary, came from the London-based *Lancet*, and subscribers from Rio de Janeiro to San Francisco, Edinburgh to Bombay, would eagerly have followed events and awaited news of a breakthrough, piecing together clues to the rivalry between Kitasato and Yersin, even as they worried over the possibility of plague splintering out from Asia and reaching their own territories.

To begin with the tone of the *Lancet* dispatches was strangely distant, even a little aloof. Such an outbreak, they seemed to imply, was the manifest outcome of a primitive way of life, too-basic hygiene, and ignorance typical of the "oriental." "The disorder," stated a report in the June 16 issue, "is said to be 'bubonic plague,' but as yet little is known beyond the fact that a most serious epidemic has occurred." Only reluctantly—stressing that "among an ignorant and superstitious population it is natural to attribute the sudden appearance of an epidemic and fatal disease to plague"—was it admitted that the disease bore "a remarkable resemblance to the plague which, some 230 years before, visited London, and of which Defoe has left us such a graphic account."

A week later, however, all equivocation had disappeared, though the *Lancet*'s tone of lofty distance was zealously maintained: The outbreak was now "oriental plague," not "bubonic plague," whose medieval European history was then described in all its bloody detail. The spread of contagion—less than an hour, according to Boccaccio—was spelled out, the symptoms lingered over with an indecorous degree of relish. "Small black pustules [were] distributed over the whole skin of the body"; "many died . . . through vomiting blood"; the term "Black Death [came] from the appearance of the skin after death." The comparison between the London of 1665—when houses were "low, unventilated and undrained," and "bulls, oxen, hogs and other gross creatures were slaughtered in the street"—and the "native quarter of Hong Kong where the coolies congregate and live" was self-evident. There was, however, occasion for hope, reported the *Lancet* on June 23. A telegram from Hong Kong—sent by James Lowson—"informs us that Professor Kitasato of Tokio [*sic*], late assistant of Professor Koch's laboratory in Berlin, has succeeded in discovering the bacillus of the plague."

Two weeks later, on July 7, the tentative reception of Kitasato's news had become unrestrained affirmation. Quoting "our correspondent in Hong Kong"—again, most likely Lowson—the *Lancet* editorial went on to state that "little doubt is any longer entertained by scientific opinion in China as to the importance of the discovery by Professor Kitasato." News of "other announcements of similar researches"—reported a month later, on August 4—was treated derisively, almost as a source of comedy. Yersin's name was even misspelled—as "Versin"—and his motivation questioned. He was noted, tongue in cheek, as having "discovered another bacillus, which he, too, claimed to be the essential cause of the disease; and others, equally anxious to discover something, had swelled the list, so that, as 'our correspondent' said, 'the varieties of plague bacilli now outnumber the leaves in Vallombrosa.'"

History, however, records no such others: The exaggeration here bears Lowson's stamp. Unquestioningly repeating Lowson's libelous asides, the journal returned to the one still point, the sole certainty: Kitasato. "The name of Kitasato is a guarantee of accuracy in observation and care in research, and when the opportunity is given for the review of his work it will probably be found to meet the severest tests." Set against such a colossus, the "local *savants* keen on discovering a specific bacillus"—the derogatory French usage making this a deliberate maligning of Yersin, the only French bacteriologist at work in Hong Kong—could be comfortably dismissed, "their" research no more threatening to Kitasato's hegemony than the posturings of a precocious child.

And yet, despite the apparent certainty—the insistence that only Kitasato was to be taken seriously—a note of confusion

Alexandre Yersin

Kitasato Shibasaburo (front row, second from left) with colleagues and assistants, Tokyo 1894

The Hong Kong cricket team. In the center of the second row, wearing a dark cap and jacket, is Dr. James Lowson.

Soldiers of the Shropshire Light Infantry at work in the Taipingshan district

Hong Kong, Taipingshan after the evacuation, photograph by Alexandre
Yersin

The temporary plague hospital in the former glass factory

"We decide that what is best for me is to have a little straw hut built next to the big straw hut hospital." Yersin is in the foreground.

A funeral procession for plague victims in Hong Kong's Chinese quarter

Hong Kong, photograph by Alexandre Yersin. "One of the special cemeteries for Chinese plague victims. There are one thousand corpses here."

June 1894. Yersin's first report to the Pasteur Institute.

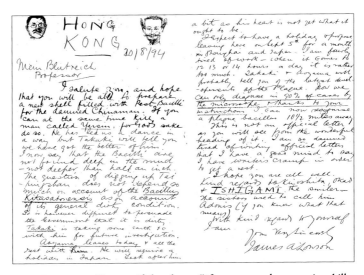

James Lowson to Kitasato Shibasaburo: "If you can at the same time kill a man called <u>Yersin</u>, for God's sake do so."

Illustration by Paul-Louis Simond. "We have to assume that there must be an intermediary between a dead rat and a human. This intermediary might be the flea."

Paul-Louis Simond, 1898, in Karachi, where the pioneering antiplague serum was first put to widespread use

Surat, 1994. Fights broke out in the railway station as people tried to force themselves into cars already solid with refugees.

Madagascar, 1998

began to infiltrate the *Lancet*. On August 11 Yersin's initial results were printed. The disease, readers learned, took four to six days to incubate, "and then [it] commences suddenly with loss of strength . . . death occurs in twenty-four hours, or it may be delayed until the fourth or fifth day." He then narrowed his description. The causal bacillus, he wrote, was "abundant in the buboes . . . and very rare in the blood at the time of death." Mice, injected with the bacillus, died within twenty-four hours.

A week later came the backlash. Of particular concern to the editors was that Yersin "claims to have discovered *the* bacillus of the Chinese plague. We think there must be some misapprehension here as Professor Kitasato is such an accurate and reliable observer that we cannot conceive that he has rushed into print without having first satisfied himself as to the accuracy of his observations and experiments." Yet doubt had reared its head: In denying that Kitasato had been precipitate, the *Lancet* was admitting that this unwelcome possibility was worthy of consideration. To scientists across the world, reading this latest update, the sudden uncertainty would have had all the weight of a whodunit: Had he been rushed, and if so, by whom? And why?

A WEEK AFTER THE HONG KONG GOVERNOR'S APPROVAL OF Yersin's request to conduct autopsies, the bacteriologist had managed to study some twenty-five cadavers. This was swift progress: After such long restraint, Yersin was working as fast as he could, collapsing into his bed only when his eyes began to fail in the candlelight. The conditions were tough: Based now in his hurriedly built grass hut, he would have had little protection from heat or mosquitoes, yet only the single reference to physical hardship survives.

Able now to focus more intently on his own work, Yersin found himself less preoccupied by news of Kitasato. Writing on July 21 to his friend Calmette at the Pasteur Institute in Paris, he noted without obvious pique that the government "heaps kindnesses on the Japanese. . . . The governor has offered them one of his villas for the duration of their stay; he sent a telegram to the Mikado to express his profound admiration for Kitasato's magnificent discovery."

Yersin, for his part, viewed this "discovery" with scorn: Kitasato's report of his findings, published in the papers the day before, was "a long screed" whose reasoning "would make La Palisse shudder." To equate Kitasato with La Palisse—a late-nineteenth-century writer synonymous with the purveyance of mindless platitudes—was the gravest insult Yersin could devise. "In short," he finished, increasingly confident that Kitasato had isolated the wrong bacillus, "it won't be difficult to do better than that."

By now, with the newspapers filled with little else but plague, and detailed discussion of the two bacteriologists' research, Yersin in his grass hut had become a target for the autograph hunter and plague tourist. Interruptions were commonplace. To Calmette he confided his mounting irritation. "People will keep coming and annoying me by asking to see the microbe. Each day unknown 'ladies' and 'gentlemen' enter my house without even being announced and ask me to show them preparations and cultures."

It was then, no doubt at least in part through a desire to escape the cascade of intrusions, that he began to intersperse his laboratory research with lone, exploratory journeys through the worst-hit parts of Hong Kong. One can picture him, notebook in hand, sketching and scribbling, standing at street corners trying to square what he was seeing with what he already knew. Early on, he was struck by the inadequacies of the drainage system: In Taipingshan, he noticed, a new (yet still insufficient) labyrinth of drains had been installed just before this same neighborhood became the crucible of plague, and so he walked the now-deserted streets, hunting for clues. Could the sewers, he wondered, actually have triggered the outbreak? "The system," he wrote to the French governor-general of Indo-China, "seems defective. . . . One cannot understand why in Hong Kong there are two very distinct sorts of drains: one wide and well conditioned for draining rainwater; the other narrow, continually getting blocked, for household water and household waste." The combination of inadequate waste disposal and the physical congestion of the area made it "easy to understand the ravages that an epidemic can make when it takes hold on such territory and the difficulty that there must be in checking its progress."

Gradually he began to hone his powers of deduction. Unlike Kitasato—whose writings contain only the scantest descriptions of goings-on outside the laboratory, and for whom the worlds of science and everyday life appear to have existed in parallel, seldom converging—Yersin was drawn to the everyday, to the clues that lay all around him. Rats, he noted, were dying "en masse"; and experiments proved that they, too, were victims of plague. By mid-July, he alone among all the scientific community was convinced that "rats are certainly the principal propagators of the epidemic," although their exact role eluded him. The drains, he postulated, may have been the link: "These animals live in drains where they maintain the illness in its sporadic state. It is impossible to disinfect or to chase them out of there, since the pipes are too narrow."

He was halfway there, tantalizingly close. All around were false leads, red herrings, chief among them the fact that

the European population has been relatively little touched by the plague. Why? Because it lives in hygienic conditions which are far superior to those of the Chinese. I know several European houses where rats have died in great numbers and where, nonetheless, no one has caught plague. That is because people always took care to remove the corpses and to disinfect thoroughly.

Having set out the rat as the main cause of plague Yersin, writing again to the governor-general, cast around for other possible culprits. Why not the common fly? he suggested:

I have experiments which prove that they can die from this disease. It is easily understood that a fly which has landed on the corpse of a plague rat and which then walks on the bare leg of a Chinese man, where there are very often abrasions and ulcers, could very easily transmit the disease to him.

"Direct contagion" also seemed "very likely." However, this theory, like so much else, left him isolated. "Several Hong Kong doctors"—almost certainly James Lowson and his entourage—opposed him. Undeterred, Yersin proceeded to devise an experiment to prove his thesis. Into the same container he placed a healthy mouse and a second into which he'd injected concentrated plague suspension. He repeated the experiment several times and the results, he claimed, were not only conclusive—"I have often seen both animals die of plague"—but indicative of the wider picture. "The Chinese who live crammed in narrow spaces are in the same position as my mice. And the other day I saw five Chinese who slept in a sort of narrow cellar catch the illness one after the other."

For the first time Yersin was stumbling. His argument was incomplete: If plague was contagious, as he claimed, what was the method of transmission? That question, at least for the moment, remained unanswered.

SOME THIRTEEN YEARS LATER, THE AUTHORITIES IN SAN FRAN-cisco—fighting to repair roads, hospitals, and schools in the wake of earthquake and fire—found themselves facing their second outbreak of plague. Never in its 130-year history had the city offered such a promising breeding ground. The earth-quake of April 18, 1906—measuring 8.3 on the Richter scale, making it ten times as powerful as the one that tore through the metropolis in 1989—lasted forty-seven seconds, by the end of which almost the entire downtown lay ruined. And then came the fires: Fractured gas mains and toppling chimneys triggered explosions of flame that the fire department, finding only bro-ken water pipes, was unable to douse. Nothing went right: Attempts at creating firebreaks by dynamiting entire city blocks only succeeded in sparking fresh fires. Seventy-two hours later, when the last blaze had finally been extinguished, four-and-a-half square miles of the city was rubble, smoldering timbers jutting from the wreckage like a broken skeleton, remains of a once-great beast. Photographs of the aftermath bring to mind post-firestorm Dresden: The outlines of the streets are jagged, the top half of all buildings destroyed; bizarre items of salvaged furniture—pianos, coffee tables—stand in the street; a soldier picks his way along a sidewalk of strewn bricks; everywhere is smoke, rising poisonous and impenetrable into the broken sky.

Some three thousand people died that first week, and more than a hundred thousand—a third of the population—were rendered homeless, squatting in tent cities in the parks and on the burned-out lot of Charles Croker's Nob Hill estate. Itinerant workers poured into the city, hired as emergency construction gangs. With the waste-disposal system no longer in operation, vacant downtown grids became vast unpoliced dumps. When plague finally struck in August 1907, it was the scenario that everyone had been fearing and anticipating: The only surprise was that it had taken this long.

As the epidemic ground on, it became apparent that, for plague to be beaten, the whole city would have to be involved, and in January 1908, with the epidemic still showing no signs of abating, a "citizens' committee" was assembled: twenty-five prominent traders, businessmen, and doctors, charged with the task of convincing the rest of the populace that they were confronting "one of the great malign forces of nature." Posters were designed and signed by every member of the committee—twelve of whom carried the reassuring suffix M.D.— exhorting the public to "Trap and Poison Rats! Obey the Sanitary Laws of the City! Have Your Premises Inspected!"

The copy, set in a dizzying variety of type sizes, seemed itself designed to engender panic:

> The dreaded "Bubonic Plague" has reappeared in San Francisco since the fire and is gaining ground. Should the Plague continue to show a marked increase, San Francisco will probably be quarantined. This would be a death blow to the industrial life of the city and would bring ruin to our people and our homes. . . . It is incumbent upon all to wage a relentless war on the Rat.

Churchillian rhetoric duly delivered, the citizens' committee set about the considerable task of public education. A meeting of butchers and fruit-and-vegetable wholesalers was called, and the tradesmen ordered to use only watertight metal garbage cans: Butchers in particular were singled out and instructed to abandon use of their open-topped wooden scrap bins. The message caught on quickly: By early February the "sub-committee of the clergy"—a five-man nondenominational team of vicars and rabbis—was issuing instructions that "every minister of a congregation, according to his own judgement, present from his pulpit to his people the necessity of continuing effort in promoting the sanitation of San Francisco"; that the same propaganda be spelled out in "Sunday school assemblies"; and that the churches themselves be ratproofed.

Determination to be rid of plague—unlike Hong Kong a decade earlier—even crossed cultural boundaries. In March the Japanese Association posted fliers demanding that all assistance be offered in the fight against the disease. CLEANLINESS IS THE

JAPANESE NATURE shouted the headline, above a list of "directions for the care of the bedroom, kitchen, porch, garbage can, etc." First of these was straightforward—"kill all the rats"— though it was necessary to read as far as point 9 before the helpful "do not kill rats with your hands" was added. Fleas were to be exterminated with equal caution: "Don't use your fingers or teeth."

And, to cover the eventuality that there might exist children who did not attend Sunday school, a crew of doctors was conscripted to spread the message in the classrooms. One contemporary account reported that "the pupils evinced a lively interest in what they were told," which hardly seems surprising, since the material cunningly appealed to their baser natures, in particular the sneak that lurks inside the heart of every otherwise blameless eight-year-old. "The rats from a neighbouring house may be dangerous to man. Therefore, uncleanly [sic] neighbours are dangerous. . . . To protect life one must watch one's neighbours and report them if they are uncleanly." But most attractive of all, one suspects, was the appeal to the pocket: "A reward of five cents will be paid for every rat, dead or alive." A trifling risk for a bag of hard candy.

· 15 ·

BOMBAY, AT THE END OF SEPTEMBER 1994, WAS A CITY BRACED for an epidemic. It had known such before: In 1896 plague hit Bombay Harbor from Hong Kong, and the disease drilled through India, killing some ten million over the next decade. Now, however, the threat was coming not from the sea, but inland, from the rotten and poisonous metropolis of Surat some two hundred kilometers to the north.

Within hours of the first Surat plague deaths, and with intelligence coming fast about the numbers fleeing by road and train, the Bombay health department ordered the immediate setting up of surveillance posts. Doctors with clipboards and bags of diagnostic equipment waited on station platforms and at bus stops and checkpoints along the highway. Cars whose license plates bore the Surat suffix—GJ5—were pulled over and searched, the occupants interrogated and ordered to drive straight to the Kasturba Infectious Diseases Hospital. In the still moments before the whirlwind, there was a surreal sense of having been here before: another time, with different people, but the same story.

A more recent traveler, navigating the choked streets of Bombay—seeing the free-for-all at stoplights; the man asleep on the pavement at ten in the morning, a scarlet flower caught in his mustache; the rat leaping the gully between two high buildings—could easily have imagined the chaos should disease strike here. As in Hong Kong in 1894, the conditions were perfect: overcrowding, dirt, inadequate drainage and clean water, ignorance, and worse.

Dr. Jehangir Sorabjee, infectious diseases specialist at the Bombay Hospital, had learned of the 1994 outbreak in Surat from a doctor friend:

He rang up and said he was getting a whole stream of patients from Surat saying they were evacuating the city because plague had broken out. He wanted to know what medicines he should be giving them, what the symptoms were. I was shocked to hear of this, but within hours there it was on the news. I was at the Kasturba Hospital at the time, and we convened a meeting and decided to discharge all patients and prepare for a really big out-break. People arriving from Surat were asked to come in for testing. It was a very strange experience—people wandering

PLAGUE

the corridors of the hospital dressed in surgical gear with their
heads covered in muslin cloths, tiny slits for their eyes. It felt
like the Martians had landed.

Sorabjee and colleagues decided to test for plague using
slides and microscopes; if they couldn't find the bacillus, they'd
refuse to confirm any patient as plague-positive. Elsewhere,
however, different diagnostic procedures were used, and doctors opting for serological testing—which gauges the presence
and volume of antibodies in the blood of an infected person,
deducing from this the exact disease responsible—came up
with dramatic positive results. Where Sorabjee's bacteriological testing had drawn a blank, the serum experiments—for reasons that were still unexplained—screamed danger.

So what was going on? In Surat, the medical superintendent
of the city's biggest hospital had insisted the disease had indeed
been plague, and subsequent work by the Atlanta-based Center
for Communicable Diseases had confirmed this. And yet here
was Sorabjee, eminent disease specialist and a man with no
obvious special interest, maintaining the opposite. Clearly
plague, of all diseases, was the very last any health professional
would wish on his country: As Sorabjee confessed, even overseas doctors began canceling trips to India. He shook his head.
"One of my colleagues had organized the world congress on
cancer-related diseases at that time in New Delhi, and 40 percent of his delegates cried off."

Among the politicians, however, the same fears assumed
more manipulative, paranoid form: Doctors, Sorabjee admitted, were under constant pressure to "suppress the incidence

of certain communicable diseases. Take cholera. There are cases all through the year but because of the worry about international maritime regulations they try and get us to record it as something else—gastroenteritis, for instance. Cholera reported in Bombay—like plague—would have tremendous economic implications. People would cancel holidays, tourism would collapse."

He weaved, avoiding direct answer, since to have done so, one imagined, would have meant admitting not only to a schism in the country's medical establishment, but also impugning the integrity of colleagues with whom he could not agree. He leaned across the desk, pressed his palms together.

'Once,' he smiled, seeming more than ever the soothing GP, "I remember walking with Mother Teresa through the slums of Bombay. These were just typical areas, the way most people live, but even she was shocked. She said, 'I've seen slums in Calcutta, but never as bad as this.' She was not a lady who was easy to shock, and the overcrowding is just getting worse. The question to ask of 1994 is not whether plague occurred at all but why it hasn't appeared more often."

NIGHT, AND MOHANLAL WAS TRAVELING NORTH. THIS, THE Ahmedabad Janata Express, was the third train he'd attempted to board, and in his growing desperation he'd abandoned every last trace of politeness and clawed and punched his way on. Even by normal Indian standards—where trains are often so crowded that grown men sit on one another's knees, squat in the luggage racks, down the steps, and along all passageways—this was farcically cramped. For ten minutes at least, he'd been hanging on to the doorjamb, the door swinging open behind him, track thundering by underneath. And then finally, and only by striking at others' ankles till they yelped and moved, had he managed to move inside enough to secure the door behind him.

Once inside, he found it impossible to get anyone to answer him. Whenever he spoke, all would turn their faces away, covering their mouths. There were other Suratis in this carriage, but they'd been barricaded into one corner and were being similarly blocked. The windows were all open, and the through-blast blew dust and scraps of paper over people's heads. A polystyrene cup came spinning through the air and was sucked out of a window on the other side of the carriage. In the press of bodies, he felt his feet lift off the floor. Silently, he prayed for the structure of the train, for the rivets and sheet steel to hold firm.

Compared with the smell and heat and crush inside, the view from the window seemed paradisiacal. Normally he'd have been happy to be inside, rather than standing under a naked sun in a landscape baked dry as biscuit, but today the solitary figures in the fields seemed unbearably fortunate. A man—shoeless, carrying two bulging plastic bags—strolled past bushes pale with dust, toward a mud-brick house. He stopped at the threshold, turned toward the train, and waved. No one waved back.

At the first stop north of Surat, a hefty man with a neck too big for his shirt collar threatened to throw Mohanlal from the train. Mohanlal turned away, knowing that any response would be read as provocation. The man began shouting. "You! Get off this train!" Mohanlal felt a hand on his shoulder, but he knew the crowd was too tightly packed to force him off, however much they might have wanted to. After what seemed an age he heard the couplings clank and the platform began to inch away from them.

He was aware of the risks of being fingered as a fleeing Surati, and was determined to hold on to his place on the train. Anand—where he was sure Hetal would have gone—was still some three hours off, and he knew that to be ejected before that meant he risked being stoned or worse by fearful territorial villagers. Already, he'd heard, a bus loaded with diamond workers had been pelted with rocks as it entered Banaskantha district. In a Rajkot village, residents had been standing at entry points with long bamboo *lathis,* fending off all outsiders: a self-appointed vigilante posse, the more terrifying for being outside the law. Alone, Mohanlal knew, he'd make an easy target.

The further they traveled from Surat, the quieter and less populous the stations became. At a small town some way south of Vadodara, five people got out, and Mohanlal found a seat arm against which to rest. He felt dazed; his brain was fogged by the heat. On the platform he noticed a prosthetic leg lying abandoned, and gazed at it blankly without wondering how it had got there. It was as if curiosity, normally his dominant trait, had died as fear had risen: With his wife and daughter still unaccounted for, he found it impossible to focus on anything else. Shop signs that normally would have caused a wry smile— "Family Fashion Point. Free Compliment on Purchase!"—now barely registered.

Though not a religious man, he found himself praying as the train approached Anand, mumbling incantations for the safety of his family. He had a good idea of the route Hetal would have taken, and could picture the long straight track through the fields that led from town to his parents-in-law's village and smallholding. What he did not know was what might have lain in wait for them along the way: the vigilantes out patrolling for plague refugees, others alert for any excuse to stir up suspicion between Muslim and Hindu, for whom the appearance of any outsider could prove the fuse for violence. These days, it seemed, it took so little to rouse hatred: the riots of 1992, the burning of temples and mosques—so many reasons not to believe, if this was the outcome of religious fervor. And yet still he prayed.

FOR INDIA THE SURAT PLAGUE OF SEPTEMBER AND OCTOBER 1994 swiftly became a test of nationhood, of its effectiveness and strength: How, with every overseas government watching and assessing, would the Subcontinent move to stamp out disease? At airports, harbors, and railway stations, the campaign was immediate, and visible to the point of high comedy: Airplanes were not only fumigated but searched by white-gloved technicians for the presence of rats, and one can picture them on their hands and knees in the airless, sweltering baggage holds, their ears to the metalwork, alert for the telltale *scritch-scritch* of rodents.

In Surat, on September 29, the plague suspects who had fled barefoot and breathless from the New Civil Hospital were warned by the district magistrate—in all newspapers and on every available radio bulletin—that unless they returned within twenty-four hours they faced "penal action." To ratchet up the level of terror, a quivering public was then informed that two "rapid action force" teams had been dispatched to track down the lawbreakers. None were ever found, but the lightning legislation did not end there: Anyone caught expectorating in a public place faced immediate arrest.

For more than a month, schools remained closed, food vendors' stands lay empty. People ventured out of doors only when their larders were bare, and then with their faces covered, heads down. Yet this picture of desolation and fear did not apply throughout the city: For Surat is above all a commercial center, and there were some for whom the lure of profit overshadowed everything else. At Hare Krishna Export, a six-floor steel-and-glass temple to the diamond industry, it became clear for the first time that this city, which had done nothing to prevent a great many from living lives of disease and squalor in their soft-floored polyethylene shacks, was also the comfortable home to a handful of very rich men.

The boss sat behind a desk of polished glass, the legs like fluted, gold-leafed Doric columns. Behind him was a painting so garish it was hard to look at anything else: a scene from an elysian Eden, with embossed silvery waterfalls and sunlight that splintered golden through the clouds.

This was the second floor, possibly the third: It was easy to lose one's bearings during the security checks, the body searches, the elevator that took forever, the uniformed guards who seemed to have been posted on every corner. A brief tour of the office had revealed floor upon floor of workers, silent and assiduous as drones. On one level, men and women had sat silently peering through magnifying glasses at diamonds, some pinprick-tiny. On another, hotter level, it was hard to focus over the whine and hammer of polishing machines. Measuring the diamonds—before they were marked and cut—was done by computer, and the operator spanned and calibrated the stone, then lifted it off its measuring wheel and drew black lines across its rough outer edge where the cutter—on yet another floor—would reveal its final shape.

The company, said the boss, stroking his phone in its cradle, employed two thousand people across five cities. "In Surat alone, there are between five and six hundred diamond companies. This is diamond city."

Diamond cutting was Surat's most profitable industry, a middle link in a chain of supply and demand that began with dealers in Belgium and ended at jewelers in Manhattan and Hong Kong. Such was the commitment of the diamond operatives that, during the outbreak of plague, not one employee fled. "At Hare Krishna Export, nobody went anywhere. We are businessmen. We have a business to run."

THE PLAGUE IN SURAT, IT WAS BECOMING CLEAR, WAS BUT A corner of a much broader canvas, and diamond cutting, just as much as the manifest degradation of the Ved Road slums, was a part. In a healthier society, the profits from such businesses would have been harnessed—even to a modest degree—and spent on street cleaning, welfare programs, low-cost housing. But not in Surat. From the earliest years of its growth as an industrial center, Surat—more than any other Indian city—had resisted direct taxation. And the resulting lack of funding had hastened decay and epidemic. As early as the 1890s, sanitation experts were advising that underground drainage should be introduced as a matter of urgency, but—despite an early-twentieth-century death-from-epidemic rate of some ninety per thousand—such a system was not built until 1956. Throughout Surat's inglorious history, any suggestion of raised taxes had met with strikes and riots: A tax on businesses in 1878 incited several days of rioting; a proposed income tax in 1890 provoked a citywide business closedown. The political community—still nascent throughout India—was in Surat close to embryonic. From builders came the same, wearingly familiar story: that construction could only begin once the appropriate government officers had been paid off, after underworld heavies had been hired for protection. The rich, it was clear, did not depend on the sewage system, the telephone network, or the public hospitals: They paid for their own, and saw little need to contribute to anyone else's.

IT WAS DAWN WHEN MOHANLAL'S TRAIN PULLED INTO ANAND. He'd not slept, but at least the train was less crowded now, and he'd been able to wrestle himself a corner of step to sit on. His heart was beating erratically: It felt like an animal, a small bird, struggling to escape its cage. With no warning, as the landscape turned from trees to burned scrub, the sun came, blinding, through the window. There was coughing all along the carriage: Those who'd managed to sleep startled suddenly awake.

Deprived of food, water, and sleep, Mohan was electrically alert one moment, seemingly drugged the next; his consciousness was playing tricks on him. With little money, he walked through the center of Anand, past *chai* sellers boiling up their first brew, waking sleeping dogs with the dust he kicked up. He rode two buses, barely having enough strength to ask the driver his destination, until the shanties of the outskirts became dusty fields and the wayside emptied of people, until only the occasional cow stopped to watch them pass. At a crossroads, the driver shouted back to Mohanlal: The bus was returning to Anand; from here he was on his own.

It felt like years since he'd been this way, though his last visit with Hetal to her parents' village couldn't have been more than six months ago. He leaned against a tree, barely cooler in the shade, and tried to remember the turnoff, distinguishing features in a landscape that now seemed to him to be utterly devoid of landmarks, flat and stripped of vegetation; the occasional goat tethered to a bony tree; some way farther on, a house that seemed too squat to be habitable, corrugated roof too corroded to reflect the sun.

His shoes had started to rub, and he took them off. For a while, his mind in neutral, he walked on in his socks until a boy, passing on a bicycle, glanced at his feet and laughed. And in that moment, the butt of the most innocent, childlike joke, he felt himself alone as never before. Fear and homesickness rose like bile in his throat. Reaching the house, he sat down against a wall, laid his head back, and closed his eyes.

He awoke sweating and uneasy. He opened his eyes but the sun was high now and his vision was blurred, tinged pale blue, as if affected by chlorine. He could see there were figures standing in front of him: a small child, two adults, though they remained in silhouette. He tried to stand, but felt his legs go weak under him, and so remained on the ground. He shaded his eyes from the sun, tried to breathe normally.

"What are you doing here?" It was a male voice, suspicious.

Mohanlal, his throat suddenly dry as sand, whispered the name of the village where he was headed. "Some water?" he added, barely getting the words out. "I am thirsty."

"Why are you going there? You have no car, no buses come this way. It will take you hours."

"My wife," Mohanlal said, suddenly close to tears again. "She is there. My daughter too." He could see their features more clearly now: the dot of sandalwood paste on the woman's forehead glistening scarlet; a wire-and-cork toy car the little boy was clutching so tight it seemed he was worried for its safety.

The man whispered something to the woman, and they both took a pace backward, pulling the boy with them.

"Get out of here," the man grunted.

"But . . ." Mohanlal began to protest, but he stopped in mid-sentence, realizing words were useless. The man was holding up a stick now, up-angled toward Mohanlal's chest as he struggled to his feet.

"Begone," the man said. 'You come back this way, and I kill you."

TO PROFESSOR SHIBASABURO KITASATO, CONVINCED THAT THE race was his, that he was the first scientist to have discovered the bacillus that caused bubonic plague, Dr. Alexandre Yersin's persistence must have seemed pointless, even impudent. Kitasato paused in his work, surrounded by the white coats of his research team, and glanced from his window. From Kennedy Town plague hospital, where he had established his laboratory, it was but three hundred yards across a strip of trampled mud to Yersin's modest *paillotte* and the more substantial straw-and-wood longhouse now serving as overflow plague ward. To Kitasato, Yersin's accommodation would have seemed ridiculous: No serious scientist would ever have settled for such pitiable conditions.

In mid-July Sir William Robinson, the governor of Hong Kong, asked Kitasato five weeks into his stay in the colony, for a research update that he could send to the British foreign secretary, the marquess of Ripon, in London. To have been able to dispatch a sample of heavyweight science signed by the peerless Kitasato would, he'd have felt, go a long way toward silencing his increasingly restless superiors, whose telegrams to Hong Kong had recently taken on an impatient air. Once they read of Kitasato's work, they would have no cause to doubt that Robinson had recruited the best, for Kitasato's name was as much a brand as that of Pasteur or Koch—a guarantee of quality.

Kitasato rose to the commission in a prose style that seems self-consciously and uncharacteristically casual. He addressed the British government as he might have a colleague; his confidence was clearly boundless; he felt unimpeachable, expansive. "This recent outbreak," he remarked, "has given us the opportunity for studying this disease—a cause of mystery for centuries—with the means which modern science places in our hands." He spoke of the autopsies carried out, the observations made, and then laid out his "proof," a three-point argument that, he'd have felt, rendered his position unassailable.

First, the bacillus he claimed to have discovered was present only in the buboes, blood, and internal organs of plague patients. Second, it was not found in any other infectious disease and was, therefore, unique to plague. Third, it induced in animals symptoms identical to those observed in humans. His conclusion left no room for doubt: "This Bacillus is the cause of the disease known as bubonic plague, therefore the bubonic plague is an infectious disease produced by a specific bacillus."

Nor did he stop there. Mindful no doubt of the prejudices of his readers, of the disinclination of the bureaucratic classes to read purely of science—however stunning the breakthrough—he then addressed himself to the practical. Experiments in which he'd managed to destroy the bacillus both by exposing it to direct sunlight and by boiling it demonstrated beyond doubt the measures necessary to keep it at bay: "General hygiene, good drainage, perfect water supply, cleanliness in dwelling houses, and cleanliness in the streets." Taipingshan—which fell short in every category—was "a suitable hunting-ground for the Plague Bacillus."

The next step for Kitasato—as for Yersin—was to investigate conceivable routes of contagion; whether it was possible to develop the disease through contact with an animal, insect, or another person; or whether plague was, rather, a disease of the soil, and that exposure to "bad" earth could lead to infection.

The latter theory dated to ancient times and—in the Hong Kong of 1894 as in the Mediterranean basin of the first century B.C.—was often allied to talk of poisoned air. First propounded by Hippocrates, the concept that meteorological conditions affected human health had proved impressively durable. Scientific thinkers as early as Jérôme Fracastor—in his 1546 *De Contagione*—had proposed a mechanism of infection whereby tissues of the body were invaded by invisible particles. And, at the end of the nineteenth century, it was this school of thought—pathogenic air and corrupted earth—that still commanded most respect.

Yersin and Kitasato would have kept up-to-date with the latest scientific papers, and so would have been aware of the weight of opinion arguing against plague as a disease that could only be caught from other humans or animals. As late as 1890, the respected British medical historian Charles Creighton was claiming that it was, in fact, a soil-borne offshoot of typhus: "When ordinary typhus has passed into a soil poison, by aggravation of conditions, as in the experience of Arab encampments in North Africa [a reference to the Tunisian outbreak of 1874], it has become at the same time bubonic fever, or, approximately plague proper." And, in Hong Kong itself, the medical establishment, led by government bacteriologist William Hunter, was working on a theory of infected food. Hunter claimed to have discovered plague bacilli in rice, in particular the low-grade grain used by the poorest Chinese; this, he said, had been infected by flies, which in turn had carried the bacillus from the diseased excreta of plague rats. He was pointing in the right direction, but no more.

Over the coming weeks, as July lengthened into August and the evacuation and sluice-through of Taipingshan had caused the rate of infection to begin to ease off, Yersin and Kitasato—under orders from the government—found themselves in the same part of the island, exploring a similar field of possibility. Their investigations took place in Taipingshan, which was now being targeted for demolition by a government anxious to be seen to be taking decisive action. Taipingshan was a compact area—just ten acres, into which three hundred and eighty-four houses had been shoehorned—and was also close to deserted. A team of Kitasato's size—six scientists, no doubt trailing a retinue of government doctors—would have been hard to miss as it gathered in the street with trays of sterile containers and loud talk, each competing for the attention of Kitasato, master of ceremonies.

By contrast, Yersin, the lone researcher, would have been close to invisible. In his August 4 bulletin to the Indochinese governor-general he explains that, like Kitasato, he had been asked by the Hong Kong government to "examine the soil of houses where there have been plague cases in order to find out whether or not they contained the germs of the illness." His language—"I sent myself to Taipingshan"—seems determinedly unself-conscious for, if the popular infection theories were correct, he was about to enter the most contagious area. And yet there is no hint of fear nor any sense that he even took precautions: His focus was solely on the work ahead.

The photograph of the plague streets pasted into the back of his *Voyage à Hong Kong au Sujet de la Peste* is taken from low down, as if Yersin, to emphasize the gradient that climbs away from him, had fallen to his knees, camera at an angle close to thirty, forty degrees. The viewer thus stands at this cross-street—a sign high up on a house corner says "Caine Lane" (now a sweeping asphalt curve between high glass-faced apartment buildings, then the heart of the plague district)—and everywhere is rubble, heaps of wood, smashed and splintered. Low down on the walls are peeling posters.

Ahead, between buildings from which shutters hang from broken hinges, climbs a narrow street, every twenty yards another steep bank of steps. From the faded print it is hard to make out where the street ends—whether it peters out into scrub or is blocked by another cross-street. Outside every door are mounds of charred debris: what remained after the soldiers threw out every last item of furniture and bedding from the houses and then set the torch to them. It is a scene that seems possible only in monochrome, as if color, faced with such desolation and abandonment, would simply dissolve.

And then Yersin packed away his camera and began to walk up the street. He carried with him a steel tin, a small trowel, a notebook, and a pencil. At the top of the first flight of steps he stopped and looked around, wondering which house to start with. All were abandoned: From each dwelling, he had been told, plague dead had been carried. The nearest door offered no chance of entry, having been roughly nailed shut; the entrances to others had been rendered near-impassable by rubble and broken timber. But two houses farther on, he could see a door swinging open. There were smashed chairs outside, the charred ribs of a bed frame, and he stepped gingerly through the debris. A dog, standing alone at the top of the street, watched him, head to one side.

He stood for a while at the doorway, letting his eyes adjust to the darkness inside. Being in midterrace, the house had no side windows; peering in, he could see none at the back either. He took a step in, turned the corner, and hammered with the heel of his hand at the shutter that was cutting out the light from the street. When it finally gave, he saw that he was standing on a floor of uneven mud; when he moved he left deep footprints. Despite the open window and door, there was a powerful and disagreeable smell. He began to hunt for a simile, for the stench reminded him of something, maybe the belch of methane as a scalpel cuts into a week-old corpse, but the search defeated him: The smell was too complex, too aged and layered, to be so easily pinned down.

He felt dampness on his shoulder. He stepped back. Something was dripping from the floor above, coming through the floorboards. It fell not like water, in bright tiny bulbs, but in long gloopy tendrils. The color—red-streaked yellow, like phlegm flecked with blood—repulsed him, for it brought to mind the gleety discharge exuded by eyes and other wet tissue at the time of death. His feet were starting to feel cold, and he knew that mud had already penetrated his shoe leather.

He wondered where to conduct his dig: Anywhere fairly central—away from the most inaccessible corners—would, he guessed, be suitable. But first, out of curiosity—and since he was starting to question how anyone, let alone the typical extended Chinese family of twenty or thirty, could ever happily inhabit such a confined and unpromising space—he climbed the stairs. The steps were narrow and creaked alarmingly; when he touched the wall for balance, his hand came away dark with soot.

On the first floor, as at ground level, there was a single window, but this was only of use to the central section of the room. The space had been divided into three cubicles about twelve feet square, each of which, he knew, would have served as the living space for a family of five or six. He shook his head, beyond astonishment, and then he spotted the source of the dripping—a decaying piece of meat, black with flies, weeping dark ooze into the surrounding floorboards. He turned for the stairs again, in a hurry now, and slipped near the bottom, his elbow grazed black against the wall.

His trowel dug easily into the floor: He'd imagined it being a vigorous work of excavation, through hard-packed earth, but it crumbled with an ease that made him ponder again the reality of living in such conditions: in near darkness, with little privacy, on an unsealed floor. With each fresh trowelful of dirt, it seemed more and more plausible that the earth itself did indeed harbor infection: He filled his tin as quickly as he could and exited into the daylight, breathing deeply, filling his lungs with morning air that now felt unusually, blessedly sweet.

FOR KITASATO THE IDEA THAT THE VERY SOIL MIGHT HAVE BEEN a plague reservoir seemed only logical. During his seven years in Robert Koch's Berlin laboratory, Kitasato had been decisively influenced by his mentor's work on the relationship between soil and disease, in particular his anthrax research, which had demonstrated how anthrax spores could lie dormant for many years before triggering a fresh outbreak. He needed little persuasion to start from the assumption that plague propagated in a similar way.

Not for the first time, he seems like a man in a headlong hurry, overtaken by the speed of events, rushed—perhaps by the constant shadow of Yersin, quietly persistent, impossible to fluster—into errant conclusions. The mention of anthrax is there from the very start: In the report he wrote for the Hong Kong governor at the beginning of July he was claiming that bacteriology had pinpointed "only two micro-organisms ... found in human blood ... the bacillus of anthrax and the spirochaetae of relapsing fever" that produced infectious diseases in humans. The connection between anthrax and plague, he believed, was intimate: Examining the way the body tissues of his laboratory animals were affected at the site of injection, he remarked that the changes were "very similar to those found in anthrax." And so, over the coming weeks, he scoured his soil samples for the spores he was sure he would find.

For the anxious residents of colonial Hong Kong, living in self-imposed quarantine on an island bereft of the usual attractions, the news from the plague front was at best perplexing, at worst suggestive of an epidemic beyond anyone's control or understanding. For, while extensive coverage was given to the endeavors and rivalry of Kitasato and Yersin, equal prominence was granted both to the Chinese theories of plague transmission and to the conflicting work of senior Hong Kong doctors. Agreement seemed impossible: According to the Chinese, plague—like some kind of putrescent gas—seeped from the soil and began its spread by attacking first those animals that lived closest to the ground, before moving upward and infecting larger animals: from rats, thus, to chickens, goats, cows, and humans. To local European doctors such as Dr. James Cantlie, these theories were no more than superstition—"native popular belief"—though he had little better to offer. In the kind of convoluted language that could have come straight from a stumbling medieval medic, Cantlie argued that "the miasma of infection seems to be soil-produced, and to flourish in filth . . . the disease is miasmatic-contagious."

UNLIKE KITASATO, YERSIN—CARRYING HIS FIRST SOIL SAMPLES— returned to his laboratory highly skeptical, and again it was this proper caution that raised him above his precipitate rival.

Writing to Albert Calmette in Paris, Yersin's lack of conviction was clear. "Between ourselves, I have a feeling that I am embarking on this research believing that I will find nothing."

Back in his *paillotte*, sitting at the rough trestle that served as his main workbench, hoping that at this of all moments he would not have to fend off the idle inquiries of another party of plague tourists, Yersin opened his sample tin. The smell—fainter now, neutralized a little by its isolation and containment—struck him immediately, and transported him in an instant to the sulfurous interior of the house from which he'd just returned. He turned away, coughed, took a deep breath, and, with his tweezers, lifted out a crumb of the black earth. This he dropped into preprepared beef broth, a culture in which the bacillus would thrive and multiply, and thus remain available for experiment. Finally, he dipped a length of platinum into the broth and pushed this into a tube of jelly. Then he waited.

He came back to his experiment expecting nothing, and there can be no mistaking the astonishment in his note to Calmette. Against every prediction he found "several plague colonies and another foreign microbe!!!" although—as he was swift to explain—this did not prove either the theories of the Chinese or the postulations of the likes of Kitasato and Cantlie. "I think the bacillus is attenuated [weakened and therefore less likely to be fatal] and today I am going to make some injections just to be sure of it." However unlikely it seemed that infected soil was the main reservoir of plague, there was now a chink of doubt. Only if his laboratory animals survived the injections would he be able to rule it out.

· 16 ·

CLOSE UP, SECONDS FROM DEATH, *RATTUS RATTUS,* BLACK RAT, seemed pitiable, toylike, too fine boned to be facing such a mechanical, heartless end. Its fur looked soft as rabbits' ears; its belly, as it attempted a last-minute corkscrew for freedom, was unexpectedly, touchingly pale. It had tiny hands—too human to be truly claws—with fingers agile as a monkey's. Its mouth was minutely pursed, its nose a blur of motion. The hands that gripped it—stretched shiny against the animal's matte luster, rubbered in surgical gloves the color of ivory—were bigger, each one, than the rat's entire length. They pressed down, pincering the rat, belly-down, against the yellow plastic until its legs, like a newborn baby's, were splayed flat, and its fingers grabbed at air. The glove holding the hips pushed hard, knuckles white through the latex, and the other hand began to pry away. For a moment the rat's back looked as if it might extend infinitely, and then came the snap: a point marked in time, like the crack of a twig underfoot, stillness followed.

Flipped on its back, the corpse was worked over with a bristle brush, the fur ground forward, against the grain. The hairs stood on end, and the pink of the skin was just discernible: a glow, like light through gauze. The rat had stopped moving; its marble-black eyes bulged; the brush was accumulating a downy fuzz. Under the animal's chin a cluster of dark specks danced to life, and another latexed hand entered the wide bowl, this one holding a pencil-thin glass tube. "There! There! There!" yipped a voice. Fingers squeezed a suction bulb; the fleas were vacuumed clear.

Three feet away, surrounded by gape-mouthed children with snail-track snot and clothes shiny with matted dirt, a woman in navy overalls and black rubber boots lifted the rat onto a chipboard slab. She, like the first two—the exterminators—was a local Malagasy, and she worked with the same air of practiced determination. She pressured the rat flat on its back, and now its incisors were visible: nicotine yellow, perfectly aligned, a miracle of miniature engineering. She forced the limbs wide, and drove long pins through its palms and then picked up the scalpel and drew a scarlet line from sternum to belly. She looped out the heart and let the blood drip onto a sheet of paper—six drops, soaking into six numbered circles. Looking closer, lifting out the innards with tweezers, she remarked that this was a female, in early pregnancy: Seven embryos, no bigger than rice grains, were connected to one another by translucent filament.

If one overlooked the jeep from the branch of the Pasteur Institute in Antananarivo, the rat technicians, and the scientists, this could have been any central Malagasy village, on any dry-heat April day. Zebu cattle were sniffing the earth in an enclosure; rice lay drying on huge raffia mats; from the top windows of red-mud houses smoke drifted, disappearing into cerulean blue. Framed by a camera, this was a scene to quicken the pulse of any jaded Westerner: Here was the simple life, pure and unadorned and close to beauty. And yet, the rats. Always the rats.

PLAGUE FIRST HIT MADAGASCAR IN 1898—DIRECT FROM HONG Kong, by way of Bombay, another staging post in the third pandemic, as the disease, rampant, leaped continents and oceans, establishing strongholds in territory where it was hitherto unknown. In this Madagascar was not remarkable. What was, however, and what was triggering such anxious activity from bacteriologists and researchers at the start of the twenty-first century, was that—after some five decades of quiescence—plague was back. Worse, it had returned not just in quantity but sporting new and alarming varieties. In 1995, in the southern highlands, scientists had isolated a strain of the bacillus resistant to all the main antibiotics used to treat plague. Since then other antibiotic-resistant strains had been identified in humans and the scientific literature on the subject—normally restrained, habitually couched in elaborate conditional clauses—was, for

once, plain talking. The resurgence of plague, and the emergence of new-variant bacilli, were of "great concern": The
reports should be taken as "warning" of the lurking danger.

In the capital, Antananarivo, there were other alarming
signs: rats, notably those that foraged in the market gutters and
sewers, were developing high levels of resistance to the plague
bacillus. Trapping was yielding rodents whose blood was
aswarm with the infective bacterium, yet that were managing to
remain unaffected and lead vigorous, healthy lives. All that was
needed for an epidemic to strike was a substantial death rate
among the rats: In a congested metropolis, rat fleas, abandon-
ing their rat hosts with esophagi engorged with plague blood,
would not have to look far for their next warm body.

In an attempt to understand a little more, the local branch
of the Paris-based Pasteur Institute—Madagascar's biggest
disease-research foundation—had started this investigation in
two villages high in the central plateaus. Today had brought a
whole raft of personnel to one hamlet, the "test" site: Dr.
Philippe Mauclère, institute director; head of plague research
Dr. Suzanne Chanteau; epidemiologist Dr. René Migliani; the
rat trappers and field workers in their blue overalls; and some
sixty or more curious children. And here, once a month for
three consecutive nights, poisoned bait boxes were set inside
houses. Similar boxes were placed in the other village, but these
contained unpoisoned placebo bait and plain white flour instead
of insecticide powder.

The design of the boxes was cunning yet simple: Rectangu-
lar in shape, length about four times each end, the interior, when
the lid was lifted, revealed three sections of equal size. The two
outer contained white insecticide powder or flour; the middle

was wedged with three blocks of bait, the size and appearance of Turkish delight. With the lid down, the ends remained open and beckoning. By enticing rats in, the idea was to monitor numbers by counting their tracks, and then assess the degree of flea infestation and the proportion of both fleas and rats that was plague infected. The placing of the insecticide on either side of the bait—before the rat took its first taste of poison— was crucial: For the experiment not to trigger its own epidemic, the fleas had to be dead before the rat hit the dirt.

Jocelyn Ratovonjato, a young Malagasy entomologist with pressed black jeans and a sheaf of laminated graphs, presented his findings. Most compelling were the rat numbers: In the six months of the trial, the totals caught were down by a factor of six, a result that paid testimony to the rat's legendary caution. The rat track records were yet more telling, clearly demonstrating that, while visits to the poisoned bait boxes had tailed off, those to the placebo boxes had accelerated. Suzanne Chanteau was smiling.

"They're clever," she said. "They've worked it out. It's a bit early to say, but that's my guess." She paused. "Rats know when they're threatened. There are records of them sending out their feeblest, oldest members to investigate something they're not sure of. If the old ones die, then the other rats know to stay clear."

SUZANNE CHANTEAU HAD SET THE BACKGROUND A FEW DAYS earlier. She'd driven her jeep through the crumbling, traffic-snarled streets of Antananarivo to a café to talk. "*La circulation,*" she'd sighed, as the taxi in front of us refused to start, and a group of men climbed out to push it to the curb, *"c'est infernale."* In the café, Parisian down to its marble-topped table and white-aproned waiters, she'd drawn an arresting, salutary picture.

To understand why plague had returned so ferociously, she said, an understanding of twentieth-century politics was necessary. Colonized by the French in 1896, Madagascar regained independence in 1960. For a decade afterward, French institutions stayed largely unaffected. The 1970s, however, heralded military government; Madagascar's own brand of isolationist socialism, "Christian-Marxism"; and a steady disintegration of the infrastructure—roads, railways, schools, hospitals—of which the French had been so proud. By the 1990s, new democratic government notwithstanding, illiteracy was hovering around 50 percent, and disease was on the rise.

Plague had first reached Antananarivo, in the highlands, in 1921, a long—and still unexplained—twenty-three years after the disease first struck the island. "Between that date and 1930," Chanteau said, shaking her head, "it killed many thousands. But then, in 1931, the first effective plague vaccine came in. There were mass vaccinations. Ten million doses were injected between 1936 and 1960."

There was a theme here, and it ran pretty much one way: The decline of plague was a colonial success, a triumph of white man's medicine. From 1950, streptomycin and the noxious pesticide DDT were introduced and, over the next thirty years, fewer than fifty cases a year were reported.

To the alert medic, it must have been clear from the late 1960s that things were going to change. "The program for ratproofing stopped, the old French institutions were left to crumble. The people got poorer and poorer, dirtier and dirtier.

And then, in 1978, plague resurfaced in Antananarivo for the first time in almost three decades."

The rat of choice in Antananarivo—as in any big city—was *Rattus norvegicus*, originally from northern China and southeastern Siberia. Unlike the smaller *Rattus rattus*, which preferred houses and, in Madagascar, kept mainly to the red-mud villages in the highlands, *norvegicus* reveled in the basest, most derelict areas of urban squalor. In the Analakely district of Antananarivo, there were vast covered markets. In one, smoky soup-and-stew stalls and meat vendors' stands lined an aisle; behind the haunches of fat-blotched purple beef was a line of cubicles, some shut, most open. Come nightfall, the vendors would bed down here, curled into a corner with their tins and plastic bags and unsold meat. In the gangway running between the stalls, blood and ooze lay in the cracks and fissures, dripping slowly into splits in the concrete that might have been expressly designed for rats. At the far end, in the darkness, was the market toilet: An open door, loose on its hinges, gave onto a heap of excrement and fruit husks, empty tins and nameless mold-encrusted objects; climbing up there, assuming one ever got that desperate, would have involved an all-fours scramble, hands and knees sinking into the mulch and movement of warm decay.

The rats that cruised these districts were showing signs of disconcerting fortitude. Across Antananarivo, Chanteau explained, up to 90 percent of all rats trapped and autopsied carried antibodies to the plague bacillus: They had, in other words, developed an inherited immunity to plague, born of so many years' exposure.

Yet for humans to live surrounded by millions of plague-infected rats was sustainable provided the rodents remained alive. If, however, another contagion or an ill-managed poisoning program caused them to be struck down en masse, then an epidemic of human plague was sure to follow.

The only option, Chanteau maintained, was to aim for a complete eradication of rat fleas with insecticide. "Unless we do that," she said, her smile gone, "we will never stop infection."

"Could that ever happen?"

"Plague was wiped out in the capital between 1950 and 1978. It can be done."

In the meantime the Pasteur Institute and the government health department had joined forces in the struggle against plague. The institute, with its background in research, was aware that, without "constant surveillance" and the swift prescription of antibiotics, an epidemic was highly likely. Doctors in the highest-risk plague areas were now under orders to take pus samples from the plague swellings of every single suspected case and send them to the institute, where they were tested for the presence and antibiotic-resistance of the plague bacillus. But the initial taking of such samples demanded a degree of delicacy that not all field medics—short on equipment and training—possessed.

Often, she said, doctors were helped least by those who should have been most eager to assist: the villagers and slum dwellers themselves. On some occasions this was unwitting: Because of increasing theft, families had begun storing grain in their bedrooms, thus tempting rats into close contact with warm, sleeping bodies. At other times, as a village doctor would later explain, it was deliberate. Entering areas he suspected to be plague infected, he'd ask the people if any dead rats had been sighted. For a long time this line of questioning got him nowhere. Then it dawned on him: He was asking the wrong question of the wrong individuals. So he tried the children. "Can you show me where you've hidden the dead rats?" he'd open, and they'd nod and lead him straight there, to darkened storerooms where there lay in heaps corpses of rodents already balding, orifices gaping and maggot filled, their fleas—the propagators of plague—long gone.

In large part this deception was triggered by fear: that the village would be targeted, that whatever human corpses there were or might be would be seized and impounded and made the target for mysterious, and certainly suspect and undignified, experiments. And few outcomes were more to be avoided, since in Malagasy culture the body of a dead relative was not an empty, worthless husk, but an object of veneration. The magnificent whitewashed tombs in which people from the Hauts Plateaux interred their dead—and from which, at regular intervals, they exhumed the remains, rewrapping the broken skeletons in fresh wild-silk shrouds—were testament to the reverence in which ancestors were held.

This held as strong today as it had some eighty years before, when the French first launched their antiplague campaign, and as early as 1920, the same deceptive techniques were used to confound the plague inspectors. In the worst cases the French were held guilty of far more than cultural insensitivity. Plague, it was claimed, was an invention of the colonizing class, the best way of maintaining ascendancy: germ warfare in its most pernicious and cynical manifestation. This claim gathered momentum until by 1936—a year of unprecedented revolutionary maneuverings—the French administration was being accused by nationalist leaders of unleashing *"une peste politique et raciste."*

MIDDAY, A HIGHLAND VILLAGE SOME HUNDRED KILOMETERS south of Antananarivo. A small crowd stood in front of an abandoned house, home to a traditional healer and part-time astrologer who, some three years earlier, had died of plague. His wife, brother, and son had died the same way too, and now the house stood empty, a large spider negotiating the cobwebs that drooped from the first-floor balcony. The door stood ajar, bottom hinge gone. It was dark inside, even though the sun was high, and it was just possible to make out the corner of a table, a plate with something on it.

The healer had been a respected member of the community—second in status, perhaps, only to the village *président*—and his methods of treatment had been given far more credence than those of the district doctor, with his obscure-sounding boxes of white pills and predilection for hospitalization, evacuation, isolation. And so it would have been only natural for the woodcutter, returning to his home village, feverish and coughing, after a long spell working in a distant district, to head first for the healer's house. On the evening of October 20, 1997, after an arduous day's walk from Ankafotra, he knocked on the heavy wooden front door. All that day he'd been hacking up blood, and when the healer finally appeared, the woodcutter weakly listed his other symptoms, in particular the pain in his chest, as if someone had taken an ax to his heart.

He must have badly wanted to get home, must have had absolute faith in this man, above all others, to cure him, since he'd endured an extremely tough journey to reach the village. He'd started out some 150 kilometers north, and would have taken endless shared taxis, each one more crowded and chicken-heavy than the last, until finally the track became too fractured and deeply grooved for even the most determined bush hand to negotiate with a vehicle.

The healer greeted him and took him inside. Not realizing that the woodcutter was in the late stages of pneumonic plague—considerably rarer than the bubonic variant, though far more infectious and swiftly fatal—he opted for his customary blanket approach. Like a medieval quack, he made a small incision in the woodcutter's chest and sucked out blood, no doubt pausing only to pronounce a healthy prognosis for his by now severely delirious patient. Early the next morning, the woodcutter died.

The healer would have done better to have kept a good distance. Two days later he was showing identical symptoms, and three days after that he too was dead. Six others—three from his own family—would be struck down before the week was out.

One man acted as narrator. He'd been digging a trench with some others and had red mud splattered like blood up his calves and forearms. He'd been a friend of the healer, he said, and had tended him when he fell ill. For six days he'd sat at the healer's bedside. He wasn't worried about catching the disease, he said.

"I didn't know what it was." He paused, looking around as if for reassurance. "And he was my friend."

After the deaths the district doctor came back. He warned the villagers of the dangers of rats, how bubonic plague can swiftly turn pneumonic, of the latter's sheer contagiousness. He instructed them, too, in the importance of hygiene, but here, as everywhere else, the houses might have been designed in direct contravention of all the most basic rules of sanitation, specifically with rats in mind: On the ground floor was a dung-trodden enclosure for the family zebu; on the first floor—up, in the gloom, an almost invisible mud-brick staircase—were the kitchen and bedroom and granary, no partitions, mats on the floor. Outside the earth was swept and there were purple flowers in beds; inside it was dusty and penumbrous with smoke; touching the walls left fingers smeared black. Despite the petitions of the doctor, nothing had changed.

And what of the healer? Was there a new one, a replacement? Where did the villagers go now for treatment?

Silence. They looked one to another. Then the healer's friend took a step forward.

"The woodcutter," he said. "He wasn't from here, you know. He came from somewhere else, someplace far away."

This was untrue: A Pasteur Institute researcher had documented the case a few months before and, after extensive interviews, had labeled Ankafotra, this village, as "native" to the woodcutter.

The healer's friend looked at the ground, scuffed his foot in the dust. Across the valley a cock crowed. He looked up again. "We'd never seen him before," he insisted. "He was a stranger to us."

THESE WERE THE STATISTICS: IN THE FIFTEEN YEARS BEFORE 1996, close to twenty-four thousand plague cases were reported to the World Health Organization by twenty-four countries; of these, just over two thousand had been fatal. The worst-affected countries were Madagascar, Tanzania, Vietnam, and Peru. Since the early 1990s, the rate of infection had been steadily increasing, which had led the WHO, in 1996, to reclassify plague. No longer dormant, it was now a "re-emerging disease." But, as troubling as this was, the figures were likely to be wild underestimates. A 1998 report in the journal *Emerging Infectious Diseases* blamed "under-reporting in remote areas" and "the lack of sensitivity of the bacteriological techniques used for diagnosis."

In the white-neon laboratories of the Pasteur Institute in Antananarivo, Chanteau was working on a small cardboard strip that, she hoped, might change all this. Like an over-the-counter pregnancy test, the prototype was marked, halfway up, with a pink line. Until use it was stored in an airtight plastic bag. When a doctor took a sample from a plague suspect, all he had to do was inject the pus—or, in the case of pneumonic plague, the blood-flecked sputum—into the bottom of the test tube. Fifteen minutes later, as the strip soaked up the sample, the result became clear: No change meant the patient was free of plague; a second pink line, however faint, spelled infection. A pilot was currently in operation: twenty-five outposts in remote areas, all under orders to test and report every suspect case, to send the finished tests to the institute, to treat infected villages with insecticide to kill the rat fleas, and, on top of that, to "educate" the inhabitants.

Until now, Chanteau said, plague had been such a problematic disease to diagnose correctly that doctors "have often preferred to wait and see what happens to the patient. If it is plague, then all that time the fleas are continuing to bite and people are dying." With a quick-result diagnostic test, she hoped, such fence-sitting would not be necessary.

Yet she was quick to stress her sympathy for the doctors in the field. "It is not their fault. They have a very hard job. One doctor will have a fifty-kilometer area to cover: That's a hundred villages. He'll have no motorbike, often not even a cycle. *C'est impossible.*"

"DR. CHANTEAU!" THE LABORATORY AGAIN. ONE OF HER ASSIStants handed over a sheet of paper. It was a printed questionnaire, ruled and boxed. Across the top was printed, "Official Declaration of Individual Cases of Plague." Chanteau scanned it in silence.

At a white-topped table in the middle of the adjoining room sat a man. There was dust in his hair. His collar was so frayed the cotton had split apart. He stared into space as if noticing nothing—the assistants pressing him in Malagasy, the walls covered with charts and pictures of rats and photographs of infected children; Suzanne Chanteau, who moved closer now, beginning her own questioning.

"*Trois morts,*" she said, eventually. "Three deaths. What happened?"

The man started speaking, his voice a quavering monotone. The assistants translated into French. He'd left early that morning, carrying—on the orders of the district doctor—a test tube with a tissue sample from one of the deceased. He nodded morosely, as if recalling the fifty kilometers of broken roads, the hours waiting in the sunshine for rides that never came, the bewildering commotion and aggression of Antananarivo, his first time in the city.

Two weeks ago, he said, one of the neighboring children, a three-year-old boy, had fallen sick. The villagers sent for the doctor, but he was not there, and no one knew where he had gone. The child died, but not before infecting his brother. Their father, tending to them, holding the boys as they muttered feverishly, watched them die and then fell sick himself. Four days after burying his children, he too was dead.

"Why," asked Chanteau—genuinely moved yet unable to hide her exasperation—"why did you not find another doctor? *Il faut vite vite voir le médecin.*"

The man did not respond. Chanteau bent closer. "If anyone has a cough—or anything out of the ordinary—they *must* go to the doctor." The man, looking down, nodded.

Chanteau looked again at the form. It had been filled in by the stand-in medic, and detailed the symptoms of all three victims. The children were both listed as suffering from classic bubonic plague—engorged lymph nodes, fever, soaring temperatures. The father, however, was not recorded as having had any abnormal swellings.

"Pneumonic plague," Chanteau muttered to herself. By now, it could have spread farther; in the hours it had taken the neighbor to reach the Pasteur Institute, most of the village might have become infected.

Chanteau was shaking her head. She pointed to the form. "Why weren't they given any medicine—the father, anyone who'd been in contact with the boys?" All the signs pointed to plague—symptoms, speed of contagion—so why wasn't it picked up?

The man shuffled off his stool, got to his feet. He brushed his hands down the front of his shirt. "We didn't have medicine," he said. "And the doctor said it was malaria. We didn't know." And he turned—his pockets empty, his message delivered—to begin the long journey home.

· 17 ·

AT THE END OF JULY 1894, ALEXANDRE YERSIN TRAVELED TO Canton. In Hong Kong, where the hose-down of Taipingshan and the flight of most of its population had seen a steady drop-off in the rate of infection, he had assembled a substantial body of data, taking soil samples from enough plague-infected houses to offer a reliable ration. "Four times out of ten," he reported, "I found the microbe." In houses where no plague cases had been recorded, the soil was clean. He went to the Chinese mainland to broaden his research, carrying out the same experiment, with similar results: The earth in plague houses carried the bacillus "as far as twenty, thirty centimeters." But the presence of the bacterium did not mean the soil was necessarily the source of infection. His next step as good as dispatched the contagious-earth theory favored not only by Kitasato and the Chinese, but also the European medical establishment: Injected with a solution of the bacillus cultured from the soil, not one of his laboratory animals died. Clearly another mechanism was at work.

The journey to Canton also confirmed the importance of what, until now, had been a brief jotting in his notebook: The epidemic on the Chinese mainland, as he explained in his August 4 letter to the governor-general, "started with rats; this fact appears indisputable." There is a surging detective thrill at this point in the letter, with Yersin underscoring "rat" so forcefully that the pen mark is still visible today on the reverse of the page. From his interviews with doctors, he learned more: that through February and March—well before the first human succumbed to plague—"rats died in large numbers . . . then the disease extended itself to men . . . The floating population— very considerable in Canton—has been almost completely spared." This was Yersin at his meticulous, observant best, noting—though he was still too close to the ground to see the whole landscape, to discern the whole relationship between the disparate elements of his investigation—the key that would eventually unlock the mystery of the spread of plague. The boat dwellers, he guessed, had been "spared" because their homes were inaccessible to rats. As yet it was only hypothesis, but he was almost there.

Back in Hong Kong, Yersin found his contempt deepening for the island colony's management of the plague crisis. In Canton, not only had he been "admirably welcomed" by the Chinese doctors—in contrast to the continual rebuff and

obstruction he'd received from Lowson—but the layout of
their hospitals and medical treatment was also markedly superior. The main plague hospital—like his own hastily constructed
paillotte—was built from straw. Yet, despite its emergency
construction, considerable thought had been exercised in the
design: each of the twelve hundred patients were accommo-
dated in separate, clean, and spacious rooms. By contrast the
Hong Kong hospitals were notable for their cramped and under-
equipped wards: In Canton, moreover, doctors claimed that
their approach had "saved fifty percent of the patients." Mortality in Hong Kong was running closer to 90 percent.

To add to his exasperation, he arrived back on the island
only to find a letter from Sir William Robinson. Inside, Yersin
noted tersely, was a brief note "demanding again, in my opinion, what would be the measures to take to prevent the return of
the epidemic." His impatience was understandable, for it had
been in an attempt to answer this very question—at the first
time of asking—that he'd initially begun his soil analyses and
then traveled to Canton.

The governor's previous request for Yersin to investigate
the soil inside infected houses had been little more than a cursory duplicate of the instructions issued to Kitasato. Now, however, there was an urgency in his communication. While Yersin
was in Canton, Kitasato—after one last "tiffin" with the loyal
Lowson—had slipped anchor and set sail for Japan. He'd
packed up his microscopes and surgical instruments, his rack
upon rack of tailored suits and dress shoes, and—anticipating a
true ticker-tape welcome, secure in the knowledge that there
would be few in Japan still ignorant of his momentous discov-

ery, or of his success against resolute competition—had ordered his research team to board their homeward vessel. He'd left with the controversy over the discovery still running in the pages of the *Lancet,* and leaving Robinson with no choice now but to petition Yersin for help. The Frenchman was now the only choice for a governor who, with one eye on the approval of his superiors in London, would have realized this one simple fact about disaster management: Activity in whatever form is always preferable, and more easily justifiable, than doing nothing. By attempting to hurry Yersin into the field again, Robinson was covering his back: With his bulletins to the Frenchman diligently copied to Lord Ripon in Whitehall, no one would have been able to accuse him of sitting idly back while the colony slid into oblivion.

It is also not impossible that Robinson imagined Yersin would have been flattered by the attention: Until now, after all, the authorities had treated him with disdain. In his note Robinson had asked Yersin to stay on for "a few months more": Only the assumption of a warm reaction could have prompted the governor to make so large a request. According to Yersin, the colony now wanted him to remain in Hong Kong "in order to research a practical procedure for disinfecting the soil and to try and prevent a resurgence of the epidemic." But his thoughts were already moving on: With news about the incursion of plague deep into the Chinese mainland, he knew that containment of the disease within the Far East was becoming increasingly unlikely. A far more radical solution was called for, one that went way beyond the myopic hygiene measures advocated by the Hong Kong government. The answer, he felt sure, lay in effective prevention, and some two weeks after Kitasato's departure Yersin sailed from Hong Kong Harbor, bound for Vietnam, where he planned to take the fight against plague onto a whole new plane. With plague now entering new territory, and the causal bacillus identified, he could risk no more time spent in research: Action was required, and vaccination, he was convinced, was the answer.

He departed as he arrived: alone. To the Hong Kong medical establishment this was the departure of the runner-up, an individual who—despite Robinson's political insistence on his continued presence—had become in the end a figure to be pitied, whose trip to Hong Kong had been one long catalog of misadventure and missed opportunity. To Yersin's admirers—a mere handful who would, over the years to come, swell to a clamorous multitude—his overlooking remained a mystery that would take another eighty-one years, some three decades after the great man's death, to be conclusively and finally unraveled.

KITASATO, ARRIVING IN TOKYO TO A SLEW OF ADULATORY newspaper profiles, launched straight into a series of lectures. The text of these—still available only in Japanese—reveals a confidence and a swagger that speaks of a man buoyed up by the adulation of others, at the peak of his powers and popularity.

Seen through the prism of his own words, Kitasato comes across as neither generous-spirited nor open-minded; at home, among peers of his own nationality, he gives free expression to his dislike of European medics in general, while at the same time stressing the bravery and clearsightedness of his own team of researchers.

Particularly dangerous, he explained, had been the post-mortem procedure. The necessary deception and secrecy was "our greatest difficulty": the moment a patient died, the corpse was nailed into a coffin and "pretended to be carried to the mortuary in front of the Chinese . . . But actually the coffin was carried to a hospital room in the police station [now plague hospital]." He continued to outline in minute detail the additional complications. "We placed the dead body on the cover of the coffin. It was a very uneven floor. This," he said, indicating the hefty lectern from which he was reading, "would shake if we placed it on that floor. The room had one window and one entrance. Since Chinese laborers would walk under the window, we had to close it even when it was hot. . . . Yes, the post-mortem examinations were the hardest part."

Kitasato swelled to fill the role expected of him: returning conqueror, dismissive of the sceptics, secure in his primacy. "Some people," he instructed his audiences, "seemed to doubt my report that I had found the cause of the disease only one week or so after my arrival in Hong Kong. . . . I would not express my view irresponsibly, since I am responsible for my field of specialty."

To his audiences, as in his *Lancet* articles, he gave details of his experiments and the processes by which he arrived at his swift "discovery." His "main goal" in Hong Kong, he explained, "was to carry out blood tests." And it was in the blood that he found small quantities of the bacillus; in the spleen and buboes a far greater volume was present. Having conducted some fifty autopsies, he was convinced. "I would like to declare, from a bacteriological point of view, that they cause bubonic plague without any doubt." His bacillus was clearly different from that isolated by Yersin: Where Yersin's was larger, more sluggish, and did not change color when stained with alkaline dye, Kitasato's was much smaller and did react to the stain.

His claim staked, he moved quickly to demolish those "European scholars [who] have mistakenly assumed that plague has vanished from the world." Such a position, he maintained, could only have come about through severe cultural myopia. Simply because plague had "ceased to exist in Europe" did not mean that the rest of the world could be regarded as similarly disease-free. "European scholars should not have come to such a conclusion," he admonished. "The world consists not only of Europe, but also Asia."

The English medics—who had offered him such whole-hearted support—came in for a forceful drubbing. The slowness of their initial diagnosis struck Kitasato as preposterous. "Even though many Chinese were dying from the plague after it reached Hong Kong, English doctors were not aware of it. This resulted in a rapid increase in the death rate of the Chinese in the spring." When they "finally realized" that an epidemic was afoot,

> they found that the symptoms of the patients were very similar to those of the bubonic plague that are mentioned in old medical books. This astonished the English doctors, and then they went to Canton to trace back to the source of it. However, they faced great difficulties, as the Chinese in Canton refused to be examined by foreign doctors and sometimes attacked them. They just beat a hasty retreat to Hong Kong, where the epidemic was raging and the situation was disastrous.

Kitasato then set about demystifying what he saw as the last veiled area of plague research: the process of contagion. Here too he entertained no doubts; the plague bacillus penetrated the body through a variety of routes: skin, lungs, stomach. His observations of the work of the British soldiers, some of whom contracted plague, had convinced him that the disease "must have entered into their bodies through the respiration of heavy dust." Cuts and abrasions were also a risk, he asserted: "The bacillus may enter . . . through an external wound, which has also been proved by many examples." What this proof consisted of he did not pause to explain, adding only that "plague can [also] infect human beings through food and drink."

And then he took his bow, hearing all around him the applause of his peers, the entire proud nation. There would, he knew, be yet more interviews, more newspaper profiles, quite likely honors from overseas medical institutions, all grateful for his bold, pioneering work. He was also expecting a visit from Lowson and—despite his cursory public acknowledgment to the Hong Kong doctor—was planning a lavish welcome, possibly even an audience with the emperor.

The very last thing he imagined, in this stellar moment, was that the coming decades would witness a gradual chipping away at his reputation and that the worst of the damage, the final work of devastation, would come from one of his own, a respected Japanese bacteriologist with whom, of all people, he would have expected his reputation to be safe.

· 18 ·

IT WAS FIVE IN THE AFTERNOON; DUSK WAS APPROACHING. Yersin, two years after leaving Hong Kong to work in his Vietnam laboratory on the plague vaccine, had been summoned back to the island. Yet, arriving in June 1896, he discovered that the state of emergency had already passed; in Canton, however, plague was running rampant. And as the sun dipped over the smoky streets of Hong Kong, he found himself filling a syringe with the plague serum, about to test it for the first time on a human being.

The patient was a young man, prostrate in the sanatorium of the French mission, with no inkling of what was to come. "At three o'clock in the afternoon," recalled Bishop Chausse, the pastor in charge of the mission, in a long letter to the *Hong Kong Daily Press,* "Dr. Yersin came to see me, as he had in 1894." They shook hands, and the bishop came straight to the point:

> I said, "Doctor, you have arrived most opportunely. A case of plague has occurred this morning in our establishment, and if you have discovered any remedy for this terrible disease since your last visit, I will be very grateful if you will employ it upon this young man. This case is very pressing, a painful bubo has formed on the thigh, the fever is intense, and the young man is completely prostrated; it is an affair of twenty-four hours.

Of all the months of preparation, the long days spent in Emile Roux's laboratory in the Paris Pasteur Institute the year before, till he was too wall-eyed with exhaustion to look at another slide or culture dish, this was the moment for which Yersin had been waiting and hoping. The vaccine had been successfully tested on animals, but he had no proof that it would be sufficiently powerful to fight plague in humans. From his case he lifted a test tube of the serum—"a limpid fluid, slightly reddish in color"—and injected "a teaspoonful . . . into the skin over one of the hips." And then he waited.

Darkness fell. Yersin and the missionary sat together awhile. Yersin—with an uncharacteristic candor that says much about his fondness and trust for the pastor—"proceeded to explain the theory of his action by saying that he was going to destroy the microbes by feeding them so to speak, on their own venom." Chausse, for his part, "was [as] excited as if going into battle."

Yersin waited all night at his patient's bedside. At dawn, confident finally that the worst was past, he went to bed. An hour later Chausse returned to find the patient no longer delirious, but looking up "with large eyes." He leaned close and asked how the man felt. The next moments—choked with biblical resonance—gave him a profound thrill. "The patient replied, 'I am cured; the bubo is no longer painful; my head no longer aches.'" Chausse told him, "Get up and show me that you are cured." The man sat up, shuffled on his shoes, and walked unsteadily around the room. It must have seemed a miracle, an overnight reversal of fortune, the kind of transformative recovery that happened only in the Gospels; and, when Yersin came back at nine o'clock, Chausse was puppyish with excitement. "It is a complete success," he enthused. "Your remedy is marvelous; a thousand times thanks." Yersin, the true gentleman-pioneer, deflected the praise. "It is I," he answered, "who have to thank you, for without you perhaps I should not have found an occasion to use it."

YET YERSIN, WHATEVER HIS TALENT, WAS ALONE: ONE MAN against newly resurgent bubonic plague. A hundred years after Edward Jenner's landmark smallpox vaccination, he may have become the first scientist to cure a plague sufferer, but time and numbers were not on his side. By September plague had leaped to India, and the Bombay government was pleading for his help. Whatever the injustices of Kitasato's fame as a plague pioneer, the success of the first twenty or so vaccinations that Yersin had carried out in China was now well known, and

Bombay's request was unequivocal: to rush as much antiplague serum to India as he could carry.

BOMBAY'S LINK WITH HONG KONG WAS CLEAR: BOTH WERE ports, between which ran frequent commercial traffic. As one government doctor wrote, "[Since] the outbreak commenced near the Docks, it appears most probable that the infection was introduced by sea and carried in their clothes or goods by traders who were themselves unsusceptible." Like the authorities in Hong Kong, the Bombay government indulged initially in some energetic wishful thinking: Despite doctors' reports of sporadic cases of patients with suspiciously enlarged glands as early as May 1896, and though these flared into an unmistakable and full-blown epidemic in September, it took a further month before the health department finally acknowledged that the city was experiencing an outbreak of "true bubonic plague." There was no need, however, for alarm: this was the disease in its "mild" form.

As in Surat a century later, little heed was paid to the voices of reassurance: Between the early-October confirmation of plague and the end of February 1897, an estimated 380,000 people, close to half the population, fled the city. At the height of the plague exodus, only one-fifth of Bombay's millhands remained at their posts. With plague fast spreading into the interior, the government cast around for help, for anyone who might be able somehow to wrest the epidemic back under control. Only one name presented itself, that of Dr. Alexandre Yersin, who since the Hong Kong plague summer of 1894 had devoted himself to a single task. For the past two years he'd been working on a vaccine, in the belief that, against a disease of this potency, mankind needed a ring fence of protection. Plague, for him, had assumed the status of enemy number one: It had to be crushed.

The early narrative of the Bombay outbreak had much in common with the way events had unfolded in Hong Kong. There was the pervasive suspicion of Europeans, born of the fact that relatively few were struck by plague. There was the use of troops to hunt down plague suspects; the widely held belief that the disease was caused by "overcrowding, destitution, deficient cubic space, ventilation, and sunlight, and a filthy and generally insanitary condition of person, clothing, habitation, and its surroundings"; the suspicion of Western medics as "callous and patent mercenaries" and hospitals as places of pollution, contaminated by blood and feces, inimical to caste, religion, and purdah. The physical examination of travelers carried out by the mostly white, male cadre of doctors compounded the atmosphere of distrust. A local paper protested in October 1897 that "Native feeling" was "most touchy" on this issue: "Native ladies will prefer death to the humiliation of having their groins examined by male doctors who are utter strangers to them." Little surprise, then, that families did their utmost to conceal the disease from the search parties. Corpses were buried clandestinely or stowed in attics, under furniture, inside specially constructed rooms.

Such an atmosphere, with its multiple sources of unreliable information, stoked by fear and hatred, bred rumors of the wildest and most arcane variety. Plague was part of a sinister evangelical plot, some claimed, evidence of a government bent on "destroying caste and religious observances, with the ultimate design of forcing Christianity on the natives of India." Others pointed to "proof" that the government was in the process of poisoning the people: According to one newspaper report, "six bags of snakes and other worms have been ground [up] and dissolved in the water-pipe at Cawnpore to bring on plague among consumers." Inside the scrubbed-white wards of plague hospitals all manner of horrors were said to be perpetrated: Workers at the Arthur Road Hospital were quoted in one article as believing that there had been "something diabolical" about a hospital "which claimed so many victims." Patients, it was said, were bled to death through the soles of their feet. There were even rumors that under every hospital bed was an "oil mill" to grind the patient into ointment for use on Europeans: The plague inspection sheds at railway stations housed, by logical and paranoid extension, "big machines" for compressing this valuable medicinal ooze from the bodies of innocent Indians. As for the early, unsuccessful attempts at vaccination, these were held to be ruthless efforts at population control: Men lost their virility and women became sterile; anyone inoculated was lucky to survive six months; the needle, others said, was a yard long.

To Yersin such gossip would have seemed close to sacrilege: Inoculation, he was now convinced, was the only sure way to curb the spread of plague, and it was to this end that he'd passed the spring of 1895 in his despised Paris. Yet the weeks spent cloistered away in the laboratory would turn 1895 into as historic a year for plague research as the one that had just passed. For it was in the Paris Pasteur Institute that Yersin— working with strains of the bacillus that he'd had the foresight to send from Hong Kong months earlier—first demonstrated that a plague vaccine was the best hope against the disease. As an official publication from the World Health Organization put it in 1954: "The modern story of vaccination against plague began in 1895 when Yersin, [and his colleagues] Calmette and Borrel proved that the rabbit could be vaccinated against this infection by the repeated injection of microbes killed by heat."

TO THE VICTORIAN BUREAUCRAT IN A BOMBAY FACING SOCIAL and economic collapse, the request that Yersin simply stockpile a boat with newly manufactured antiplague serum—and head without delay to India—must have seemed reasonable enough. But even for an expert bacteriologist, the manufacture of the serum was fraught with uncertainties: It was a delicate process, hard to calibrate, with a raft of unpredictable factors. To begin with, it was dependent on animals.

Back in Nha Trang at the end of 1896, the telegrams from Bombay mounting unanswered on his desk, Yersin returned to the laboratory he'd set up the year before. Stabled on the grounds were horses, all of which—following the technique first pioneered by Jenner—were in the process of being injected with increasing doses of the plague bacillus. It was the task of Yersin and his team of assistants then to draw off serum—the bile-yellow fluid that separates from blood—that would by now be ripe with plague antitoxins. Yersin worked as swiftly as he could, writing to his mother on January 20, 1897, "As soon as I arrived we did a test bloodletting on two mares who seemed to me the best immunized. If their serum is good I will do big bloodlettings and go immediately to India." But it was a hazardous process: Horses frequently died, and the varying quality of the serum samples brought Yersin on occasion close to despair.

A month later he had collected seven hundred doses: cure, if the strengths were correct, and providing they survived the sea crossing, for an equal number of Bombay patients. By choice Yersin would have stayed longer at his laboratory, but now he decided to capitulate, ground down by pressure from Bombay. The texts of India's telegrams to Yersin do not survive, but some significant leverage must have been applied to persuade the Frenchman—who rarely allowed outside pressure, from however elevated a source, to hurry him or force a change of plan—to leave Vietnam before he was ready. Writing again to his mother on February 20, he did little to hide his resentment. "It's not seven hundred but seven thousand doses that I should have been able to take with me, and then my serum would have been active and effective." Reluctantly, however, and despite his misgivings, he began to pack his equipment for the journey.

· 19 ·

BY THE TIME MOHANLAL REACHED THE VILLAGE, THE SUN WAS
dipping below the trees. The color in the sky was fading, turning to an aquarelle wash. Mohanlal, on the road for almost two
days now, was having difficulty focusing. He rested against a
fence post and squinted ahead, down the dirt track toward the
scatter of low dwellings that was Hetal's parents' home. When
he'd first visited he had been astonished that a girl of Hetal's
delicacy and urban ease could have been raised somewhere so
basic and backward. He, who'd spent his childhood in Bombay
and his teens on Chowpatty Beach, found it hard to believe that
anyone intelligent could have been satisfied with so little. But
he liked her parents: They would speak with hushed reverence

of their son-in-law's "newspaper job," and though they were poor they were hospitable. Now, though, he approached their village in fear: for their reaction to his arrival, for what might have happened to Hetal and his daughter over the past two days, for the future.

He pushed himself upright, and, overhead, the vulture that had tailed him for the last hour lifted heavily from the top branches of a skeletal eucalyptus. In the calm evening air he could hear the noise of its wings, and a slow clicking sound that he imagined was its beak, the knock of bone on bone.

The village was silent, and he was having trouble recalling its layout—which house belonged to his parents-in-law. He remembered scarlet flowers, some kind of perimeter fence, but that could have been any one of these houses. All were equally humble: cracked mud walls, corrugated aluminum roofs. There couldn't have been more than twenty or thirty at most, and he was already halfway through. Twenty yards farther, a tethered goat marked the limit of the village: Beyond were the same terracotta dust fields through which he'd spent the last hours walking, the same concrete-hard earth into which seed, somehow, had been sown.

Someone coughed. Through the darkened window of the nearest house he could see a still candle flame and he turned, called out. No sound. He walked to the door, knocked against the frame. "Hello?" In the half-light inside he could see two figures sitting motionless on the floor, watching him. A man spoke: "Further on." And Mohanlal, seeing them lift their hands to their mouths, retreated as fast as he could, half tripping over a dog in his scurry to reach the safety of the track.

He wanted to cry but felt too used up and desiccated for

tears. He stood motionless and felt the cool of darkness come. Now he could see candle glow in all the windows, but no one ventured outside their doors. Normally the newcomer to any village faced questioning, invitations from more than one household. The silence now scared him, though he knew it stemmed from their fear of him: They were cowering, as if from a predator, huddled in their farthest, safest places.

And then an older face appeared at a window. In the shadows he could see white hair, a beckoning arm.

"Son!" a voice called out.

Mohanlal broke into a run. Then he was at the door, the blood rushing in his ears. His father-in-law was nodding, smiling. His teeth were betel red, eroded at the roots, and his skin appeared gray, as if he'd not seen rest, much less sleep, in days. "Son," he said again, more softly now. "You've come."

He ushered him inside and, when Mohanlal had crossed the threshold, took one last glance outside, then shut and bolted the door.

His mother-in-law was sitting on the floor in front of an open fire. Mohanlal fell to his knees. "And Hetal?" he said. He could smell the starchy tang of almost-done rice. She raised her pale eyes to meet his. "Do not worry," she said. "You must not."

The old man walked slowly to the far corner of the room. He had a limp, and was lifting one heel, dragging his toes. He reached the storeroom door, murmuring to himself, and Mohanlal could see his hand moving in his pocket. He pulled out a key and angled the base of the padlock toward him, then pushed the key home. He opened the door and whispered inside.

Mohanlal found himself on his feet. His mother-in-law was

holding up a hand, but he pushed past her, over the heat of the fire, and in one stride was at the door to the storeroom.

He heard a whimper and knew the noise at once. His father-in-law called for a match, and then, with a phosphorous fizz, the storeroom loomed before them. Hetal was before him, sitting on a grain sack. Their daughter was lying in her lap, and Hetal's eyes were closed, her hand resting on the baby's forehead. Mohanlal's voice came out a croak.

"Hetal, sweetheart. All right?"

His wife nodded, and slowly she opened her eyes and looked up at him. Her face was blotchy from crying.

"I thought you would not come." She put a finger to her temple; her breathing was shallow, quick.

He knelt beside her and breathed her scent: of the sun, sweet and warm, undercut by something else, something sharper and less familiar. He touched her arm. "You just left," he said. "What was I to do?"

The match died, and the storeroom fell to black again. He got to his feet, lifting Hetal with him. She felt lighter than he remembered, almost insubstantial, even though she was holding the baby.

"Why are you here?" he asked. "Why are you hiding away like this?"

She allowed herself to be led to the door; the light from the fire softened the smear of dirt on her cheek, the signs of crying. In her dark eyes he saw the jagged reflection of the flames.

She rested her head on his chest. "No one knows I'm here," she murmured. "It can't get out."

He nodded, held her, and said nothing. He knew this was wishful thinking, had understood the moment he'd arrived in the village and there'd been no one to greet him that her presence was no secret. He stretched down to touch the baby, but Hetal held the infant tighter, turning away so he could not reach her.

"What has happened?" he said.

But she did not answer or even now meet his eye. Her father put a hand on Mohanlal's shoulder and guided him toward the fire. "We will eat," he said.

The rice was overdone, and the curry too heavily flavored with cardamom. Halfway through he set down his bowl and put out his hand for the baby again. Hetal's mother whispered something to her daughter, and Hetal, eyes down, lifted the baby for him to take.

Laying the child in the crook of his lap he immediately noticed a dark ridge of dried blood just above one eye. He touched it, and she moaned in her sleep. He could feel the ridges and grooves of the hardened scab, but he pulled his hand away, feeling suddenly unsteady. He wanted to wake her, make her cry out and show him she was undamaged.

"What's this?" He tried to sound sympathetic but could hear the accusation in his voice.

With no warning, Hetal started to speak. She talked fast, as if defying interruption, and her voice rose as she went on, cracking with the release of tension.

They'd been stoned, she said. Like Mohanlal, she'd ridden the train to Anand, but from there no buses would take them, and even though she knew she was more of a target on foot, she'd had no choice but to head on. The first night she'd slept in the open, and then, midmorning, entering a village and desperate for water, had been set upon by a gang of teenagers.

She'd shouted that she was holding a baby, but the boys, ignoring her cries, began hurling stones. She yelled back, frightened and bellicose, but that only seemed to fuel their aggression. She was hit on the arm, between the shoulders, and she started to run. She was almost in open country again when a woman stepped out from behind a house and pelted her with a hail of gravel. It was as if in slow motion, events suddenly suspended, that she saw the skin split on her baby's forehead, the bone-white cut, then the first blister of blood; after that it came fast, rich and dark, warm against the cotton of her sari, and she cried out like an animal, a howl that made the other woman, her aggressor, turn and flee.

She ran until she was out of sight of the village and then, under cover of a small spinney, laid her howling baby on the ground and tended to the wound. She tore a strip of cotton from her sari and bandaged the head and for an hour, eyes closed, she pressed a hand to it, feeling the blood under her fingers begin to grow sticky, and eventually the child slept and she was able to strap her again to her chest and move on.

"I will never go back," she said quietly. "Not to Surat."

"Plague will die down," Mohanlal said. "Life will carry on."

She pushed her plate away, shook her head. "How many people have died? How many?'

He looked from Hetal to her parents: All were waiting, expectant. "I don't know," he answered. "No one seems to know."

"They wanted to kill me," Hetal went on. Her eyelids bulbed with tears again. "Just because I came from Surat."

"But everything we have is there. Our lives, everything."

She lifted a sleeve to wipe her eye. "I can't go back."

"It's plague," Mohanlal said, trying to soothe her. "It's not AIDS, or some terrible African virus. There is a cure."

"Plague," she repeated. "How much worse can it get? It is 1994, and our city is struck by plague. Doesn't that tell you something?"

Her parents were nodding in agreement now, murmuring encouragement to their daughter, their only child. And Mohanlal knew that, against them, he had no words.

"Mohanlal," she said after a while. "Mohanlal, my sweet. Do you want to live in a place where the doctors run away the moment disease strikes?'

He held up his hands, as if in surrender. Less than a week before his world had seemed certain, knowable, unassailable. Now his wife was saying that she wanted no further part of it.

"I don't——" he began to say, but she interrupted him.

"Gandhiji was right. We are a dirty people. We care for our own families, but we are blind to what happens even just outside our own front doors. We do not care."

Mohanlal suddenly had a picture of similar struggles occurring at that very moment in villages all over Gujarat, wherever Suratis had fled: wives, husbands, grandparents, all arguing over their futures. He did not yet know that, on the world stage, India itself was being shunned, or that airlines had ceased flights to Indian cities and that some countries had begun imposing embargoes on Indian imports. All he knew was that he would not be the one to run.

"We cannot stay away," he told her. "We must go back. Surat is our home, and if we are not to help make it a better place, then who will?'

She reached out, took back the baby. "That is not my job. I am a mother, and I will not raise my child there." There was steel in her voice, and he understood that, for them to remain together, only one course of action remained open to him.

"I am tired," he said. "I have never been so tired. Tomorrow, we will talk, and we will decide." He paused. He had no more certainties any more, nothing on which to rest: He could no longer see the future.

"Yes," he finished, trying to sound as if he had it all worked out. "Tomorrow it will all be decided."

THE OUTBREAK OF PLAGUE IN SURAT REMAINED A SUBJECT THAT left no one neutral, that still provoked the fiercest opinion. No aspect of the story escaped controversy; and from diagnosis to treatment, from the intervention of the United States to the fearful reaction of India's trade partners, no single narrative emerged. If there was any agreement at all, it was that a whole slew of culprits was responsible: the federal government, Surat's crumbling infrastructure, the media, America, modern farming methods, the collapse of plague surveillance.

Once again, even the most extreme theories found sympathetic ears. According to the wilder conspiracists, all evidence pointed to a U.S. germ warfare experiment—a claim loudly rebutted by Washington. The "proof," so it was said, was various: the presence in Delhi, even before the start of the epidemic, of a team from Atlanta's world-renowned Centers for Disease Control; the "unusual" features of the outbreak, in particular the lack of an immediately preceding ratfall—that is, the death of many rats—and the fact that fewer than a hundred people died, both factors that raised suspicions that this was a "plague bacterium mutated in some germ warfare lab"; the disappearance of vital serum samples from the laboratories of Bombay's respected Haffkine Institute; and the presence in the Surat bacillus of an extra band of protein, too "fat" to have been the result of natural genetic selection.

Yet the whys, as ever, proved more elusive: As the *Calcutta Business Standard* put it:

> What is beyond the comprehension of Indian scientists is why anyone would engineer a non-virulent strain if it was meant for intentionally introducing plague. . . . Some scientists who think the Surat outbreak was an experiment believe that the aim could have been to study how the government, the people and the scientific community would react in the event of a real attack.

If the conspiracy theorists had fingered the United States as the source of the epidemic, a broader consensus also accused America—in the words of one newspaper—of "manipulating public health matters for political ends." At the heart of this charge was the alleged glee with which the U.S. media had reported the epidemic, typified in headlines such as THOUSANDS FLEE INDIAN CITY IN DEADLY PLAGUE OUTBREAK, and MEDICAL EXPERTS FEAR REFUGEES MAY SPREAD INDIA PLAGUE, both from the normally circumspect *New York Times*. America, countered India's commentators, was itself a reservoir of plague, with a steady increase in the number of cases during the latter half of the twentieth century. And so to witness its return in India, ran the argument, was an occasion of some satisfaction to the West: "The general portrayal of the USA (and Western Europe) as a superior repository of rationality and civility in a seemingly chaotic world, and hence ordained for world leadership, is supported by every successful embarrassment of the Third World."

Voices of moderation were rare, uncommon the newspaper commentator who strove for balance. Fewer still were those who chose to look not abroad but inward: Plague, these brave voices claimed, was no one's fault but India's. And only one writer pointed out, for instance, that the World Health Organization had warned as early as March 1994—six months before the Surat epidemic—of a global resurgence of plague.

It took less than a week for India's top doctors and scientists, faced with a collapsed economy and a populace in flight, to begin bickering over the cause of the chaos. In Surat itself there was unanimity: The disease *was* plague, and the city had acted with all speed and efficiency. In Bombay infectious-disease researchers at the Haffkine Institute were less convinced, and drew darker conclusions as to the speed of Surat's self-diagnosis, since for the city to have admitted to anything less would have meant that flight had been unnecessary, and the entire disease control program a shameful overreaction. By December the health department of the Swiss government—which, like so many other overseas authorities, had nervously analyzed the chain of events—announced that the outbreak had been nothing less than an "epidemic in the media. . . . It appears that the 1994 outbreak did not take place." The WHO, it went on, found no evidence of the plague bacillus in humans or animals during the plague weeks, news of which, "an attentive reader would have observed . . . disappeared from the press on October 5, 1994, the day of the massacre of the members of the [Swiss religious cult] Temple of the Sun."

Consensus seemed impossible. Shortly before the Swiss rebuttal, the Center for Disease Control posited the exact opposite, that the outbreak had indeed been plague. The American research had come as a result of an invitation from the Indian government, baffled by two months of contradictory findings—first, from Delhi's National Institute of Communicable Diseases and the Surat Medical College, that the disease was plague; second, from the National Institute of Virology and Pune's B. J. Medical College, that it was no such thing, rather a distinct and unrelated infectious disease called melioidosis, whose symptoms conveniently matched those of plague. The CDC report, the government hoped, would be the end of the controversy, and a spokesman for the health department instructed reporters that those "certain institutions" that registered a nonplague diagnosis had now been ordered to fall into line and "publicly deny the [earlier] reports."

To the ordinary resident of Surat, or the inhabitant of any one of the cities to which terrified Suratis were fleeing, these arguments must have seemed at best arcane, at worst an irresponsible diversion from the main business of fighting a disease that was manifestly among them. And from the start—while the scientists sniped at one another—the message to the public had been unswerving and direct. Throughout October, billboards across the neighboring state of Maharashtra had carried "an appeal" from Information Minister Sharad Pawar. Under a snapshot that made Pawar look bruise-eyed from lack of sleep, the public was exhorted "to stand solidly behind the government." His language was steady, his certainty unshakable. The disease was "Plague," and originated in the unnamed "neighboring state." In Maharashtra, by contrast, "the situation is under control. . . . Prophylactic measures are being undertaken on a war footing. . . . No room should be given to rumors of any type." And as for refugees, he lied, "their number is minimal."

BUT THERE WAS STILL NO RESOLUTION. AT THE HAFFKINE INSTI-tute in Bombay, the country's first dedicated plague center, the very mention of September 1994 brought sighs of exasperation, hands clapped percussively to foreheads, from the director and his deputies. Here were men who six years earlier had scorned the increasingly desperate communiqués from Delhi's National Institute of Communicable Diseases to "use mask, wear knee-high socks and gloves, even while sleeping" and who now openly ridiculed those, like the head of Surat's New Civil Hospital, Dr. Shailendra Vajpeyee, who persisted in talk of plague.

Like the best-schooled politicians, all senior Haffkine staff toed the same line, using identical terminology to describe the outbreak. To director Dr. Barsu Khadse, as to his deputy, Dr. Narendra Chanderkar, and every other Haffkine scientist, the Surat epidemic was "so-called plague." There should have been, growled an unsmiling Khadse—a small man dwarfed by a presidential desk, sunk low into a chair whose back loomed a good eighteen inches above his head—no argument. "You should know that the Haffkine Institute has very many depart-ments: chemotherapy, pathology, zoonosis, pharmacology, bio-chemistry. But it was the bacteriology department that in 1994 played such a crucial role in detecting whether the so-called plague epidemic was really plague or not. And we found out that it was not, that it was biochemically different. It was some-thing similar, but not plague. Definitely not plague."

YET ELSEWHERE IN THE INSTITUTE, DESPITE KHADSE'S PROTES-tations, a very different impression was abroad. Every day, under a plague-monitoring program that had been running for fifty years, around fifteen hundred dead rats were swept off the back of the health department trucks, combed for fleas, and autopsied for evidence of the bacillus.

In the autopsy room, midmorning, the smell was already overripe with blood and excrement, and the technicians in white coats and masks, slicing open rodents in a line along a long concrete counter, seemed to have their heads raised as high as possible, as if in an attempt to evade the stench. By the door were the most recent deliveries: five full buckets of rat corpses, their bodies twisted around one another, mouths yawning open, their clogged and matted fur the only sign of the drowning that had been the cause of death.

Every night, from the urban heart of Bombay to its dis-heveled suburbs, teams of ratcatchers baited cages, returning each dawn to collect and drown the rodents and deliver them to the institute. From each district, too, a small number were always kept alive and here, in the center of the autopsy room, was a cylindrical concrete holding tank, about eight feet across, where the animals were allowed to run free until fresh blood was required. In the corner of the room were filmy yellow garbage bags, full of old test tubes, banana skins, discarded masks, dismembered and discarded rats that pushed fatly against the translucence like an intruder in a nine-denier mask.

A technician looked up. "I hope," he murmured, "that no one still believes that there was any kind of controversy."

"Here at Haffkine there is no disagreement. Bombay had no plague, nor the whole of Maharashtra State." He was silent awhile, then shook his head as if in stern disapproval. "There was no plague in Bombay," he repeated dully. "This city, our city, did not have plague."

AN UNSETTLING PICTURE WAS EMERGING, ONE IN WHICH A MIS-placed kind of regional loyalty had become more important than truth, however unpalatable. It was as if even to raise the subject, merely to pose the question, was seen almost as willful provocation. Only in the broadest historical or theoretical discussion, it seemed, was one safe, and later a technician led the way through the laboratories where serum was tested for plague, outlining the three tests that "ensure that no case goes undetected."

"The first two tests," he announced eagerly, "the first two are staining and microscope analysis. You know what the bacillus looks like? Like a safety pin, exactly. So we look for that. Also we see if there is bipolar staining. And finally, just so we are completely sure, we take serum samples direct from the hearts of the rodents and test for plague antibodies."

Through another microscope he showed me a slide of

Xenopsylla cheopis, the rat flea. Under magnification the flea looked bigger than the lens, suddenly swollen monstrous. Its legs were most striking: long, muscular, and hairy, multi-jointed.

"That is the real villain," he said. "That is why we say that people should not sleep on the ground during plague. When rats die, the fleas search for other hosts. But they cannot fly, so during epidemics people should make their bed at least one foot above the ground."

Slowly, out of earshot of the offices of the Haffkine management, the technician was getting back into territory that no longer smacked of news management. Plague, he went on, was a disease that required constant monitoring. The fact that Bombay had not seen "classical plague" since 1966 counted little.

"It is out there in the forest, in the countryside, all the time. We have different people from the health department killing the rats there, doing surveys. If plague spreads from the countryside to the city it will create havoc. It is," he said, his jaw set, "a very dangerous disease which is always just around the corner."

He was out of the cool of the laboratories now and was standing on the first-floor balcony, overlooking the main sweep of drive where once, when this had been the governor's residence, elegant landaus ferried white-suited civil servants and their soft-voiced consorts to endless receptions, but where now, a century later, the only sign of life was a single gardener desultorily directing an aimless hose at the poinsettia. The technician had begun to talk more widely about plague, its spread in the modern world.

"No one talks about America, do they?" he burst out. "They've had outbreaks of plague in the twentieth century. There are reservoirs of plague in the wild rodent population in the western United States, but how much do you read about that? Every year people get plague in America, but does it get reported? A single outbreak in India, and the whole world is canceling holidays, boycotting our products, and stopping our planes from landing."

· 20 ·

OVER THE CENTURIES THAT PLAGUE HAD LAIN QUIESCENT, remaining always an opaque threat, it had acquired the status of some kind of diabolical sorcery. According to one chronicler, it was the "Flying Dutchman of disease" because of its seemingly magical ability to traverse the earth and explode in areas and at times when it was least expected. In the last two years of the nineteenth century, plague—from the flashpoint of Hong Kong, in 1894—flared in Arabia, Mauritius, Japan, Algeria, Mozambique, Turkey, Russia, Egypt, Africa, Paraguay, Turkestan, Austria, Brazil, and Madagascar. In 1900 it hit the Philippines, Hawaii, and the United States.

Its spread across America—and the resultant lingering

threat that it poses even today—remains one of the nation's most effectively buried pieces of medical history. From the first U.S. human plague death in March 1900 in San Francisco, the disease spread steadily, until by 1905—after successive San Francisco epidemics—it broached Oregon and Washington State. In 1906 it struck Louisiana; eight years later the city of New Orleans fell victim; and, by the end of the decade, Florida and Texas were also affected.

PNEUMONIC PLAGUE WAS NOT RECORDED IN THE UNITED States until it hit Oakland, California, in 1919. Five years later, in Los Angeles, the pneumonic variant struck with such startling force that the entire county was mobilized in an effort at containment. Once again—and gratifyingly for the vocal white majority, which held that disease was something that happened only to the primitive other, to people of different colored skin and beliefs they made no effort to understand—plague overlooked the Caucasian districts, igniting in an area inhabited almost wholly by Mexican immigrants.

The first to die was Lucena Samarano, owner of a boardinghouse at 742 Clara Street. With no epidemic suspected, no inquest was held. But three days later, October 22 , her husband, Guadalupe Samarano, and Jessie Flores, a nurse who had cared for Lucena, both fell sick, complaining of high fever, back pains, and "expectorating'—in the words of the California State Board of Health report—"a profuse bloody sputum." They died soon after, and in the days that followed, many others in their neighborhood were also struck down.

It took a good week for the correct diagnosis to come

through, and the response of the city was immediate and determined. Eight city blocks—comprising most of the Mexican population—were cordoned off and quarantined. Seventy-five police officers patrolled the perimeter; sentries were also posted outside houses where cases had occurred and further infection was predicted. Ration packages were delivered to all houses under quarantine, and the Macy Street Baptist Church was made a temporary laboratory for rat dissection. With quarantine enforced and daily house inspection under way, the focus moved toward rat extermination, since for two decades rodents had been established as the primary carriers of bubonic plague, from which pneumonic plague then sprang. According to the health board: "Trapping operations were started, the entire local supply of traps was obtained, telegraphic orders sent to San Francisco for all available traps and arrangements [were] made with eastern firms to rush their entire supply to Los Angeles. A total of forty thousand traps was thus obtained."

It was an all-American operation, carried out with an uncomplicated sense of moral purpose and more than a hint of pious self-congratulation: The weekly meetings of the Health and Sanitation Committees, the numberless subcommittees busying themselves with ever-more-civic-minded "recommendations," the creation of a dedicated Rodent Control Department, the generous $750,000 "budgetary appropriation" for fighting plague—all this and more spoke of a state government in reassuring and masterful control. Plague suspects were dispatched to the same hospital, Los Angeles General, where they, their wards, and charts were tagged with prominent red labels. The hospital—an archetypal early-twentieth-century institutional edifice, its windows vast and square, its slab sides zig-zagged with cast-iron fire escapes—issued a daily "plague bul-letin," detailing numbers of deaths.

The health board report divides into dark and light, black and white. Nowhere is this more evident than in the selection of photographs. Dark is disease and the neighborhood from which it came: It is the "shack used as sleeping quarters" at the back of 742 Clara Street, shot at sundown, the rough-boarded dwellings in deep, brooding shadow; it is the "typical interior of [a] Mexican home," bed and chairs strewn with clothes, upturned chests serving as kitchen cabinets, bucket as garbage pail filled to overflowing with empty cartons of Camel ciga-rettes; it is the blurred focus of "premises, North Anderson street, where two bubonic plague cases occurred," the whole scene redolent of ribbon development along a railroad track, unplanned and unchecked, from which the well-heeled, riding toward open country, would carefully avert their gaze.

Light, through a choice of photographs that was no doubt largely subconscious, is associated with whites and their right-eous endeavors to curb disease. While "the Mexican," like "the Oriental" in Hong Kong, was seen as a homogeneous racial type, who "always, when ill, calls the Priest, and generally [is] prompt in securing medical aid," pictures of the American doc-tors and the gleaming-floored wards "where pneumonic plague cases were cared for" encouraged an impression of a world where malign forces could hold no sway. The white medics were portrayed as resourceful and innovative. In the absence of readymade supplies, masks were made from pillowcases, with "celluloid eye pieces" and "gown fitting closely about the neck": They were latter-day Ebola paramedics, every inch of skin concealed. And so, with perfect propagandist logic, America's worst outbreak of pneumonic plague—though small in fatalities, accounting for just thirty lives—was transformed, to become a totem of hope for the future.

One image prevails: that of a Mexican boy, six-year-old Raul Samarano, sole survivor of 742 Clara Street and, according to the caption, "the only child known to have recovered from an attack of pneumonic plague." But what is most striking is not the plain fact of his survival, but rather the photographer's knowing juxtaposition: the startling white bars of his hospital cot against the tan of his face, his tiny form surrounded by the very image of the modern world, the confident, healthful future—a place where plague would find no home.

YET IF HISTORY HAS ANYTHING TO TEACH US ABOUT PLAGUE, it is that it refuses to be reined in. If diseases have personalities, plague is an escape artist, a criminal Houdini, tunneling from highest-security confinement to trigger new outbreaks, to wreak escalating havoc. Its quiet periods are illusory, time during which—as the antibiotic-resistant strains in Madagascar have shown—it is mutating, regrouping for fresh attack.

After the 1924 Los Angeles outbreak, the disease consolidated its position, digging in as if for a long siege. Through the first half of the twentieth century, there were few years that plague was not reported in the United States, and as the disease spread eastward, through the midwestern prairie states toward Florida, Texas, and Louisiana—crossing the Sierra Nevada mountains in 1929 and the continental divide in Montana four years later, to reach Canada by 1942—so the numbers of infected animal species multiplied. In 1902 three species of U.S. rat were known to be carrying the plague bacillus; by 1940 the figure was forty.

Today, hikers and hunters in the western states are at risk from a bewildering number of animals: infected mice were found in Louisiana in 1915; ground squirrels in California in 1908; groundhogs some twenty years later in Oregon; and prairie dogs, marmots, Tahoe chipmunks, and kangaroo rats have also all tested positive. And it is this ever-present, constantly refilling reservoir of plague that continues to pose a danger into the twenty-first century: In New York, a city thus far free of plague, the health department has gone to the trouble of posting a page on its Web site detailing the symptoms of plague, and the current best treatment routes. Lessons have clearly been learned: With plague nothing less than constant vigilance, unflagging surveillance, will do.

YERSIN, CARRYING HIS SEVEN HUNDRED DOSES OF PIONEERING antiplague serum, docked at Bombay Harbor on March 5, 1897. A scene of eerie calm would have greeted him as the hills of Bombay emerged from the heat haze: The dock, normally chaotic with activity, clamorous from the hollering of fishermen and cargo hands, was now absolutely still; not a boat moved. Stepping ashore, he'd quickly have discovered the reason: The imposition of quarantine, intended to prevent the further spread of plague, had resulted in the effective closedown of the port, of all international trade.

The atmosphere in the city itself—the simmering loathing

that Europeans and Indians reserved for each other—would have brought back uncomfortable memories of Hong Kong. This time, however, Yersin, at least in French eyes, was no longer the unknown ship's doctor and part-time jungle explorer that had arrived to such indifference in Hong Kong Harbor that June evening in 1894. Here was now a man who—if one left aside the ongoing tussle for the title of true plague pioneer—had proved himself fully in the field. It was he who'd spent the last two years working on a vaccine, he who quietly assumed that, given time, he would emerge from Kitasato's overblown shadow, and now it was he who was once more risking his life on the front line.

For the next two months he was the guest of the French consul, and his days and nights cannot have struck a greater contrast. By day he sought out the most abandoned and diseased parts of town; by night he returned to the butlers and polished hallways of the consulate, his foie gras and chilled Chablis awaiting him, the sheets of his bed pressed and freshly scented. Aided this time by the authorities—rather than, as in Hong Kong, willfully obstructed—he pushed on with his vaccination program. But the results were disappointing: Barely half his patients survived. The arrival from Paris of a batch of Pasteur Institute vaccine—a process initiated by Yersin in France the year before—saw his spirits rise, and something of his old optimism return. With the Paris preparation, closer to 80 percent recovered.

Yet, as the weeks wore on, a familiar pattern began to emerge. The Bombay government, reacting no doubt in part to Yersin's often blundering negotiating manner, started restricting his access to plague patients: To Yersin's frustration he was too often allowed to carry out injections only when the patient's infection had become irredeemably advanced. Fury, then exhaustion, set in, and when in July he received orders from the Pasteur Institute to return to his laboratory in Nha Trang, he did so almost gratefully, with no hint of rivalry in the welcome he gave Dr. Paul-Louis Simond, the bacteriologist sent to replace him. And so "the intrepid Yersin"—as Louis Pasteur had dubbed his young disciple—settled back into life in Vietnam, concentrating on establishing a specialized immunization laboratory and heading the small community of cattle-hands, technicians, and farmers required to keep such an enterprise in operation. In his own mind he was convinced of the credit that—as the first to isolate the cause of plague and the pioneer of the first antiplague vaccine—was rightly his, yet he must have wondered, as he forged on alone in his fight against the disease, whether he was destined to live out his days unacknowledged and overlooked, in the eyes of the scientific community no more than the dramatic foil for the true hero, Shibasaburo Kitasato.

SIMOND, FELLOW PASTEURIAN, WAS ONE OF THE FEW FOR WHOM Yersin's reputation was unassailable, and he arrived in Bombay flattered and thrilled to have been asked to take over the senior bacteriologist's work. What he had not prepared for, however, was the volatile parabola of plague, and his first few weeks in the city, in May 1897, brought an unexpected—albeit temporary—quiescence. Yet this lull also carried an opportunity, and Simond, demonstrating a hunger for the big prize that might have been learned at Yersin's knee, seized the chance to home in on the one major remaining unknown of plague research: the process of transmission.

Until then, the boldest rat-plague connection had been made by Yersin himself, three years earlier in Hong Kong: "It is probable," he had written in his notes, "that rats constitute the main vehicle." Yet this was hypothesis, and had been taken no further. It was also, to judge from prevailing opinion in Bombay, a theory that was pitiably wide of the mark.

On the Indian west coast, all efforts were focused on disinfection, segregation, and quarantine: logical consequences, in the eyes of Bombay medics, of the discovery of a specific bacillus of plague. Consensus was in favor of human-to-human transmission, and maximum energy was being expended in attempting to track down and isolate infected persons: Along all railroads and main arterials checkpoints were set up, and fugitives searched and medically examined. The disinfection operation was equally formidable, with some thirty-one thousand Indians hired by the government as emergency street, house, and sewer cleaners. Such was the volume of carbolic acid used in the sluicing of houses that health inspectors would cower under umbrellas as they entered buildings, as protection from the corrosive spray from the upper stories. Every day three million gallons of disinfectant were pumped into the sewers; grain was either burned or laid in the open to "breathe." And, in the midst of all this poisonous commotion, the rat escaped the city unnoticed, spreading infection as it went.

Simond, settling in, brought himself quickly up to speed with the latest research and hypotheses of the international plague missions stationed in the city. In large part these were substantial posses of government-sponsored scientists—from Russia,

Germany, Britain, Austria—all of which had staked out firm, and for the most part equally erroneous, claims about the mechanism of the disease. According to the German Plague Commission, parasitic insects were manifestly not to blame: If they had been, ran their argument, the plague hospitals would surely have been worse hit by new infections. The Austrians' blind fumble toward a solution concluded that any kind of irritable scratching of the skin might lead to infection. The British, while conceding that infection normally happened through the skin, rejected the notion of blood-sucking insects as vectors of plague: Usually, they suggested, soil was the area of highest danger, with exposed microbes the likely agents of transmission. Rats were mentioned but briefly, and when they were it was in a tone of almost flippant dismissal.

And yet the rat—to judge from plague accounts from previous epidemics—clearly merited closer attention. In the East the connection had been made as early as the tenth century: The noted Arabian physician Avicenna, who lived in Persia between 980 and 1037, had described how the appearance of plague would cause an unsteady, stumble-footed exodus of rats and other subterranean animals from their burrows. In London in 1665, observers noticed a similar chronology: Nathanael Hodges's *Loimographia*, an account of the London plague of 1665, gave as "a sure sign that pestilence is at hand" the startled and sudden emergence of moles, mice, serpents, and foxes from underground. In China, a century later, the first suspicions of a causal chain were beginning to emerge: Of the Yunnan outbreak of 1792, Hung Liang-Chi wrote that it was rats that died first; human deaths came later. The rodents, he added, were everywhere and unavoidable, appearing as never before in broad daylight, vomiting blood as they staggered their final steps.

Simond's first observation was startlingly different from those of his peers, and indicative of a man refreshingly unencumbered by the herd instinct that distinguished the thought processes of most of the international plague commissions. Examining the symptoms of plague patients in an epidemic hotspot some way up the coast, he noticed the occasional presence of a tiny blister on the feet and lower limbs. This in itself was a fairly workaday observation, and one that had moreover been made by numerous other plague researchers: Where Simond differed was in his level of curiosity. Taking the trouble, as no one had before, to examine microscopically the fluid drawn from the blister, he found a swarming abundance of plague bacilli. His resulting hypothesis was the beginning of a theory of plague transmission that would cause him to suffer ridicule for the rest of his life and for which he would receive credit only posthumously.

Working under conditions uncannily reminiscent of those endured by Yersin—to Yersin's grass hut, Simond had just a small tent to protect him and his experimental instruments and animals from the onslaught of the Indian monsoon—he demonstrated the kind of bravery for which Yersin was already well known. As he learned more about the likely mechanism of transmission, a fearful recoil would have been understandable enough, yet his behavior betrayed no such trepidation. He would have known that science conferred no immunity from plague—one of Kitasato's team had died from an infected scalpel cut in 1894—but this did not deflect him. He was closing in and would not turn back.

Insects had already been implicated in disease transmission, and Simond would certainly have been conscious of Patrick Manson's 1877 experiments in China, which showed that the mosquito was a factor in the spread of systemic filariasis, just as he would, some four years later, have read of Carlos Finlay's proposal that the causative agent of yellow fever was also carried by mosquitoes. Yet, though time would vindicate their theories, such thinkers were as yet considered near-heretical by the scientific mainstream, with Finlay's work, for instance, earning him the sobriquet of "theorizing old fool." For Simond even to consider and begin investigating such a mechanism for plague—so setting himself up in opposition to the accepted wisdom of international science—was courage in itself.

Researching alone, he determined to ignore the encroaching barrage of conflicting hypotheses and concentrate instead on his own observations. Working from no one's notes but his own, he observed and distilled, sifting relevance from red herring. His notes are simple, unadorned: He wrote down only what he could see and what he was told. He was baffled, intrigued, utterly focused.

From the start it was clear that the most popular theories of contagion—through either air, food, or infected feces—merited no further respect. Most striking, for Simond, was the almost spectral, random manner in which the disease appeared to surface, often finding new victims at considerable distance from those already infected. He recorded instances of plague flaring up in houses a good half mile from the next nearest case, whose inhabitants claimed to have had no contact with other plague sufferers. A carrier, Simond posited, was at work, and, like Yersin before him, he fingered the rat.

Drawing on his experience in the field, he recalled that, in China's Yunnan Province, people fled their homes on the first sight of a dead rat; in Taiwan, any contact with dead or dying rats, however fleeting, was believed to lead to plague. As he traveled the worst-hit plague districts of Bombay and beyond, evidence was building: His notebook contains a description of one house in Karachi in which no fewer than seventy-five dead rats were found. Standing in the street, wondering where to position this latest piece of the jigsaw, he witnessed the trademark drunken, shambling stagger of the plague rats, animals uncommonly oblivious, their usual nimbleness gone, dragging their limbs, dying in front of him in the dust.

Yet if rats were to blame, it remained uncertain exactly how the plague bacillus made the leap to humans. At issue, Simond judged, was chronology: Some kind of sequence was in operation. A Bombay wool factory offered up a crucial clue, recorded by Simond in his characteristically exact prose: "One day, employees arriving in the morning noticed a large number of dead rats on the floor. Twenty laborers were ordered to clean the floor of the dead animals. Within three days, ten of them developed plague. None of the other employees became ill."

Simond had broken from the pack, and from this point he was on his own. Deliberately, now with only half his mind on the vaccination program, he sought out survivors, juicing them for information. Increasingly his questions followed a similar track: Did rat mortality precede human deaths? What contact had the deceased had with dead rodents? In some villages, like one he visited in April 1898, the people appeared to intuit the process at work with far greater accuracy than did the theorizing luminaries assembled in Bombay: In this particular village, Simond noted, the population had fled their homes the moment news spread of the first dead-rat sighting. "Two weeks later, a mother and daughter received permission to go back to the village to bring clothing from their house. They found several dead rats on the floor of the house. They picked up the rats by their tails and threw them out on the street and then returned to the camp. Two days later, both developed plague." These are a detective's notes, written hastily, anticipating no further readership: There is a winning modesty, too, as well as the kind of self-restraint exhibited by Yersin. And so Simond, using the same deadpan prose he might have used to murmur confidences to a colleague, listed "one more observation: on 13 May 1898, in Bombay, a man walked into a stable to take care of his horse and found there a dead rat on the floor. He picked up the rat by the tail and threw it out. Three days later he developed plague."

A perplexing picture was beginning to emerge, one in which a dead rat, contrary to expectations, appeared to be far more dangerous than one captured alive. There was clearly a missing link, and Simond already had more than enough evidence to implicate the rat flea, *Xenopsylla cheopis*. In the Karachi house, reluctant home to the corpses of those seventy-five rats, fleas were found darkly swarming, shadowy swells of movement. "On the rats captured alive, and on the rats which had just died, the fleas," wrote Simond, "were thicker than I had ever seen them." And so, tentative at first, came the hypothesis: "We have to assume that there must be an intermediary between a dead rat and a human. This intermediary might be the flea."

Step by step his research was becoming more and more perilous, and the next move toward proving his hypothesis was the most hazardous yet. In order to establish whether the flea was the go-between, he first had to discover whether it was capable of absorbing and transporting the bacillus. In Cutch-Mandvi, a town north of Bombay in the maw of a ferocious outbreak of plague, and to which Simond had just been posted, he devised an experiment that was as fearless as it was direct. Trawling the back alleys until he found a rat that had died recently enough to still be blood-warm, he seized it with long forceps, dropped it into a paper bag, and rushed the whole parcel back to his tent laboratory. There he sank the bag into a tub of warm soapy water, scissored it open and combed a scattering of drowned fleas from the rat's matted fur. Compared to insects taken from a healthy rat, whose intestines showed nothing abnormal, fleas from the plague rat were bloated with the bacillus.

The final section of the search for proof—carried out in Karachi in the spring of 1898—bears the genius stamp of simplicity. With limited materials and laughably basic clinical surroundings, Simond devised an assay so unpretentious, so Boy Scout straightforward, that it was only inevitable he would attract ridicule from the regiments of sophisticated science. One can almost picture him arranging on a bench his few tools and experimental objects, explaining the process step by step, as if he were the easy-smiling host of a parentally approved children's television show. He laid out a wide-mouthed glass bottle, some sand, a strip of fine wire mesh and the same length of cotton fabric, a metal cage small enough to fit into the bottle, and finally two rats, one obviously ailing, one in bouncing health.

Simond "was fortunate enough" to have caught a plague rat in the home of a plague victim. In the rat's fur there were several fleas running around. "I took advantage of the generosity of a cat I found stalking the hotel premises, borrowing some fleas from it." He emptied the sand—a urine absorber—into the bottle, dropped the rat in on top, and "deposited the cat's fleas on it from a test tube. I was thus quite sure the rat would be covered with parasites."

Like a dispassionate seven-year-old frying ants with a magnifying glass, Simond then watched as the rat began its final contortions. Twenty-four hours later, the animal had "rolled up into a little ball. With its hair standing on end it seemed to be in agony." Knowing that death was now near, and that the rat's plague-engorged fleas would, as soon as they sensed the rodent's body begin to cool and stiffen underneath them, be looking to move off in search of warmer and fresher blood, Simond then

> introduced into the bottle a small metal cage containing a perfectly healthy young Alexandria rat caught several weeks before and kept sequestered from any danger of infection. The cage was suspended within the inside of the bottle several centimeters above the layer of sand. The cage had three solid sides, but the other three sides were covered by wire screen with a mesh size of about six millimeters. The rat inside the cage could not have any contact with the sick rat, the wall of the bottle or the sand.

The next morning the first rat was lying cold on the sand. Simond left it another twenty-four hours, then removed it for autopsy. "The blood and organs all contained an abundance of [plague] bacilli." And again, notepad at his elbow, he sat down to watch. For four days the caged, healthy rat continued to feed and sleep normally. Then, on "about the fifth day, it seemed to have difficulty moving. By the evening of the sixth day it was dead. An autopsy of this one revealed buboes, both inguinal and axillary. The kidney and the liver were swollen and congested. There were abundant plague bacilli in the organs and blood."

From theory to practice, from hypothesis to first proof, Simond's experiment and its robust conclusion were like an adrenaline punch to the heart. His involuntary yelp of realization, in all its unrestrained and maximum-decibel joy, deserves to be printed in full. *"Ce jour-là, le 2 Juin 1898, j'éprouvai une émotion inexprimable à la pensée que je venais de violer un secret qui angoissait l'humanité depuis l'apparition de la peste dans le monde."* "That day," he fizzed, "I felt an inexpressible emotion at the thought that I had just uncovered a secret that had tortured humankind since the appearance of plague on the earth."

Simond's findings, under the title *La Propagation de la Peste*, were published in the Pasteur Institute journal that same year. His recommendations were as penetrating and unstinting as the accounts of his research. Key to controlling plague, he said, was keeping rat populations in check: Port authorities should do everything in their power to prevent rats jumping from ship to shore; any vessel coming from an infected area should be fumigated with sulfuric acid. In these strictures, as in his findings, he was the lone voice, the prophet without honor: Not one scientist, from any of the assembled international commissions, held up his work for anything but scorn. Typical was an editorial comment in the *Indian Medical Gazette* some four years later that referred to similar—but crucially flawed—experiments by the distinguished Cambridge parasitologist

George H. F. Nuttall as "having pretty completely demolished Simond's . . . worthless . . . flea hypothesis."

History has treated Simond little better: He remains a forgotten hero whose name is often conspicuously absent from works of medical history, in which chapters dealing with the race to find the cause of plague refer to those who built on his pioneering work, and seldom to the trailblazer himself. In part this may be ascribed to Simond's personality: Uncommonly disinterested in the egotistical scramble up the ladder of doctorates and professorships, he was described by a pupil as being "without ambition, indifferent to things he knew only too well to be vain, devoting himself [in old age] to his friends and giving himself over to social work for the betterment of his neighbors."

Yet he was equally likely to have been overlooked as the deliberate result of professional jealousy. This is more than fancy: In Victor Heiser's best-selling travelogue *An American Doctor's Odyssey: Adventures in Forty-Five Countries,* the peripatetic medic referred to "a hypothesis conceived by P. L. Simond of Spain [sic] that plague was conferred by fleas. He had no supporting proof for his theory; he merely imagined this was the way it happened. His claim was tested first by the First Indian Plague Commission which, after investigation, announced that no connection could be found between the flea and the rat." Heiser's information came from a visit to India in 1902, during which he was befriended and escorted around the plague hospitals by one of the most senior members of the Indian Medical Service. No doubt to the sweet satisfaction of his source, he made no attempt to seek any response from either Simond or the Pasteur Institute.

And yet, amazingly, nowhere in any of Simond's papers can one detect a hint of resentment. Awarded the Légion d'Honneur in Paris in 1901, he went on to study yellow fever in Brazil, found a medical school in Marseilles, and serve as director of the Imperial Institute of Bacteriology in Istanbul. He retired to Valence, in a house on whose walls were skins from a Bengal tiger and a leopard—talismans from his travels. He wrote and published short stories, could run off an accomplished piano sonata, and was, until old age, a patient and intuitive trout fisherman. He died on March 18, 1947, aged eighty-seven. On his gravestone is carved but a single line: "Docteur P.-L. Simond, 1858–1947." No bombast, no plea for immortality. Just a profession, a name, some dates.

· 21 ·

BY 1907 THE WORK BEGUN BY SIMOND IN 1898—AND EXPANDED, consolidated, or just plain plagiarized by each wave of successors—had become established scientific fact, as uncontroversial a notion as the orbit of the earth around the sun. For the Citizens Health Committee of San Francisco, struggling to beat back plague after the earthquake and city fires of that spring, the aim, in the words of committee historian Frank Morton Todd, was simple: "to organize the community for the starving and destroying of rats." Yet for this to succeed among a populace wholly ignorant of Simond's rat-flea thesis, some significant reeducation was required. The city, Todd explained in his colorful prose, "had to go to school and study zoology, bacteriology, and fleas. The whole community had to learn about plague as a disease and an epidemic. In general, this is what it learned. Bubonic plague is not a filth disease—it is a rat disease."

The war on the rat was waged with a specifically military lexicon. Photographs of the "regiments of health" show ranks of black-suited, trilby'd conscripts, brooms shouldered as if they were .303s. Every day they set up scores of poison-baited traps. The poison—a mixture of "phosphorus or arsenic baited with lard, cheese, sugar or other food preferred by rats"—was "spread on stale bread" and placed inside nineteen-inch wire-cage snares, and circulars were rushed out describing in detail how and where the traps should be most effectively set. These instructions were clearly intended for householders not much accustomed to rat destruction—"Before setting, the lever on the trap should be tested to see that it works properly"—and gave considerable space to the rodent's catholic taste in scraps:

> The rat is more or less of an epicure; therefore the bait should be changed at frequent intervals. Also, he should be given food which he is not in the habit of getting. For example: in a meat market, vegetables are the best bait, while in a location where vegetables are plentiful, fresh liver and fish heads or a little grain are best. The following may be suggested as good bait to be used: fish, fish heads, raw meat, cheese, smoked fish, fresh liver, cooked corn beef, fried bacon, pine nuts, apples, carrots and corn. When trapping in chicken yards a small chick or duckling is remarkably good.

Dealing with an animal with the boundless cunning of the rat required a degree of sly forethought. Females could even be used as lure to "call in the young or the males." Final touches were equally important: "Before leaving the trap, it should be smoked with a piece of burning newspaper to kill the smell of the human hands or rats which have been in it." The rat, ran the subtext, was a notable adversary, and exterminators were instructed to be ever alert, moving successful traps regularly in order to confound the rat's formidable survival-instinct memory. Finally, snared animals should be taken to another place to be drowned or have their necks broken: To kill them on the spot might result in "squealing," which would "frighten the other rats away."

A boom in manufacturing followed: Each year brought a whole slew of new inventions, innovations in trap design, poisons promising immediate effect, absolute handling safety. By the end of the 1920s, books such as Alfred Moore Hogarth's London-published *The Rat: A World Menace* were carrying substantial sections of advertisements—for Zelio paste, "the new method of exterminating rats and voles ... approved by the Ministry of Agriculture and Fisheries"; for the "one-night wonder" toxin Rodine; for the ruthless-sounding Cyanogas, which to judge from the illustration knocked rats immediately insensible, their tongues lolling stupidly from the sides of their mouths; for the downright sinister Lloyd's Rat Exterminator, "a new discovery embodying the use of a powerful Eastern Drug, which has a specific action on the peculiar structure of the rodent"; and powerful adhesives such as Dak Ratlime, an "amazingly tenacious birdlime [which] ensnares the wiliest and holds the strongest as easily as a sticky flypaper traps flies."

Hogarth's text further expanded the theme, furnishing succulent detail on a whole variety of traps and methods of snaring. Here Hogarth counseled, a certain profligacy was called for: "Do not be sparing in the number of traps, as money spent in traps is a small item compared to the cost of the damage done by the rats." The choice was bewildering: snap traps, jaw traps for use in burrows, any number of different kinds of cages. But most appealing—no doubt in part for the anguished end it inflicted—was the "varnish trap," honorable forebear of the glue trap so beloved of modern-day New York exterminators. Onto a strip of eighteen-by-twelve inch cardboard was spread "lithographer's varnish of a certain consistency . . . the rats are practically always found dead in the morning. . . . Most die of suffocation as a consequence of the mouth and nostrils being closed with the varnish when the rats attempt to free their limbs." Yet just occasionally, Hogarth concluded approvingly, the most effective traps were those that evolved by accident, and at the end of the chapter he reprinted in full a letter first published in the *London Daily Mail*, headed "Floating corks in a pail of water," and signed "Helpful." The discovery of this near-flawless device, explained the gleeful correspondent, had taken place in a wholesale grocer's warehouse, where a bucket of water, with a thick layer of corks floating on top, had been left overnight beside a sack of peas. Come Monday morning, the bucket—the surface of which would have appeared a straightforward stepping-stone to the meal beyond—was "almost full of drowned rats of all sizes." Thenceforth the trap was set deliberately; within a week, "the stores were rid of rats."

Of all extermination methods, however, the longest established appear to have been straightforward arsenic poisoning, and the setting up of basic baited traps. English chroniclers record rats being caught as long ago as 1297, and Chaucer in his

"Pardoners Tale" became arguably the first poet to include poison in a rhyming couplet: "And forth he gooth, no lenger wolde he tarie,/Into the toun unto a pothecarie, /And prayde hym that he hym wolde selle/ Som poyson, that he myght his rattes quelle." Yet the fact that Shakespeare's *Romeo and Juliet,* written in 1592, included a reference to a ratcatcher did little to induce ordinary people to willingly turn exterminators and, by the early decades of the twentieth century and despite the rat's outlaw status now having been incontrovertibly established, bribes were still deemed necessary in order for dead rodents to begin appearing on health-department doorsteps. Here, though, the level of the payment, according to one rat-destruction textbook, was critical: "If too low the premium attracts children only; if too high it tempts fraudulent persons to try their cunning." All of which made it vital for unpaid predators—owls, kestrels, stoats, even weasels—to be given

the fullest protection. . . . They are most valuable allies and destroy large numbers of rats. It is not a sound argument to object, as some do, that a weasel will not attack a full-grown rat—they will kill large numbers of young ones, and young rats are far more dangerous than old ones. If these beasts and birds of prey occasionally help themselves to a young game bird or a rabbit it is not of much consequence; the rats they destroy will do far more damage.

RATS. THEN AS NOW, RATS WERE FEARED AND REVILED: PARIAH creatures, known to bite babies, to fight blindly when startled, subjects of myth and nightmare. A century after the discoveries of Yersin and Simond, the rat has become properly recognized as the health hazard it truly is. It has found its level, earned due recognition as mankind's most persistent and unshakable parasite, a shadow presence to every careless and wanton human activity, a reminder of our own greed and weakness. The tourism industry, of course, would have one believe that the rat remains a problem only in cities where civic pride has no place—sprawling conurbations synonymous with squalor and degradation, such as Calcutta, Bombay, Surat—and yet the tenaciousness of the creature is such that it can contentedly make its home anywhere there are people. In Manhattan—the very quintessence of the modern city—the war against the rat has never been waged with more manpower or zeal, and yet it has never looked closer to being completely lost.

ON MANHATTAN'S WEST TWENTY-THIRD STREET AND NINTH Avenue, nearing midnight on an April night in a driving east wind, a tall, stooped African American was shuffling behind what looked like a steel-tube Kmart cart rendered three times its original width by bulging black sacks, each filled and clanking with empty soda cans. Despite the cold he was wearing beach sandals, the rubber soles worn as thin as cardboard. He wore headphones and talked over the hiss of his music.

"'Round here," he said, chopping his hands through the air as if leading some imaginary orchestra to crescendo, "we get rats big as this." And he abruptly ceased his conducting, measuring a space in front of him the length of a domestic cat.

He beckoned: an infinitesimal—and unsettling—one-finger gesture. He indicated a steel grille in the sidewalk. "You ain't seen none? They watching you. They not stupid. They live down there." From a tunnel below came the loose rattle of the subway. "Sewers, too," he added.

He looked suddenly over his shoulder, as if worried someone was following him. "They burrow through wire, concrete. They everywhere, and at night I hear them a-scufflin' and a-scrapin'. Sometimes I have to beat them off with my fists."

He shook his head. "There's lots of stuff people will tell you about rats, lots of stuff you won't believe. But let me tell you now, it's all true."

NEW YORK CITY IS HOME TO THREE SPECIES OF RAT: *RATTUS rattus*, also known as the black, or ship, rat; *Rattus norvegicus*, the brown, or Norway, rat; and the Alexandrian, or roof rat, which is vastly outnumbered by the first two. None of these is indigenous. The black rat originated in India and, most historians agree, disembarked on American soil with the first explorers, having spread to Europe along trade routes during the Middle Ages. The brown rat began life still farther east, in Central Asia, and started its westward migration early in the eighteenth century. It is a formidable athlete: eyewitness reports from 1729 tell of vast hordes swimming the Volga, then shaking themselves down and shouldering their way into the houses of Astrakhan. Once in western Europe, its advance was rapid: By the time of the American Revolution, it had penetrated North America and is now by far the most numerous, dirty, and visible of the U.S. rats.

Rattus rattus is smaller, measuring about seven inches nose to rump, with an extra nine for tail. It has bluish-black fur that appears to rise in one long hackle along its spine. Its ears, at least compared with those of the brown rat, are noticeably large, their shape reminiscent of radar bowls. It is less likely to be aggressive than the brown rat but, as if aware of this, seldom allows itself to be cornered: It can rapidly shin up curtains, slick-painted drainpipes, elevator cables, or telephone wires. It is a formidable acrobat, and can gnaw a hole in a ceiling while at the same time gripping tightly an electric wire.

It is hard to speak of these creatures without a good measure of awe, and even those who have spent a lifetime in their pursuit—men one might expect to have become blasé about the threat rats pose—can be heard lowering their voices, attempting jokes about the animal's prowess that only serve to highlight their own respect. Sitting around a conference table in New York City's Department of Health, some eight floors above the streets of Lower Manhattan, the city's pest control experts competed to outdo one another in extreme rat tales. The creature was the enemy; their vocabulary spoke, as in San Francisco in 1907, of military maneuvers against a guerrilla force—rodent inspectors were "exterminators"; rat infestation they dubbed "total involvement"; a building overrun from basement to roof terrace was judged to be "totally compromised."

The most experienced—and the most compelling—of the witnesses was Larry Adams, a rat exterminator of some twenty-five years' standing and currently the city's "senior supervisor for extermination." When he spoke of rats it was with a distinct relish: Recounting details of rat behavior made him smile ruefully, and the more impressive the animal's feat of endurance or strength or resistance the more his amusement grew. He had the excited air of a man faced with a worthy adversary, with an enemy who was always just out of range, constantly moving, more than a match for him in both strategy and cunning.

But it was the animal's physical capabilities that struck him as most continually astonishing. The Norway rat, he said, was an "excellent swimmer, good climber. Poor vision but pretty fair sense of smell. They're adaptable to anywhere that humans can live. They're attracted to the food we eat, to anything that smells good to us. A double cheeseburger," he said, smiling slowly, "smells just as good to them as it does to us."

He warmed to his theme. "Rats can penetrate darn near anything outside of galvanized steel. They can cut through mortar, brick, wood, even concrete." He paused, put a finger to his front teeth. "It's their incisors. If they didn't keep gnawing, their two front teeth would carry on growing, curve back under their chin, drill into the brain, and kill them."

He stopped talking, folded his arms, leaned back. His chair creaked ominously. "I've seen rats all my life, and I can't stand them. No one who has any idea of the number of ways they can affect you will ever get used to them. You ever seen a baby bitten by a rat? Well, now, that's a very unsettling thing, to go into a place and see a child that's been bitten, who's got a chunk of his face missing. Maybe the kid's asleep, maybe got a bit of food or milk on his face. Bam! The rat goes for him."

And it wasn't just plague that rats carried, he said, though plague of course was the best known, the most agonizing, and by far the most dangerous of all rat diseases. Others included spirochetal jaundice, ratbite fever, trichinosis, Brill's disease, and tularemia.

"The reason they're so difficult to control is that they multiply so fast." His initial good humor had dissipated; in its place was a stiff-necked resolve.

"A female," he was saying, staring glaze-eyed out of the window, "will drop a litter of eight to eleven rats. Give her a couple of months and she'll do the same again." The consequences of this were astonishing: it had been calculated that a single pair of rats could—given three litters a year, with ten young in each, abundant food, shelter, and zero mortality—increase in five years to something over more than 940 billion (940,369,969,152). In New York City, the record reproductive rate—achieved by a single captive pair—stood at seven litters in the same number of months.

Nonetheless he believed that it was largely thanks to human beings that the rat population was currently so healthy: If it weren't for the overstuffed Dumpsters filled with half-eaten Whoppers and pizza crusts, "rats would control their own population by cannibalizing one another. Since there's always more than enough food to go around, this doesn't happen."

And so all this bold talk of extermination proved after all to be a smoke screen for a more salutary reality: Rats would always be with us, and as the human population increased, so would the numbers of rodents. Most chilling for Adams was the knowledge that there existed in the city locations to which people no longer had access but that rats had made their fiefdom, areas in which they would always be safe, unreachable by trap, poison or fire. "In this very district right here," he said, rapping heavy knuckles against the table, "there are buildings with third-level subcellars, structures that date back to the Revolutionary War. I've seen the underground maps of the city, and you'd be astonished what's down there. You can betcha that rats have made a pretty sweet home in those places. And we'll never reach them. Not ever."

IN NEW YORK CITY, AT THE TURN OF THE TWENTY-FIRST CEN-tury, ratcatching had become a badge of courage, a stamp of manhood. Gill Bloom, who described himself, unprompted, as a "hero ratcatcher"—ran the same company his grandfather had started in 1929. At nine sharp he was standing outside the Queens office of Standard Exterminating Co., Inc., headed in his pickup for a job that was "pretty much typical": an overrun warehouse, where the rats had become so brazen that they had begun openly foraging for food during daylight. Like most New York exterminators, he spoke of rats with a tone of mea-sured respect. All the way to the job he pointed out factories, front porches, and abandoned lots, each of which might have been expressly designed with the rat in mind.

"Look at that," he said, gesturing with his thumb as the pickup idled at a stoplight. "Food-packaging plant. Candle fac-tory. Empty lot. Right next door to each other. Rodents love to gnaw on wax. No shortage of food, either. And there," he added, as he began to head off, "an overgrown garden. Right next to it, there's garbage spilling out of a Dumpster. See the problem? The moment you clean rats from one place, they just go right ahead and move across the street, where it's just as nice as where they were before."

He drew the truck to a halt. Ahead was a yard with an open warehouse at the far end. There were heaps of wooden pallets, steel tubing, a Dumpster that seemed to glisten in the pale sunlight as if slimed with cooking fat. "And check that out," he said, pointing to a high brick wall topped with jags of broken glass. "I was teaching a class on extermination one time in Manhattan. I was telling the students about all the latest exclusion techniques, and then we looked out the window and saw a whole line of rodents running along the top of a cyclone fence. That's the way it goes."

IN A WINDOWLESS PLYWOOD OFFICE OFF THE MAIN YARD, THE warehouse manager was waiting. He wore a denim shirt stretched tight over his belly and had skin as pale and smooth as kneaded dough. The phone was ringing; he ignored it, stood up from the desk.

"We kept the dog food in the lockbox out in the warehouse, and the rats got in under the padlock. Don't ask me how. Then the dog got rat fleas, and we had to put him down. That's why we called you guys in. One rat ate so much dog chow he couldn't get out again." He coughed drily. "And now they're coming in here, into the office. One of them has grown so large he's the size of my arm. When I'm working late he comes in through the doorway, stands on his hind legs and stares at me. It's like he's daring me to chase him."

Outside the office again, in the watery April light, Bloom stopped and knelt down. There was a manhole-size fissure in the concrete. He looked up again, nodded at the manager. "That's a broken sewer you got down there."

Inside the warehouse, out of earshot of the manager, Bloom murmured, "Open sewer. Rats live in sewers. They come out the hole, find food, start their little colony. Why don't they get the sewer capped?"

He and his deputy were scouting around the darkness now, flashlights held over their heads dagger-style, aimed downward. There was evidence of rats everywhere: Shredded Styrofoam and silver foil; rat droppings the size of toothpaste squirts and the color of diseased-dog excrement; corners where the dirt floor had been worn into patterns by rat footfall.

"Sometimes," he went on, "you get rats coming up out of the toilet bowl. Alive."

He began setting up bait stations—sizable green plastic triangular boxes, with rat-size entrances at each point. Inside were blocks of poisoned bait: anticoagulant toxins that, once ingested, took twenty-four hours to kill. The dog food, to which the rats had been enjoying such free access, contained coagulant, a blood-clotting agent added in part to protect canines from rat poison. And so, for the toxins to be effective, clearly the rats had to be denied their rations of dog food.

He was concentrating hard, poking the flashlight under piles of pallets, behind the metal-slab workbenches into which colossal circular saws were set.

Back in the daylight again, he said, "The rats in New York, they're pretty healthy." He waved an arm toward the barrel of dog food inside the warehouse. "They get a lot to eat."

He'd decided against using traps for this job, and no glueboards, either—large cardboard slabs painted with glue and protected, until use, by protective peel-off strips. The glue was so strong rats had been known to chew off their own legs trying to escape. But Bloom, fearing that glueboards would be rendered useless in the wet, had opted solely for poisoned bait.

On the way back he was pensive, dismissive of the claims of the municipal authorities to be winning the war against the rat. He was not alarmist, merely realistic.

"There was a novel written a few years back," he said as he drew to a stop outside his building. He killed the engine; his clipboard was on his knee. "It was a pulp book, about plague breaking out in New York City. I guess most folks thought it was ridiculous, that this kind of thing was real unlikely. But I read it, and it didn't seem that crazy to me. It's a 'what if?' scenario. It *could* happen."

UNLIKE SAN FRANCISCO—AND, IN THE EARLY YEARS OF THE twentieth century, Los Angeles, Seattle, and New Orleans— New York has been fortunate and vigilant enough never to have had an outbreak of plague. On two occasions, however, the city has come extremely close. The first time was in 1900, at the peak of the third pandemic. Ports across the world were reporting major and sudden inflagrations of plague and, one night, infected rats were discovered on ships in New York Harbor. On that occasion, quarantine restrictions were ordered quick enough for the disease never to make it ashore. The second time, however, some forty years later, was an altogether closer call.

On January 10, 1943, a French freighter, the *Wyoming*, carrying a cargo of wine and tobacco, docked from Casablanca. According to the *New Yorker* writer Joseph Mitchell, who was told this story sometime in 1944, the events that unfolded threatened the safety of the city to such a degree that the public health officials who dealt with it kept the affair secret for more than a year. In the end Mitchell managed to glean the details from Dr. Robert Olesen, medical director of the city health service's quarantine department.

Olesen began by explaining to Mitchell the method used for inspecting ships engaged in foreign trade: A five-strong boarding party was dispatched, including a sanitary inspector, whose main job was to determine the degree of rat infestation. This involved a thorough search—looking for rat tracks, signs of gnawing, evidence of droppings and nests. Rats, Olesen went on, "have a smell that is as distinctive as the smell of cats, although not as rank, and an experienced inspector can detect their presence that way."

If a ship was judged to be infested, fumigation was ordered. This was an extreme—and often poorly targeted—procedure: Early attempts using hydrocyanic acid resulted in the death of a number of stowaways. After this, precautionary tear gas was always released before the poison, and it had, by 1944, become commonplace to see lines of weeping and spluttering refugees staggering from the hatches of South American freighters. After about ten hours, the holds would be opened up and aired and searched for dead rats. Whatever fleas were combed from their fur were ground into pulp and injected into guinea pigs, and the condition of the laboratory animals was monitored carefully and not without a measure of trepidation.

Casablanca, the *Wyoming's* port of origin, was on the "plague list" at the start of 1943, and so its crew was examined with special care. There was no sign of illness. "Then," Olesen said, "the captain brought out a deratization certificate stating that the ship had recently been fumigated—in Casablanca, if I remember correctly—and was free of rats; looking back, I feel sure the official who signed this certificate had been bribed." Nonetheless, on the strength of the certificate, the ship was allowed to dock. A few bags of mail were unloaded, and then the longshoremen boarded and were on the point of beginning to discharge the cargo when one of them noticed some dead rats. It was not until January 18, more than a week after the *Wyoming* had first pulled into port, and with most of the cargo emptied from the hold, that the first rats were finally autopsied. A guinea pig was injected with mashed-up rat fleas. Four days later it died.

For the next two weeks, a major covert program of rat-trapping was conducted on and around the Brooklyn, Manhattan, and Staten Island piers. Early in February the first rats were sent for autopsy. Olesen and his colleagues awaited the report with "considerable anxiety. It was negative on every rat, and we began to breathe easier." Trapping continued for the next two and a half months, and not one infected rat was found. By some miracle, and not for the first time, the city had escaped plague.

The ever-present potential, however—and the prospect of unchecked carnage in such a confined and densely packed population—remains a rich source of novelistic melodrama. To pick just one: *Epidemic!*, an obscure and long-forgotten 1961 procedural about a plague outbreak in Manhattan; author, one Frank G. Slaughter. "The Chilling Account of a Great City's Battle Against the Black Death!," hollers the subtitle. On the cover a woman stumbles, hand to her forehead; behind her in the shadows, a man can just be seen scurrying away, shoulders hunched, collar up.

It is a tale of sudden and virulent contagion, hysterical

panic, granite-hearted villains and cool but "brilliant" doctors, of a city suddenly out of control, open to seizure by the most malign criminal forces. It is also—despite being unashamed pulp—unexpectedly gripping, as well as unintentionally comic.

It starts slowly and ominously, with a feverish tramp-steamer captain bravely struggling his vessel into New York Harbor. As he changes out of his oilskins, the extent of his infection becomes clear. "His superbly muscled body dripped with perspiration while he fumbled into slacks and a sports shirt." As he and his shivering crew stagger ashore, they are closely followed by diseased rats, creatures "not listed on the ship's manifest, but . . . a sinister part of the cargo she had taken [on] in the Cameroons."

By the end of chapter 2, "the destiny of New York was truly in the balance. . . . The pattern of destruction established by *Pasteurella pestis*, erratic as the finger-painting of a demented child, was now virtually complete." And at this point "brilliant immunologist" Eric Stow steps manfully into the frame. Faced with a city in sudden and apocalyptic meltdown—"Apartment dwellers had already snapped on their burglar chains and locked their windows. . . . Theaters and movie houses had seen their audiences reduced to a trickle"—his prescription is blunt. Manhattan has to be sealed off, and he addresses his subordinates in a crowded hospital ward, the general before his troops, roused to Churchillian rhetoric by the thrill of the emergency before him. "*Pasteurella pestis* has established its beach head. We can defeat it within these boundaries. If we hesitate, we'll have two thousand cases tomorrow in Greater New York. The day after, there could be ten thousand in the metropolitan area alone. Don't think I'm romancing. I've seen this bug in action."

It is exhilarating stuff that—due largely to the liberal use of hyperbole, the stagy dialogue, and inevitable descent into an Ian Fleming–style struggle between white-knight scientists and an underworld bent on global domination—screams, "Fantasy!" from every page. And yet all Frank G. Slaughter did was properly research his field. As preposterous as the thriller undoubtedly is—with its cartoon-impassive immunologists, its square-jawed and resolute police chiefs—there is little that one could decry as implausible. Without the Ernst Stavro Blofeld subplot, *Epidemic!* simply draws on what is already established about the nature and effect of plague on society. And this is known: that few diseases are more contagious or feared, that terror triggers flight, that among those who remain, the worst of humanity results—riots, victimization of the infected, the gradual collapse of order. It had happened in London in 1665, across Europe in the 1340s, in Hong Kong in 1894, and in Surat a century later. Why not in New York?

IN HONG KONG THE CATACLYSM OF 1894—AND THE INTERMITtent plague outbreaks that continued until the 1930s—triggered a systematic rat-destruction program that lasted the entire twentieth century. The first and most controversial move was the leveling of Taipingshan, the central Hong Kong district from which plague had first flared. From the start of the epidemic, establishment opinion, happy to have been able to scapegoat an entire cultural enclave, pushed for demolition and, while the argument spiraled into barely concealed racial jousting, a prison-high brick wall was hurriedly constructed as interim containment. The government, increasingly enthusiastic about the idea of erasing not only disease but any memory of the terror of that early summer, began angling forcefully for the whole area to be first torched, then razed. In Kitasato, as it had no doubt hoped, it found a compliant ally. "If one desires to properly clean the contaminated houses to make them free of plague," ran his reply to the letter from the colonial surgeon, Dr. Philip Ayres, "it is recommended to proceed radically . . . [and] it is best if at least the inner parts of the houses are burned." Yersin, whose research into the soil of infected houses had revealed no such certain course, stopped way short of Kitasato. Setting entire streets to flame, he said, was overkill: The microbe in the soil was "no longer virulent."

Yet destroyed Taipingshan was, and today only the street names and precipitous incline remain the same. The memory of plague, however, died harder, and that rare Hong Kong commodity, an undeveloped city block, now squats in the center of the neighborhood in the form of Henry Blake Park, named after the governor who took over in late 1894 from the benighted Robinson. This unprepossessing rectangle of shorn grass and concrete walkways had been intended, so a shopkeeper explained, as "a kind of lung, to help us breathe," but it seems now that few ever used it, that in fact the Chinese of Taipingshan preferred a claustrophobic proximity, as they had always done, living at the turn of the twenty-first century in 1950s slab-built concrete tenement apartments, balconies festooned with washing and cooking pots.

Walking this quarter it was not hard to spot rats, too, lumbering out of the gutter before dusk had even fallen, but shopkeepers, the moment the subject was broached, would noisily deny their existence. Voices from the buried dark of television repair shops shouted, "No rats! No rats here!" And yet, just across the street, stapled to a telegraph pole, was a forty-eight-point warning poster: "Food and Environmental Hygiene Warning—Poisonous Rat Bait Is Being Laid in This Vicinity." Another counseled, "A clean environment prevents rats. Eliminate hiding places for rats. Do not leave food for rats. Prevent rats from entering your premises."

Senior Hong Kong health figures told a different story: the triumph of order over chaos, of modern science over what had been a continual cycle of pestilence and disease. Dr. Gerald Choa, physician and medical historian—and one of those anglicized Hong Kong Chinese, now in his seventies, whose pronunciation was more regal than even the Queen's with its throwaway "actuallys" and "mind yous" and "whatnots"— remembered how the 1940s, with plague still a too-recent memory, had seen ferocious cleanup campaigns. Householders, he said, "were encouraged to catch rats and dump them in boxes full of carbolic acid on the street." Every three months, "tanks of disinfectant were put in the middle of the street and people were told to dump their furniture, utensils, clothing, and whatnot in there for disinfection."

Until the late 1980s rat collection in Hong Kong was pursued on a ceaseless and vigorous basis, the most obvious signs of which were the countless "rat boxes" secured to lampposts throughout the city. Little more than ten years later, this seemed a comically quaint custom, though with the clear volume of rats on the island it was also surprising that the practice had ever been halted. Responsibility for collecting the rodents, explained consultant health department pathologist Wai Ping Mak over the telephone—his manner wry, loftily amused—

had been in the hands of government technicians, who emptied the boxes and took the rats for autopsy. Rat collection, he confided, had never been the most popular job and now the boxes no longer existed only the most committed operatives were to be found waiting with their fetid plastic bags for the morning doors to Bacteriology to be thrown open.

He turned abruptly serious, and one could picture him holding the receiver away from his ear and frowning, as if the very object suddenly caused him displeasure. "The real worry," he said, his voice quieter, "is the border with China. That is hard to police, and refugees might bring rats and disease with them. But try persuading anyone to pick up rats on the border. The soldiers won't do it, no one will do it. It's becoming a practical problem."

Which is where it would no doubt remain, at least until plague or another rat-borne contagion erupted once more. No one wanted to admit the scale of the rat problem in Hong Kong, much less be part of a collection or destruction program, and on at least one occasion the now-defunct scheme of paying premiums for each rat tail delivered had ended in low farce. This story came from Dr. Dan Waters, a long-retired colonial service physician and local history enthusiast who doubled as president of the Royal Asiatic Society.

"The thing is," he said, his voice startlingly loud, "the Chinese will always find a way to make money." In another room of his tiny high-rise apartment a Chinese woman—his wife? housekeeper?—was preparing tea. She brought peanut-brittle cookies and he nodded acknowledgment, his conversation unbroken, volume undiminished.

"Over the years there have been various programs to curb

the rat population," he went on. "At one time you could be paid ten cents for every rat tail you brought in. Now, it didn't take long for the Chinese to see that there was money to be made from this, so they started importing rats' tails from Canton." One could picture convoys of trucks, waved breezily through customs, then the bewilderment on the faces of health department officials as they handed out ever-increasing wads of dollars.

"This," Waters said, "went on until they were found out." He smiled. "Yes, great entrepreneurs, the Chinese. *Great* entrepreneurs."

· 22 ·

THE YOUNG DOCTOR WAS PREPARING TO TREAT A PATIENT
when the bomb exploded. Some twenty years later, he recalled
color, flame, a world hellishly inverted.

The sky was dark as pitch, covered with dense clouds of smoke;
under that blackness, over the earth, hung a yellow-brown fog.
Gradually the veiled ground became visible, and the view
beyond rooted me to the spot with horror. All the buildings I
could see were on fire. . . . Electricity poles were wrapped in
flame like so many pieces of kindling. Trees on the nearby hills
were smoking, as were the leaves of sweet potatoes in the fields.
To say that everything burned is not enough. The sky was dark,

the ground was scarlet, and in between hung clouds of yellow-ish smoke. Three kinds of color—black, yellow, and scarlet—loomed ominously over the people, who ran about like so many ants seeking to escape. . . . It seemed like the end of the world.

Nagasaki, August 1945. Survivors, the doctor continued, somehow found their way to his office. "Half naked or stark naked, they walked with strange, slow steps, groaning from deep inside themselves as if they had traveled from the depths of hell. They looked whitish; their faces were like masks. I felt as if I were dreaming, watching pallid ghosts processing slowly in one direction—as in a dream I had once in my childhood."

It was into this scene—already on the scavenge, crawling red eyed from sewers and culverts—that the rat slowly and deliberately advanced. It has become folklore that, after the obliteration of Hiroshima and Nagasaki, only the rats, among all mammals, continued to thrive. More likely they were pro-tected from the blast by being hidden away underground; in the aftermath, as the earth cooled, great packs would have coursed down the abandoned, ashen thoroughfares now bordered by the skeletons of buildings and the burned spikes of trees. And everything still smoking, still dangerous.

Radiation hits humans and rats—mammals both—with equal ferocity, but in the Japanese city–targets it was the people, in daylight, going to work or waiting outside shops, that were fastest destroyed, their skin melting from their bones from the heat of the blast and the extreme gamma and neutron exposure. Rats, emerging later, would have suffered from fall-out, but not before they had feasted on the ruptured corn silos, the wheat flour still spilling from bakers' storerooms. And when they died, to the collapsed cities' lists of postattack perils would have been added the worst: the threat of plague.

For Cold War scientists, commissioned by fearful governments into researching the effects of nuclear war upon the cityscape and its population, it was contagious disease that loomed largest in the catalogue of aftermath catastrophe. According to the 1987 World Health Organization report *Effects of Nuclear War on Health and Health Services:*

> Infection would emerge as a major problem. It is a leading cause of death in victims of burns as well as of radiation. The epidemiological pattern of disease would be altered drastically in the aftermath of a nuclear war, by impairment of the immune response of the body, by malnutrition, by the lack of sanitation, by the proliferation of insects and microorganisms, which are much more resistant to radiation than human beings, and by the collapse of epidemiological surveillance and disease control. Outbreaks of diarrhea and respiratory disease would be likely to occur in the surviving population and be intensified by the overcrowding and insanitary conditions of the shelters in which people would have taken refuge.

In the event of "all-out nuclear war"—a scenario that, in the mid-1980s, seemed far from implausible—"millions of putrefying human and animal corpses and mounds of untreated waste and sewage would provide a perfect breeding-ground for flies and other insects that are more resistant to radiation than human beings. The uncontrolled growth of insect populations would favor an increase in the numbers of insect vectors of disease."

Chief among which, of course, was the rat flea, *Xenopsylla cheopis*, bearer of plague, and it was to gauge the likely severity of this disease in the event of nuclear attack that, in 1966, the U.S. Atomic Energy Commission published an exhaustive report. "Even now," wrote the authors in conclusion,

> there is only a thin protective wall which guards the human population against [plague]. As the record shows, the wall has been breached occasionally in very recent years. . . . The universal hardship that might have to be endured with the debilitating effects of radiation exposure and other injuries are very likely both to hasten the conversion of bubonic to pneumonic plague and to increase measurably the chances for an explosive epidemic.

Plague squats on our doorstep, no longer a disease of the Far or even Near East, no longer elsewhere but very much here. In the United States, the plague bacillus has been found in some thirty-eight wild rodents and rabbits and their fleas; it is endemic among wild rats in the eleven westernmost states; in 1981, a typical year, thirteen people were infected, four of whom died. A nuclear attack, according to Eric Chivian in *Last Aid*, a 1982 investigation into the medical implications of nuclear war,

> would create almost ideal conditions for breaching the thin protective wall against plague. Large areas of the western United States now relatively devoid of inhabitants might receive an influx of refugees from threatened or devastated urban areas. . . . Millions of urban refugees, unable to obtain shelter in

existing dwellings, would build earth-covered "expedient" shelters in undeveloped areas. Such shelters might provide good fallout protection, but they would create ideal conditions for transmission of plague from rodents.

In the weeks following a nuclear attack, plague would dig in, establish itself, become an intimate part of the landscape. As radiation subsided in leveled cities, survivors would return to the streets that had once been their home. Most likely they'd discover only a shell, artifacts melted beyond recognition: Ninety percent of housing would be destroyed in a nuclear attack. The only certainty is that they would encounter disease in unexpected and medieval forms, of which the most distressing and manifest would certainly be plague. And, like the most malign parasite, plague bites harder the worse the circumstances. "Under post-attack conditions," Freeman concludes coolly, "radiation and stress would raise the conversion rate of bubonic to pneumonic plague to twenty-five percent." And, with no drugs available and most hospitals destroyed, death would come quickly and without pity to the surviving homeless, huddled in the few remaining roofed buildings, black rain falling all around.

EPILOGUE

IN THE FIRST WEEK OF SEPTEMBER 1894, DR. JAMES LOWSON—loyal champion of Professor Shibasaburo Kitasato, and painstaking enemy to the best scientific endeavors of Dr. Alexandre Yersin—travelled to Japan as an honored guest of the imperial government. He received a tumultuous welcome. A note in his diary, added some time later, reads, "In Japan . . . was made a national 'hero.' Valuable presents numerous, and suite of rooms at the Imperial Hotel." He was receiving his due, proper payment for his role as starmaker.

The visit was also proof, in the world's eyes, of Kitasato's status as sole plague pioneer. But it was not the end of the matter for, over the coming decades, Kitasato's claim to have discovered the cause of plague began to look increasingly shaky and—though he never publicly set the record straight—he too in time would come to realize that his findings were crucially flawed, the victim of hurried research and a precipitate rush for publication. Now, more than a century after the two men faced each other over their microscopes in Hong Kong, the plague bacterium is officially classed *Yersinia pestis*. Yet for most of this time, and certainly during the lives of the two rivals, it was Kitasato who enjoyed the glory.

The conventional narratives—either that Kitasato and Yersin simultaneously discovered the bacillus, or that Kitasato, as he would always publicly maintain, beat Yersin to the goal—have been particularly resilient. Such models of careful scholarship as William Bulloch's 1938 *History of Bacteriology* state that "in 1894 Kitasato and Yersin discovered the plague bacillus," while the alternative line has been propounded by books like Richard Shyrock's 1947 *History of Modern Medicine*, which saluted Kitasato as having "added to his fame in 1894, when he discovered the cause of bubonic plague during an epidemic at Hong Kong, and thus exposed one of the historic enemies of man."

Returning from Hong Kong, Kitasato lost no time in declaring that he had discovered the "virus" of the disease, an announcement that was faithfully and prominently relayed in the medical press: According to one journal, the "people of Nagasaki sent a gold cup to Dr. Kitasato for the honor of his discovery of the pest-bacilli." In his publications, Kitasato was no less forthright, and seldom passed up an opportunity to highlight the differences between his and Yersin's observations, most obvious of which was the fact that Yersin's bacillus did not react to Gram-staining, while his colored easily. Science, he concluded, needed to come to a "definite conclusion" as to which of the two bacilli was the plague pathogen: Only then could therapy and prophylaxis "be initiated on a truly rational basis."

Yet as the old century drew to its close, Kitasato's claim began to be eroded not by allies of Yersin—as he might have anticipated—but by his own contemporaries in Japan. The first stone was thrown by Masanori Ogata, who in 1896 published a paper describing plague research in Taiwan during which he had managed to isolate a bacillus identical to Yersin's from infected humans, rats, and rat fleas. Any suggestion, he concluded, that the bacillis of Yersin and Kitasato were identical was plain wrong: "They are two quite different kinds of bacteria." And it was Yersin's, not Kitasato's, that caused plague.

By the last months of 1899, Kitasato must have known that his claim was untenable, and yet he persisted not only in doing his best to shore up his own earlier shaky research, but in seizing every opportunity to trash the work of his rival. That year the Japanese government sent Kitasato and three other researchers to investigate outbreaks of plague in Kobe and Osaka, and the subsequent report, with its numerous references to plague bacilli, surely ranks as one of the great masterpieces of omission. Nowhere, despite the work of Simond in Bombay, did he mention rat fleas, or hint at any point that there had ever been any disagreement over the identity of the plague bacillus. The only reference to Yersin was a brusque put-down, a dismissal of his antiplague serum as therapeutically and prophylactically useless.

There seems no charitable way to read Kitasato's actions: The unavoidable conclusion is that he was trying step-by-step to erase his previous error in order to protect his reputation. With each publication, his position subtly changed. In 1900 the publication of *A Textbook on Plague* by Kitasato's assistant Tohiu Ishigama—a member of the Hong Kong team—stated that there were differences in the bacilli found in the blood and buboes of plague patients. The book—"revised" by Kitasato, Ishigama's "revered teacher"—came down heavily and unsurprisingly in favor of the blood bacillus. "Professor Kitasato was of the opinion that those [bacilli] which existed in the glands and other organs were pleomorphic involution forms and . . . attached greater importance to those existing in the blood."

This convoluted slice of scientific jargon was evidence of Kitasato further shifting his ground: Previously, he had asserted that the bacillus found in the plague swellings "was an entirely different species from the one that exists in the blood." Now, six years after his initial research, his own bacillus had undergone a remarkable and most unscientific metamorphosis, to become an "involution form" of Yersin's bacterium, which first "invades the blood" as such, and then "assumes, as it were, a second nature during the septicemic stage of the disease." This magnificent piece of fudging enabled Kitasato to surrender to the weight of evidence now supporting Yersin's discovery without having to admit the errors in his own findings.

When Kitasato died in 1931, his reputation—as he would have hoped—was safe. Every obituary acclaimed him as the hero who had uncovered one of science's greatest secrets, the cause of plague. Only once did he admit his error, that the bacillus he had found was not the one that caused plague—and this in private, during plague investigations in Japan in 1899 that unfolded increasing evidence discrediting his earlier descriptions. In public, in the words of Norman Howard-Jones's intricately argued 1973 retrospective article in the U.S. journal *Perspectives in Biology and Medicine*, for the rest of his life Kitasato "tacitly shared with Yersin paternity for *Pasteurella pestis*." To have admitted his mistake—that what he claimed was the plague bacillus was in fact Streptococcus pneumoniae, a similar-looking bacterium that causes pneumonia, itself a common secondary infection of plague—would not only have been a crushing loss of face—a humiliation particularly grievous for a Japanese scientist—but would most likely have spelled the end of his dream of winning backing for a private research institute. And so he dodged the issue, kept his head down, and did nothing to discourage those who persisted in proclaiming him the plague pioneer.

But there is another player in this too, whose shadow in Hong Kong cast such a pall over the work of Yersin, and whose influence was critical in Kitasato's acceptance as discoverer of the plague bacillus. The figure was James Lowson, for whom there was no question which scientist deserved his loyalty: Kitasato was celebrated and venerated—hailed in the press as "perhaps the greatest bacteriologist in the world"—while Yersin, at least outside France, was unknown. When on August 4 the *Lancet* broke the news that "Dr. Kitasato has discovered and described a specific plague bacillus," it was Lowson who had acted as delivery boy by telegraphing the journal, and no doubt he was the source for the paper's extraordinary coda that "there will probably be many local *savants* keen on discovering a specific bacillus, and it is necessary to caution against accepting all the statements which will no doubt be put forward in this respect." Lowson kept the venom he felt toward Yersin carefully hidden, but in a private—and previously unpublished— letter to Kitasato written after the Japanese scientist had returned home, the strength of his feelings is made clear. Under sketches depicting Kitasato with an unwavering visionary gaze and Yersin as an elf-eared, spade-bearded devil, he wrote, "If you can . . . kill a man named Yersin, for God's sake do so. He has led us a dance . . . but Takaki [Kitasato's assistant] will tell you we have got the better of him."

Lowson followed up his first telegram to the *Lancet* by rushing a selection of Kitasato's slides to London, which were reproduced in the *Lancet* on August 11 and in the equally prestigious *British Medical Journal* a week later. That day, however, both journals carried a news item about Yersin's letter to the French Académie des Sciences claiming discovery of "*the* bacillus of the Chinese plague." Yet this was dismissed by the *Lancet*, which cited Kitasato's famed caution and accuracy.

It seemed that Kitasato had rushed into print without having thoroughly tested his assertions. His announcement may have come a good six days before Yersin's, but his descriptions lacked the same forensic precision and, crucially, were unable to confirm how the bacillus reacted to the alkaline Gram stain. His subsequent reports were contradictory and confusing; all signs pointed to a headlong rush to publication, which—though Kitasato had other failings—had never until now been characteristic.

Which leaves just Lowson, the wild card, whose friendship

with Kitasato was from the start unreserved and headstrong, his admiration unbounded. Not only did he contribute some of his own slides to the package mailed to London, but the choice of first outlet must have also been his: Kitasato had never published in the *Lancet* before, and would never do so again.

For the rest of his life Lowson remained convinced that he had backed the right man. Never one to favor diplomacy over brute honesty, he would—at a meeting of London's Epidemiological Society in 1896—declare with explosive bombast that "all" Yersin's work was "suspicious," and that both he and Kitasato had "little faith in Yersin's serum treatment." For Lowson, the determination to see proper recognition for his hero—and not for the thirty-one-year-old upstart Frenchman—overrode all proper caution.

Two years before his death in 1935, now back in Forfar, the granite-austere northeastern Scottish town of his birth, Lowson took up his 1894 diary one last time. With an unsteady hand, he set about making the annotations he knew would be read by future historians; the final editorial touches that would, he hoped, leave no room for doubt. By now even he would have realised that Kitasato's claim was untenable and yet he—like his recently dead hero—had gone too far to back down. With hefty pen strokes he underscored what he considered the vital dates and movements—"Kitasato discovered bacillus" from June 14, the next day's "wired Lancet" and, under July 10, "Kitasato's paper—transmitted to Lancet." At the very end of the diary is a page smaller than the rest, a once-loose notepad leaf, now pasted into the inside of the back cover. Here he repeated the dates, adding "Yersin found bacillus on 23 June," before concluding with spite and untruth, "He would not work in the same building as Kitasato and it took him some time to get up a mat-shed."

MOHANLAL STAYED A WEEK, AND EACH DAY WAS HARDER THAN the last. He had started compliant, offering Hetal a choice— either to return to Surat or to stay in her parents' village—and promising that whatever she decided, he'd stick with her. Secretly, though, he'd hoped that emollience might soften her to his will, for he could not imagine life in such a dusty backwater, could not see how he could survive such boredom and hardship, even with his beloved wife and daughter.

And so he returned to the city, and he knew the moment he'd done so that he'd taken the right course. The authorities were already setting about a vigorous campaign of demolition and street cleaning, instituting fines for anyone spotted jettisoning garbage outside of proper receptacles. It felt like hope, and he wrote Hetal to tell her of his excitement at being part of it. Come, he told her: It is not only I who needs you, but the city also; your city.

He received no reply, and it was another month before his editor allowed him the week he needed to make the trip north and back again. Shorn of his duties as husband and father those few weeks back in Surat, he'd rediscovered an earlier self: He'd worked late most nights, part of the team of reporters now permanently assigned to plague. He, though, had thrown his net wider than had his colleagues: Where they spent their days tailing the new municipal commissioner, he'd felt drawn to the wider investigation, the threat of resurgent plague in a world that had for decades assumed the disease was of only historical interest.

In London, he learned, a duo of scientists was working on a greater understanding. From a former colleague, now on the staff of the London Independent newspaper, he gleaned more: names, research details. Dr. Mike Prentice, senior lecturer in medical microbiology at St Bart's Hospital, was aiming to demonstrate how the disease had changed over time and how it might alter in future. Dr. Brendan Wren, professor of pathogenicity at the London School of Tropical Medicine and Hygiene, was looking to the imminent completion of the DNA sequence of *Yersinia pestis* as a way of isolating those sections of the bacillus that were subject to change and that, in turn, could be targets for new vaccines or antibiotics. Plague, Wren claimed, was "down but not out." Prentice went further: "Given the resurrection of whatever conditions allowed plague to spread in the first three pandemics, there's always the potential that it could come back."

As a journalist these comments intrigued Mohanlal, and proved the starting point for a series of front-page stories about the global threat of plague that thrilled his editor and provided a much-needed circulation boost. As a man with a family still in hiding, however, he knew the articles would do little to encourage their return and so, as he arrived in the village once more, he reminded himself again to accentuate the positive.

Hetal was cooking when he looked in through the open door. Another woman, of about the same age, was holding his daughter. Hetal was talking and laughing, wagging a finger in the air as she reached the climax of her story. And then she glanced up, at the darkened figure in the doorway, and fell silent.

"Mohanlal," she said quietly.

"You're looking well," he answered. He nodded a greeting to the other woman and entered the house. When he bent to kiss Hetal she turned her head and offered her cheek. It was not until late evening that he was able to be alone with her.

Walking outside, the warmth of the earth rising into the cool black night, she put her arm in his; he felt himself loosen. She talked, and it was immediately clear to him which way this was going. She'd forgotten the simple pleasures of rural life, she said: the focus on crops and animals and the preparation of food. She'd rediscovered a friend from childhood, too, who had a baby the same age. She looked up at him, expectant.

"And Surat?" he said eventually. "You've asked me nothing about Surat, or our home."

She did not reply. Away from the dim lights of the village, the black of night was absolute, and he could not read her face. He stopped walking, and spoke out loudly till she stopped and turned and came close to him again.

"We're rebuilding the city," he said. "Plague was the lowest point, but things are getting better."

"I love you, Mohanlal," she replied, taking his arm again. "But what I saw then scared me. For the moment, I feel safest here."

And so he returned to Surat alone. Six months passed. He saw Hetal once every six weeks, sometimes less, and could sense estrangement growing. At times she seemed close to surrender, to swallowing her fears and coming back with him. At others her resolve felt stronger than ever.

His daughter stopped recognizing him, began crying when he reached out to hold her. Most days, as he worked on yet another investigation into the disease that had split his family, he found himself drifting into reverie, imagining that he'd one day look up from his desk to find them standing at the door, that he suddenly possessed the power to rewrite the past. And he knew where he'd start: with that 1:30 A.M. phone call. With that gone they could start over. And on this new morning they'd wake up late and in each other's arms, their baby sleeping still, sunlight streaming through the windows. A day just like any other, simple and perfect and full of possibility.

SELECTED BIBLIOGRAPHY

KEY BOOKS AND JOURNAL ARTICLES

Airlie, Shiona. *Thistle and Bamboo: The Life and Times of Sir James Stewart Lockhart.* Hong Kong: Oxford University Press, 1989.

Albrecht, H., and Ghon, A. *Denkschr. Kgl. Akad. Wiss. (Math.-naturw. Klasse), Wien,* 66. Part 1, 1898. Parts 2, 3, 1900. *Über die Beulenpest in Bombay,* 1898–1900.

Anonymous. 'A Cure for the Plague'. *British Medical Journal* (1896);2:1760.

Anonymous. 'The Life and Achievements of Shibasaburo Kitasato.' In: Mizunoe K,, ed. Collected Papers of Shibasaburo Kitasato. Tokyo: Kitasato Institutes and University, 1977.

Anonymous. 'The Plague at Hong Kong'. *British Medical Journal* (1894);2:201

Aoyama. Ueber die Pestepidemie in Hong-Kong im Jahre 1894. *Mitteil. a. d. med. Fakult. D. Kaiserlich. Jap. Universität, Bd.* (1895) *3. H. 2.*

Arnold, David, ed. *Imperial Medicine and Indigenous Societies,* Manchester University Press, 1988.

Arnold, David. *Colonizing the Body: State Medicine and Epidemic Disease in Nineteenth Century India.* Berkeley: University of California Press, 1994.

Ayres, P. B. C. 'Colonial Surgeon's Report for 1872'. *Hong Kong Government Gazette,* 1873.

Bannerman, William Burney. Statistics of inoculations with Haffkine's anti-plague vaccine, 1897–1900, compiled from records in the Plague Department of the Secretariat and the Plague Research Laboratory, Bombay. Bombay: Govt Central Press, 1900.

Barrett-Hamilton, Gerald E. H., and Hinton, Martin A.C. *A History of British Mammals,* Part 18. 'The Black or Ship Rat'. London: Gurney & Jackson, 1916.

Bartholomew, James R. *The Formation of Science in Japan: Building a Research Tradition.* New Haven: Yale University Press, 1989.

Bibel, D. J., Chen, T. H. 'Diagnosis of plague: An Analysis of the Yersin-Kitasato Controversy'. *Bacteriol Review,* (1976);40:633–51

"Black Plague in Hong Kong: Discussion in the Sanitary Board." *Hong Kong Telegraph,* (May 10, 1894).

Blanchy, S., et al. "Epidémiologie clinique de la peste à Madagascar." *Archives Institut Pasteur Madagascar* (1993);60:27–34

Boisier, P., et al. "Urban Epidemic of Bubonic Plague in Majunga, Madagascar: Epidemiological Aspects". *Tropical Medicine and International Health* (1997);2:422–27

Boghurst, W. 'Loimographia, or an Experimental Relation of the Last Plague of London'. Ed. By J. F. Payne, 1894. *Supplement, Trans. Epidem. Soc. Lond.* (1666); 13: 1–99.

Bradley, Richard. *The Virtue and Use of Coffee with Regard to the Plague.* London: E. Matthews and W. Mears, 1721.

Brygoo, E. R. "Epidemiologie de la Peste à Madagascar." *Archives Institut Pasteur Madagascar* (1966);35:7–147

Bruce Low, R. *Reports and Papers on Bubonic Plague.* H.M.S.O., London, (1920).

———. *The Progress of Plague, Cholera and Yellow Fever throughout the World, 1914 to 1917.* London: HMSO, 1920.

Buchanan, Andrew. *Cats as Plague Preventers.* Allahabad: Pioneer Press, 1909.

Cantlie, James. *How to Recognise, Prevent and Treat Plague.* London: Cassell & Co.

———. 'The Plague in Hong Kong.' *British Medical Journal,* (August 26, 1894), 423–427.

Cantlie Stewart, Jean. *The Quality of Mercy: The Lives of Sir James and Lady Cantlie.* London: Allen & Unwin, 1983.

Camus, Albert. *The Plague.* London: Hamish Hamilton, 1948.

Castro, Josué de. "The Geopolitics of Hunger." New York, London: *Monthly Review Press,* 1977.

Catanach, I.J. 'Fatalism? Indian Responses to Plague and Other Crises.' Delivered at the 5th New Zealand Asian Studies Conference, Aug. 1983. Extract from: *Asian Profile* (Apr. 1984), vol. 12, no.2.

Chanteau, S, et al. 'Current epidemiology of human plague in Madagascar'. *Microbes and Infection* (2000);2:25–31

Childe, L.F. *British Medical Journal* (1897); 1: 1215

China Mail. 'Discovery of the Plague Bacillus.' (June 20, 1894.)

Chivian et al, ed. *Last Aid: The Medical Dimensions of Nuclear War.* San Francisco: W. H. Freeman, 1982.

Choa, G. H. 'A History of Medicine in Hong Kong'. In: *Medical Directory of Hong Kong, 2nd edition.* Federation of Medical Societies of Hong Kong (1970): 11–27

———. *The Life and Times of Sir Kai Ho Kai, a Prominent Figure in Nineteenth Century Hong Kong.* Hong Kong: The Chinese University Press, 1981.

Condon, J. K. *The Bombay Plague, Being a History of the Progress of Plague in Bombay Presidency from September 1896 to June 1899.* Bombay: 1900.

Coulanges, P. 'Situation de la Peste à Tananarive [Antananarivo], de Son Apparition en 1912 à Sa Résurgence en 1979'. *Archives Institut Pasteur Madagascar* (1989);56:9–35

Crawfordd, E. A. 'Paul-Louis Simond and His Work on Plague'. *Persp Biol Med* (1996);39:446–58.

Creighton, C. *A History of Epidemics in Britain.* Cambridge: Cambridge Univ. Press (1891); 1: 202, 632–3.

Defoe, Daniel. *A Journal of the Plague Year.* London: F & J Noble, 1720.

'Dr Kitasato on the plague bacillus'. *Hong Kong Weekly Press* (July 10, 1894).

Dyer, Dr Isadore. 'The Rat, the Flea and the Plague: Some Plain Facts for the Public'. Prepared for the Medical Plague Conference of New Orleans. Published in the bulletin of the New Orleans Plague Conference. Undated, but likely to be early 1900s.

Dyer-Ball, J. 'A Chinese View of the Plague'. *Hong Kong Government Gazette* (1895):423–5.

Eitel, E.J. *Europe in China.* Hong Kong: Oxford University Press, 1983.

Endacott, G.B. *A History of Hong Kong.* Hong Kong: Oxford University Press, 1995 (second edition).

Eskey, C. R., and Haas, V. H. *Publ. Hlth. Bull., Wash.* (1940), No. 254.

Fracastor, J. (1546), *Les Trois Livres de Jerome Fracastor.* Trans. L. Meunier. Paris: 1893.

Gaffky, Pfeiffer, Sticker and Dieudonné, *Bericcht über die Thätigkeit der zur Erforschung der Pest im Jahre 1897 nach Indien entsandten Kommission.* (Report of German Plague Commission). *Arbeit. Kgl. Gesundheitsamte.* (1899); 16: 1–352.

Galimand, Marc, et al. 'Multidrug Resistance in *Yersinia pestis* Mediated by a Transferable Plasmid'. *New England Journal of Medicine* (Sept 4, 1997). Vol. 337, No. 10.

Garrett, Laurie. *The Coming Plague: Newly Emerging Diseases in a World Out of Balance.* New York: Farrar, Straus & Giroux, 1994.

Ghosh, Archana. 'Plague in Surat, Crisis in Urban Governance', Archana Ghosh, S. Sami Ahmad. New Delhi: Institute of Social Sciences, 1996.

Granta, *India!* 57. London: 1997.

Gregg, Charles T. *Plague! The Shocking Story of a Dread Disease in America Today.* New York: Charles Scribner's Sons, 1978.

Guiyoule, Annie et al. 'Transferable Plasmic-Mediated Resistance to Streptomycin in a Clinical Isolate of *Yersinia Pestis*'. *Emerging Infectious Disease* (Jan–Feb, 2001); Vol. 7, No. 1.

Guiyoule, Annie et al. 'Recent Emergence of New Variants of *Yersinia Pestis* in Madagascar'. *J Clin Microbiol* (1997);35:2826–33

Haffkine, Waldemar Mordecai Wolff. *Serum-therapy of Plague in India, reports by Mr. W. M. Haffkine and various officers of the Plague Research Laboratory, Bombay,* edited and with an introduction by W. B. Bannerman (1860–1930). Calcutta. Office of the Superintendent of Govt. Print., India, 1905. (Series: Scientific memoirs by officers of the Medical and Sanitary Departments of the Government of India. New series. No. 20).

Hampton, B. C. *Publ. Hlth. Rep., Wash.* (1940); 55: 1143.

Hankin, E. H. *Ann. Inst. Pasteur, Paris* (1898); 12: 705.

Hecker, J.F.C. *The Epidemics of the Middle Ages.* Trans B.G. Babington for Sydenham Society. London, 1859.

Heiser, Victor. *An American Doctor's Odyssey: Adventures in 45 Countries.* New York: W.W. Norton & Co., 1936.

Hinton, Martin A.C. *Rats and Mice as Enemies of Mankind.* 3rd edn. Brit. Mus. (Nat. Hist.) Economic Series (1931), No. 8, London.

Hirst, L. Fabian. *The Conquest of Plague: A Study of the Evolution of Epidemiology.* Oxford: Clarendon Press, 1953.

Hodges, Nathaniel (1672), *Loimographia, or an Historical Account of the Plague in London in 1665.* Trans from Latin by John Quincy. 2nd edn. London, 1720.

Hogarth, Alfred Moore. *The Rat.* London: John Bale, 1929.

Howard-Jones, N. 'Was Shibasaburo Kitasato the co-discoverer of the plague bacillus?' *Perspect Microbiol Med* (1973);16:293–307

———. 'Kitasato, Yersin and the plague bacillus.' *Clio Med* (1975);10:23–7

Hunter, W. *A Research into Epidemic and Epizootic Plague.* Hong Kong: 1904.

Jones, Maurice E., Platt, Arleen Kay, and Platt, Jerome J. *The Whitewash Brigade: The Hong Kong Plague of 1894.* London: Dix, Noonan, Webb, 1998.

King, H. H., and Pandit., C. G., *Indian J. Med. Res.* (1931); 19: 357.

Kitasato, S. 'Fighting Plague in Japan', *New York Medical Journal* (1906); 84: 1–29.

———. Research reports on bubonic plague, 1894–1897. Collection of articles and texts of speeches, published in *Tokyo Medical School Journal.* Translated for author by University of Bath Foreign Languages Department, UK.

———. 'The Bacillus of Bubonic Plague'. *Lancet* (1894);ii:428–430.

———. 'Combating Plague in Japan'. *Philipp J. Sci.* (1906);1:465–481.

———. 'Fighting Plague in Japan'. *New York Medical Journal* (1906);84:1–29.

———. Obituary of. *British Medical Journal* (1931); 1:1141–2

Klein, E. *Studies on the Bacteriology and Etiology of Oriental Plague.* London: Macmillan & Co., 1906.

Kohn, George C., Ed. *The Encyclopedia of Plague & Pestilence.* New York: Facts on File, 1995.

Lagrange E. 'Concerning the Discovery of the Plague Bacillus.' *Journal of Tropical Medicine and Hygiene* (1926);29: 299–303

Lamond, Margrete. *Plague and Pestilence.* New York: Allen & Unwin, 1997.

Lancet reports on Hong Kong plague of 1894. Vol I:
June 16 issue p. 1518 and p. 1538;
June 23 issue p. 1581–1582. Vol II:
July 7 issue p. 40 and p. 59;
August 4 issue p. 266 and p. 269–270;
August 11 issue p. 346, p. 325 and p. 369–70

Latham, Baldwin. *The Climatic Conditions Necessary for the Propagation and Spread of Plague.* Edinburgh: R. & R. Clark, 1900.

Lien-The, Wu. *A Treatise in Pneumonic Plague.* League of Nations Health Organization. Geneva, 1926.

Liston, W. G. *Indian Med. Gaz.* (1905); 40: 43

Lloyd, B. J. *J. Amer. Med. Assoc.* (1925); 85: 729

Lowe, J. 'A Note on the Work of Dr P.L. Simond on the Transmision and Epidemiology of Plague by Fleas.' *Indian Medical Gazette* (1942);77:418–21

Lowson, James A. *Report on the Epidemic of Plague from 22 February to 16 July 1897.* Miscellaneous Official Publications, Presidency of Bombay. London, 1897.

———. 'The Bacteriology of Plague'. *British Medical Journal* (1897);1:237–8

———. 'The Epidemic of Bubonic Plague in Hong Kong, 1894.' Hong Kong: Government Printer, 1895.

———. 'The Outbreak of Bubonic Plague in Hong Kong, 1894.' Speech to the Eighth International Hygiene Congress, Budapest, September 4, 1894.

———. Obituary of. *British Medical Journal* (1935);2:880.

Marr, John S. *The Eleventh Plague: A Novel of Medical Terror.* New York: HarperCollins, 1998.

McCoy, G. W., *J. Hyg., Camb.* (1910); 10: 589

McNeill, William. *Plagues and People.* Oxford: Blackwell, 1997.

Millot-Severin, A. G. 'A Note Concerning the Discovery of the Bacillus Pestis.' *Journal of Tropical Medicine and Hygiene* (1927);9:208–9

Mitchell, H. H. *Plague in the United States: An Assessment of its Significance as a Problem Following a Thermonuclear War.* Rand Corporation, Santa Monica, California. Published for the U.S. Atomic Energy Commission.

Mollaret, H. H. 'La Découverte par Paul-Louis Simond du Rôle de la Puce dans la Transmission de la Peste.' *Rev. Prat.* (1991);41:1947–1952

Mollaret, H.H., and J. Brossollet, 'Alexandre Yersin ou Le Vainquer de La Peste.' *Les Inconnus de l'Histoire:* 320. Paris: Fayard, 1985.

Morton Todd, Frank. 'Eradicating Plague from San Francisco,' report of the Citizens Health Committee and an account of its work with brief descriptions of the measures taken, copies of ordinances in aid of sanitation, articles by sanitarians on the nature of plague and the best means of getting rid of it; facsimiles of circulars issued by the Committee and a list of subscribers to the health fund (March 31, 1909). San Francisco: C.A. Murdock & Co., 1909.

Moseley, Jack E. "Travels of Alexandre Yersin: Letters of a Pastorian [sic] in Indochina, 1890–1894." *Perspectives in Biology and Medicine,* (Summer 1981). Pp. 607–618

Nathan, R. *The Plague in India,* 1896, 1897. Simla: Government Central Printing Office, 1898.

Niles, Mary. 'Plague in Canton'. *The China Missionary Journal* (1894);8;116-119

Nuttall, G.H.F. *Brit. Med. J.* (1899); 2:. 642

Nuttall, G.H.F. *John Hopkins Hosp. Rep.* (1900); 8: 1–154

Ogata, M. "Über die Pestepidemie in Formosa." *Centralbl. F. Bakteriol.* (1897);21:769–777

Oullette, Pierre. *The Third Pandemic.* London: Hodder & Stoughton, 1996.

Papon, J.P. 'De la Peste ou Epoques memorables de ce Fleau.' Paris: Vol. I, p.115 [*2]

Pariset, E., *Mémoire sur les Causes de la Peste et sur les Moyens de la Détruire.* Paris (1837).

Pasteur, L., Chamberland, and Roux *C. R. Acad. Sci., Paris* (1881); 92: 429

Paterson, E. H. *A Hospital for Hong Kong: The Century History of the Alice ho Min Ling Nethersole Hospital.* Hong Kong: Alice Ho Min Ling Nethersole Hospital, 1987.

Procopius of Caesarea (550), *De Bello Persico, Works of Procopius of Caesarea,* vol. 2. Trans. by H. B. Dewing. London: Loeb Classics.

Rahalison, L., et al. 'Diagnosis of Bubonic Plague by PCR in Madagascar under Field Conditions'. *Journal of Clinical Microbiology* (2000);38:260–263

Rasoamanana, B. et al. 'Surveillance de la sensibilité aux antiobiotiques des souches de Yersinia pestis à Madagascar de 1989 à 1995.' *Archives Institut Pasteur Madagascar* (1995);62:108–10

Rasolomaharo, M. et al. 'Plague in Mahajanga, Madagascar.' *Lancet* (1995); 346:1234.

Rat and its Relation to Public Health, The. Various authors. Washington. Govt Printing Office, 1910.

Report of Austrian Plague Commission (1899).

Report of the Commission appointed by the Secretary of the Treasury for the Investigation of Plague in San Francisco, under instructions from the Surgeon General, Marine-Hospital Service. Washington: Govt Printing Office, 1901.

Report of German Plague Commission (1899).

Report of Indian Plague Commission, vols. 1 to 5. London, 1900–01.

Report of the Municipal Commissioners on the plague in Bombay, with charts and diagrams. Bombay: Municipal Commissioners Office, 1899–1901.

Reports of Plague Investigations in India, No. 13 (1907), *J. Hyg., Camb.,* 7. 373

Reports on Plague Investigations in India, No. 25 (1908), *J. Hyg., Camb.,* 8. 266

Reports on Plague Investigations in India, No. 22 (1908), *J. Hyg., Camb.,* 7. 724

Report of the Plague Research Laboratory, Bombay. Bombay. *Government Central Press,* 1905–1906.

Robb, Peter. Ed. *Rural India: Land, Power and Society under British Rule.* (includes essay by I.J. Catanach, 'Plague and the Indian Village' London, 1942

Roux, E. *Bull. Acad. Méd., Paris* (1897); 37, 91.

Sanitary Convention, 1897. Simla. *G.C. Press.* 1897.

Scott, H. H. 'Conquest of Plague.' *British Medical Journal* (1953);ii:1327.

Shah, Ghanshyam. *Public Health and Urban Development: The Plague in Surat.* New Delhi: Sage Publications, 1997.

Simon, Sir J. *English Sanitary Institutions.* London: Cassell & Co. Ltd. 1890.

Simon, J. C. *Public Health Reports.* Ed. by E. Seaton, London: Sanitary Inst. of Great Britain. 2 vols., 1887.

Simon of Corvino, *Bibl. De l'Ecole des Chartes,* 1840–41 Ser.I, Vol.2, p.241

Simond, Marc, et al. 'Paul-Louis Simond and His Discovery of Plague Transmission by Rat Fleas: a Centenary'. *Journal of the Royal Society of Medicine,* (Feb 1998);91:101–104.

Simond, P.L. 'Comment fut mis en évidence le rôle de la puce dans la transmission de la peste'. *Rev. d'hyg.* (1936);58:5–17

————. 'La propagation de la peste'. *Ann. De l'Inst. Pasteur* (1898); 12:625–687.

————. 'La question du véhicule de la peste.' *Rev. Médico-Chirug Brésil Am. Lat* (1905);5.

Simpson, W. J. *A Treatise on Plague.* Cambridge: Univ. Press, 1905.

Sinn, E. *Power and Charity: The Early History of the Tung Wah Hospital, Hong Kong.* Hong Kong: Oxford University Press, 1989.

Slaughter, Frank G. *Epidemic! The Chilling Account of a Great City's Battle Against the Black Death!* New York, 1961.

Solomon, Tom. 'Hong Kong's Eastern and Western Medical History'. *Journal of the Royal College of Physicians of London,* (July/August 1997). Vol. 31, No. 4.

————. 'Alexandre Yersin and the Plague Bacillus'. *Journal of Tropical Medicine and Hygiene* (1995);98:209–12.

————. 'Hong Kong, 1894: The Role of Dr James A Lowson in the Controversial Discovery of the Plague Bacillus'. *Lancet* (1997);350:59–62.

Sontag, Susan. *Illness as Metaphor.* New York: Farrar, Straus & Giroux, 1978.

Styler, Herman. *Plague Fighters.* NY: Chilton Company, 1960.

Sutphen, Mary P. 'Not What, but Where: Bubonic Plague and the Reception of Germ Theories in Hong Kong and Calcutta, 1894–1897.' Oxford University Press, Oxford, 1997.

Sydenham, Thomas. *Tractatus de Podagra et de Hydrope.* pp. 58–9. London, 1685.

Thomson, G. *Loimotomia or the pest anatomized.* London, 1666.

Thomson, George S., and Thomson, John. *A Treatise on Plague.* London: Swan Sonnenschein, 1901.

Thompson, C.J.S. *Magic and Healing.* London: Rider & Co., 1947.

Thompson, J. A. *Report to the Board of Health on the Second Outbreak of Plague at Sydney, 1902.* (with F. Tidswell). Sydney: Government Printer, 1903.

Thorne-Thorne, R. (1894), *Ann. Rep. Med. Officer, Local Government Board, for 1898–9.* London: H.M.S.O.

Tindall, Gillian. *City of Gold: The Biography of Bombay.* London: Temple Smith, 1982.

Twigg, Graham. *The Black Death: A Biological Reappraisal.* London: Batsford, 1984.

Veith, Ilza. 'Plague and Politics', *Bull. Hist. Med.* (1954); 28:409.

Voelckel, J. 'La vie et l'oeuvre de P.L. Simond' (1858–1947). *Médecin Tropicale* (1969);29:428–441.

Wherry, W. D., *J. Infect. Dis.* (1908); 5:485

White, Andrew. *A Treatise on the Plague; More Especially the Police Management of That Disease.* London: J. Churchill, 1846.

White, Norman F., 'Twenty Years of Plague in India, with Special Reference to the Outbreak of 1917–1918.' Simla. *Government Central Press* (1920).

Williams, James E., and Cavanaugh, Dan C. 'Measuring the Efficacy of Vaccination in Affording Protection Against Plague'. *Bulletin of the World Health Organization* (1979); 57:309–313.

Wood, Winifred A. *"A Brief History of Hong Kong."* Hong Kong: *South China Morning Post*, 1940.

World Health Organization. 'Human Plague in 1995.' *Weekly Epidemiological Record* (1997);46:344–8.

———. 'Effects of Nuclear War on Health and Health Services'. *Report of the WHO Management Group on Follow-up of Resolution WHA36.28: 'The Role of Physicians and Other Health Workers in the Preservation and Promotion of Peace . . .'* Geneva, 1987.

Wyssokowitz and Zabolotny, *Ann. Inst. Pasteur, Paris* (1897); 11: 663.

Yersin, A. Letter to mother, June 24, 1894.

Yersin, A., Calmette, A., and Borrel. *Ann. Inst. Pasteur, Paris* (1895); 9: 589

Yersin, A. 'La peste bubonique à Hong Kong,' *Ann. Inst. Pasteur, Paris* (1894); 8:662–7

Yersin, Alexandre. *Yersin et La Peste*. Lausanne, 1944.

Yule, W. L. 'A Scottish Doctor's Association with the Discovery of the Plague bacillus'. *Scot. Med J* (1995);40:184–6

Zeigler, Philip. *The Black Death*. Stroud: Sutton, 1997.

PUBLISHED SOURCES ON SURAT INCLUDED THE FOLLOWING:

The Times of India (Bombay)

The Hindu (Madras)

Business Standard (Calcutta)

New Wave

Indian Express (Bombay)

The Pioneer (Delhi)

The Telegraph (Calcutta)

'Forget the Symptoms and Tackle the Disease'. *Mainstream*, (January 14, 1995).

'It Was the Plague. Or Was It?' by Vijay Jung Thapa and Smruti Koppikar. *India Today*, (November 30, 1994).

'The Morning After' by Kai Friese. *India Today*, (October 31, 1994).

'Plague Posers Persist' by R. Ramachandran. *The Economic Times*, (July 20, 1995).

South Asian Affairs 'Plague in India: Are Epidemics Being Turned into International Political Weapons?' (Dec. 1995)

The Week 'Military Microbe: International Scientists Confirm the Week's Investigative Report on the Plague in Surat. The Germ was Genetically Engineered and Indians Were Used as Guinea Pigs'. By R. Prasannan (July 23, 1995).

KEY UNPUBLISHED SOURCES:

The Colonial Records Office, Public Records Office, Kew, London, holds the original correspondence between the British government in London and the colonial government in Hong Kong during the 1894 epidemic. Also internal memoranda, etc. Mostly filed under CO/129, CO/131, CO/132.

The Public Records Office also holds microfilm copies of contemporary newspaper coverage of the Hong Kong plague of 1894, from which such quotes as those on p.57 and p.64 are taken.

Crawford, Edward A. *The Life of Paul-Louis Simond and His Work on Plague.* Unpublished thesis in collection of Pasteur Institute, Paris.

James Alfred Lowson's unpublished diary for 1894 is held on microfilm by the Hong Kong Museum of Medical Sciences.

Lowson, J. A. Handwritten report, May 16, 1894, enclosed in Robinson to Ripon, May 17, 1894. Colonial Offfice. Original Correspondence: Hong Kong 1841–1951; series 129/263: CO10982.

Ratsitorahina, Mahery. 'Rapport de Mission: Epidemie de Peste Pulmonaire à Soanierana et à Merikanjaka dans le Service de Santé de District d'Ankazobe entre le 26 Novembre et 1 Décembre, 2000'. *Pasteur Institute, Madagascar,* 2000.

Yersin, A. Manuscripts of reports to French governor-general of Indochina, 1894. Also manuscript letters from Yersin to friends and colleagues at the Pasteur Institute, notebooks, etc. Held in collections of Pasteur Institute, Paris.

Yersin, A. 'Mon Voyage à Hong Kong au Sujet de la Peste, 1894'. Manuscript (with Yersin's own photographs) held in archives of *Pasteur Institute, Paris.*

Most of the quotations from Yersin's letters to his mother come from Mollaret, H. H., Brossollet, J. 'Alexandre Yersin ou le vainquer de la peste.' *Les Inconnus de l'Histoire.* Paris: Fayard, 1985.

Much of the material in the Surat, New York, Madagascar, and modern-day Hong Kong sections is taken from tape-recorded interviews and first-hand research by the author.

DIALOGUE IN YERSIN SCENES:

Most of the dialogue in the scenes featuring Yersin—for example, that on p.29 and pp.82–83—comes verbatim from his own unpublished notebooks, in which he often jotted down the actual words used in a conversation. Only the meeting with Lowson on pp.88–89 is a dramatization. This, however, is based closely on Yersin's own notebook description of the events.

SCENES FEATURING MOHANLAL AND HETAL:

Mohanlal and Hetal are the only fictional characters in the book. Their story, however, was constructed using the first-hand accounts of many of the real refugees from the Surat plague of 1994.

TEXT OF LETTER WRITTEN BY JAMES A LOWSON TO SHIBASABURO KITASATO (UNPUBLISHED, HELD IN ARCHIVES OF KITASATO INSTITUTE, TOKYO, JAPAN)

Dated Hong Kong, 20/08/94

Mein Blutreich* Professor,

I salute you, and hope that you will be able to prepare a new shell filled with Pest Bacilli for the damned Chinaman. If you can at the same time kill a man called *Yersin*, for God's sake do so. He has led us a dance in a way but Takaki will tell you we have got the better of him. I now say that the Bacilli are not

*Ruddy (literally, "blood-filled").

found deep in the mud – not deeper than half an inch. The question of digging up Taipingshan does not depend so much on account of the *Bacillus Kitasatonensis* as on account of its general dirty condition. It is however difficult to persuade the government that it is dirty. *Takaki* is taking some earth &c with him for future investigation.

Aoyama leaves today & all the rest with him. He will require a holiday in Japan. Look after him a bit as his heart is not what it ought to be.

I expect to have a holiday and propose leaving here on Sept 5th for a month in Shanghai and Japan. I am fairly tired of work—when it comes to 12, 13 or 14 hours a day it is rather too much. Takaki and Aoyama will probably tell you of the latest developments of the plague. Now we *can only diagnose in 90 per cent of cases by the microscope & thanks to your instructions* I can now recognise a plague bacillus 10½ miles away.

This is not an official letter as you will see from the wonderful heading of it. [Cartoon sketches of Kitasato, looking learned in spectacles, and Yersin, looking diabolical with long elfin ears and a pointed beard and moustache] I am so damned tired of writing official letters that I have a good mind to say I have writer's cramp in order to get a rest.

I hope you are all well . . .
Yours very sincerely
James A Lowson.

ACKNOWLEDGMENTS

The research for *Plague* was complex, and I owe grateful thanks to a great many for their patience and generosity:

In Britain: G. P. Amrick and the students at the University of Bath Foreign Languages Centre who translated Kitasáto's writings from the Japanese for me; Simon Andreae; Will Beck for his Hong Kong advice; Jane Bradish-Ellames whose agenting expertise is sadly no longer available; the polymathic Petra and Paddy Cramsie; Bernice Davison at the London *Evening Standard* for her generosity and flexibility; John Dryden; Jane Durham at Okavango Tours and Safaris; Jan Euden; Jake and Keiko Hobson; Dr. Douglas Holdstock for his advice on rats and nuclear radiation; Derek Johns; Ben Jones; Hester Marriott; Richard Milner; Dr. Mike Prentice from St. Bartholomew's; Denise Prior from the Royal Geographical Society as well as the staff of the society's library, where much of this book was written; Susanna Scouller; brother-in-arms Jeremy Seal; Becky Senior; Sally Shalam for helping me get to Madagascar and much else besides; Peter Straus; Dr. Brendan Wren from the School of Tropical Hygiene and Medicine; the staff of Hay-on-Wye public library; and Pat from Castle Video for her lunch-hour patience. I also owe a very special debt to Patricia de Mesquita for her tireless and good-humored translation work.

In Japan: Takeshi Sugiyama from the Kitasato University East Hospital and Ruiko Oiwa from the Kitasato Memorial Museum of the Kitasato Institute.

In Hong Kong: Dr. Gerald Choa; Dr. Robert Collins; Ringo Ng and the staff of the Hong Kong Museum of Medical Sciences; and Dan Waters.

In Madagascar: Dr. Suzanne Chanteau; Lambo Herizo and his 'bus trés fort'; Dr. Philippe Mauclère; Glenda Puente; and the staff of the library in the Tana Pasteur Institute.

In New York: Gil Bloom from the Standard Exterminating Company; Russell Galen; Riva Hocherman; and Greg Zareck from Metro Pest Control.

In Paris: Elizabeth Carnier, Daniel Demellier, Dominique Depenne, and Denise Ogilvie of the Pasteur Institute, who were always helpful and courteous. During my first visit to the archives I also benefited from the consummate translation skills and wonderful companionship of Camilla Elworthy.

My biggest thanks, however, are for a single comment made by the novelist Raj Kamal Jha at the end of an interview I conducted with him for the arts page of the *Evening Standard*. It was he who started the whole thing off.

INDEX

Avicenna, 235
Ayres, Dr. Philip, 21–22, 33, 35, 37, 82, 84–85, 136–37, 263

bacteriology, 3–4, 190, 223–24. *See also* plague bacillus
serological diagnosis vs., 159
Banjeri, Mr., 44, 45
BBC World Service, 51
Bible, 112
B.J. Medical College, 220
Bloom, Gill, 255–58
Boccaccio, Giovanni, 114, 147
Bombay
Europeans in, 206
health authorities and outbreak of 1995, 157–60, 219–25
outbreak of 1896–1898, 113–14, 122, 157, 204–9, 231–33
Simond investigates transmission in, 234–44
Yersin in, with vaccine, 231–33
Borrel, 208
Bourgeois, chancelier d'ambassade, 82–83, 85
Brazil, 226
Brill's disease, 253
British Medical Journal, 277
British Parliament, 113
British Plague Mission in Bombay, 235
Bulloch, William, 273

Calcutta Business Standard, 218
California, 125, 231
Calmette, Dr. Albert, 40, 82, 150, 177, 208
Canada, 231
Cantlie, Dr. James, 176
Canton outbreaks of 1894–1896, 23–26, 58, 194–96, 202
Cardiff, 123
Casablanca, 259–60
Center for Communicable Diseases, 159
Centers for Disease Control (CDC), 217, 220
Chadwick, Osbert, 21
Chanderkar, Dr. Narendra, 221–22

Chanteau, Dr. Suzanne, 181–84, 190–94
Charlemagne, 125
Chaucer, Geoffrey, 114, 248–49
Chausse, Bishop, 202–4
Chavassieux, Laurent, 38–39
China. *See also specific regions*
history of plague in, 26, 112–113
outbreak of 1792, rats and, 235–36
outbreak of 1894, 2, 15, 122
Yersin's vaccinations in, 204–5
China Mail, 132
Chinese doctors, 33, 71, 83, 195–96
Chivian, Eric, 270
Choa, Dr. Gerald, 264
Cobbold, Rev. R.F., 61–62
contagion and transmission theories, 12–14. *See also* rats; rat fleas
animals or humans, 152–53, 171
filth, 62–64, 103, 144–45
insect, 235, 237–44
foods, 171
Kitasato and, 170–71, 201
Lowson and, 116
poisoned air, 12–13, 170
Simond discovers secret of, 234–44
soil, 170–77, 194–95, 235
Corrientes, 123
Creighton, Charles, 171
Croker, Charles, 154
Cutch-Mandvi, India, 240

DDT, 183
De Contagione (Fracastor), 170
Defoe, 147
Delhi National Institute of Communicable Diseases, 220, 221

Edward VII, King of England, 86
Effects of Nuclear War on Health and Health Services (WHO report), 269
Egypt
outbreak of 1834–1835, 13–15
outbreak of 1843, 91
outbreak of 1898–1900, 226
Emerging Infectious Diseases, 190

plague bacillus (cont'd)
  Kitasato claims to find, 86, 89, 90,
    120–21, 131, 132, 169–70,
    199–200, 276
  Kitasato's vs. Yersin's, 98–99, 121,
    132–33, 142–50, 200, 274–77
  officially classed *Yersinia pestis*,
    273–74
  Simond finds, in fleas, 236, 240
  Yersinia pestis, DNA sequencing
    of, 280
pneumonia, 49, 276
pneumonic plague
  antibiotics to combat, 52
  in California, 227–30
  clinical features of, 50
  in Madagascar, 188–89, 192–93
Prentice, Dr. Mike, 280
press
  Hong Kong and, 29–30, 87
  San Francisco and, 125
  Surat and, 51, 76–77, 218
Private Hygiene Society of Japan,
  65–66
Propagation de la Peste, La (Simond),
  242

Qui nonh, Vietnam, 39

Rat: A World Menace, The (Hogarth),
  247–48
ratbite fever, 253
rat fleas (*Xenopsylla cheopis*), 156,
  181–82
  diagnosing disease in, 190–91
  eradication of, 185
  under microscope, 224
  nuclear attack and, 270
  Simond investigates, 239–43
Ratovonjato, Jocelyn, 182
rats, 1–2, 26, 80
  Alexandrian, or roof rat, 251
  Bombay and, 234–36, 238–39
  contagion theories touch on, 171
  diseases carried by, 253
  extermination of, 228, 245–50,
    252–58, 262–66
  fear of, 249–50

Haffkine Institute and, 222–23
Madagascar and, 178–82, 184–86,
  188–89
New York City and, 250–58
nuclear attack and, 268–69
Rattus norvegicus or Norway rat,
  184, 251, 253
Rattus rattus, black or ship rat, 178,
  184, 251–52
San Francisco and, 154, 156,
  245–46
Simond and, 234–44
Surat and, 108–9, 110
traps, 248–49, 257
types and behavior of, 251–55
U.S. and, 231, 270
Yersin and, 127, 151–53, 195, 234
Rennie, Dr. Alexander, 62
Ripon, marquess of, 129–30, 169, 197
Robinson, Sir William, 36, 62–63,
  85–87, 92, 129–31, 142, 169–70,
  196–98
Romeo and Juliet (Shakespeare), 249
Roux, Dr. Emile, 3, 203
Russia
  outbreak of 1879, 91
  outbreak of 1898–1900, 122, 226
  Russian mission in Bombay, 234

Saigon, 38–39
St. Bart's Hospital, 280
Samarano, Guadalupe, 227
Samarano, Lucena, 227
Samarano, Raul, 230
San Francisco
  outbreak of 1894–1901, 123–26,
    227
  outbreak of 1907–1908, 153–56,
    245–46
San Francisco Bulletin, 124
San Francisco Citizens' Health
  Committee, 154–55, 245–46
San Francisco Japanese Association,
  155–56
San Francisco Medical Society, 125
sanitation studies, 21–22, 189
Schmitz, Eugene, 126
Schwartzenbach, Mina, 5

ABOUT THE AUTHOR

Edward Marriott is the author of *Savage Shore* and *The Lost Tribe*, recipient of the Banff and John Llewelyn Prizes, a Thomas Cook Award finalist, and chosen as a *New York Times* Best Travel Book. He lives with his wife and son in London, where he writes for the *Evening Standard* and the BBC.